Routledge•Cavendish Questions & Answers Series

English Legal System
2009–2010

Routledge·Cavendish Questions & Answers Series

English Legal System
2009–2010

Gary Slapper, LLB, LLM, PhD, PGCE
Professor of Law, and Director of the Centre for Law
at The Open University
AND
David Kelly, BA, BA (Law), PhD
Principal Lecturer in Law, and LLM Course Director
at Staffordshire University

Routledge·Cavendish
Taylor & Francis Group
LONDON AND NEW YORK

Eighth edition published 2009 by Routledge-Cavendish
2 Park Square, Milton Park, Abingdon, Oxon, OX14 4RN

Simultaneously published in the USA and Canada
by Routledge-Cavendish
270 Madison Avenue, New York, NY 10016

*Routledge-Cavendish is an imprint of the Taylor & Francis Group,
an informa business*

© 1993, 1995, 1999, 2001, 2003, 2006, 2008, 2009 Slapper, G and Kelly, D

Previous editions published by Cavendish Publishing Limited
First edition 1993
Second edition 1995
Third edition 1999
Fourth edition 2001
Fifth edition 2003
Sixth edition 2006

Previous editions published by Routledge-Cavendish
Seventh edition 2008

Typeset in Garamond by
RefineCatch Limited, Bungay, Suffolk
Printed and bound in Great Britain by
TJ International Ltd, Padstow, Cornwall

All rights reserved. No part of this book may be reprinted or
reproduced or utilised in any form or by any electronic,
mechanical, or other means, now known or hereafter
invented, including photocopying and recording, or in any
information storage or retrieval system, without permission in
writing from the publishers.

British Library Cataloguing in Publication Data
A catalogue record for this book is available from the British Library

Library of Congress Cataloging in Publication Data
Slapper, Gary
English legal system, 2009–2010 / Gary Slapper and David Kelly.—8th ed.
p. cm.—(Q&A Routledge-Cavendish questions and answers series)
Rev. ed. of: Q&A English legal system, 2007–2008 / Gary Slapper & David Kelly. 7th ed. 2008.
1. Law—Great Britain—Examinations—Study guides. 2. Law—Great Britain—Problems,
exercises, etc. I. Kelly, David. II. Slapper, Gary. Q&A English legal system,
2007–2008. III. Title.
KD663.S58 2009
349.42—dc22
2008032725

ISBN 10: 0–415–48032–9
ISBN 13: 978–0–415–48032–1

CONTENTS

Preface	vii
Table of Cases	ix
Table of Statutes	xv
Table of Secondary Legislation	xxviii
Table of International Instruments	xxiv

1	Sources of Law and Legal Reform	1
2	The Courts and the Appellate Process	35
3	Judicial Reasoning	67
4	Judges and Juries	91
5	The Criminal Process	115
6	Civil Process and Legal Services	167
7	Alternative Dispute Resolution	197
8	The Rule of Law, Judicial Review and Human Rights	217
Index		243

PREFACE

This book has been written to assist students in their study of the English legal system. It has been composed for students of this subject, in general, and for undergraduates and those studying for professional examinations, in particular. The text is not a substitute for course books, law reports and legal journals, but aims to complement them by showing how typical examination and assignment questions can be answered.

The subject matter of the English legal system requires students to be familiar with our legal institutions and procedures, the criminal and civil processes, some substantive law, legal theories and debates in the realms of morals and politics. One thread running through all these topics is the requirement that students be evaluative and critical in their approach to the issues. It is also essential that answers take account of recent developments. Our answers in this book aim to show examples of such technique.

These answers will, perhaps, be most appreciated by students who have already acquired a good working knowledge of the relevant issues, principles and law and who desire clarification on the techniques that can be used to best present their knowledge in response to typical questions. The questions are modelled on those from a variety of English legal system courses, including the University of London (External) LLB. We have chosen a mix of essay and 'problem' questions and concentrated on issues which have current significance.

There have been many changes made to the apparatus and processes of the English legal system since the seventh edition of this book was published in 2008. There have been changes to civil and criminal process, the court system, the funding of legal services, the jury, human rights law, and several important common law decisions in the Court of Appeal, the House of Lords, and the European Court of Human Rights. These have all been digested in this edition.

We are very grateful to our families for their forbearance in not asking too many questions while we were answering those in this book.

We have endeavoured to state the law as at August 2008.

Gary Slapper
David Kelly
August 2008

TABLE OF CASES

A and others v Secretary of State for the Home Department [2004] UKHL 56,
  [2005] 3 All ER 169 .... 21, 224, 241
ABC case (1978) The Times, 18 November 109
Addy and Sons v Dumbreck [1929] AC 358 .... 39, 40
Adler v George [1964] 1 All ER 628 77
Agar [1990] 2 All ER 442, CA 160
Algar [1954] 1 QB 279 58
AM&S Europe Ltd v EC Commission (1983) Case 155/79 185
Angry Brigade *see* R v Greenfield
Antaios Compania Naviera SA v Salen Redereiarna AB [1985] AC 191;
  [1984] 3 All ER 229 212
Associated Provincial Picture Houses Ltd v Wednesbury Corporation
  [1948] 1 KB 223; [1947] 2 All ER 680 .... 170, 171–2, 232
Attorney-General's Reference (No 3 of 1999) [2000] 4 All ER 360 88
Aziz [1996] AC 41; [1995] 3 All ER 149 126

B v Auckland District Law Society [2003] UKPC 38; [2004] 4 All ER 269 185
Badham [1987] Crim LR 202 .... 139, 140, 141, 142
Bellinger v Bellinger [2003] 2 WLR 1174 .... 17, 31
Bentley v Brudzinski [1982] Crim LR 825 .... 143, 144
Bird [1977] 67 Cr App Rep 203 160
BLCT (13096) Ltd v J Sainsbury plc [2003] EWCA Civ 884; [2004] 2 P & CR 32 212
Boardman v DPP [1974] 3 All ER 887; [1975] AC 421 .... 84, 86
Bolitho v City and Hackney Health Authority [1998] AC 232;
  [1997] 4 All ER 771 195
Bromley LBC v GLC [1983] 1 AC 768; [1982] 1 All ER 129 233
Broome v Cassell [1972] AC 1027; [1972] 1 All ER 801 69
Brown [1988] 87 Cr App Rep 52 88
Burmah Oil Co Ltd v The Lord Advocate [1965] AC 75 83

Cain [1976] Crim LR 464, CA 158
Campbell v UK (1992) 15 EHRR 137 185
Chaffers, Re, ex parte A-G (1897) 45 WR 365, 76 LT 351 48
Chandler [1976] 1 WLR 585, CA 134, 136
Christie v Leachinsky [1947] AC 573 148
Churchill [1989] Crim LR 226, CA 142
CILFIT Srl v Minister of Health (No 283/81) [1982] ECR 3415 28
CMA CGM SA v Beteiligungs KG [2002] EWCA Civ 1878; [2003] 3 All ER 330 212
Coombes (1960) 45 Cr App Rep 36, 125 JP 139 85
Corkery v Carpenter [1950] 2 All ER 745; [1951] 1 KB 102 78
Council of Civil Service Unions v Minister for the Civil Service (GCHQ Case)
    [1984] 1 WLR 1174, CA 232
Culver (infant) v Beard [1938] 2 KB 292n; [1937] 1 All ER 301 61
Curry v DPP (1994) 144 NLJ 498 .... 72, 74

D v M [1983] Fam 33; [1982] 3 All ER 897 61
Danvers [1982] Crim LR 680 108
Davidson [1988] Crim LR 442 130
Davis (1959) 43 Cr App Rep 215 .... 119, 134
Dimes v Grand Junction Canal (1852) 3 HL Cas 759 .... 101, 103
DPP v Hawkins [1988] 1 WLR 1166 148
DPP v Schildkamp [1970] 2 WLR 279; [1969] 2 All ER 835n 81
Director of Serious Fraud Office ex p Smith [1993] AC 1; [1992] 3 WLR 66, CA 118
Donnelly v Jackman [1970] 1 WLR 562, CA 143–4
Doolan [1988] Crim LR 747 88
Duncan (1981) 73 Cr App Rep 359 126
Dunford (1990) 91 Cr App Rep 150; [1991] Crim LR 370, CA 131

Eagil Trust Co Ltd v Pigott Brown [1985] 3 All ER 119 61
Earl of Oxford's Case (1615) 1 Rep Ch 1, 21 ER 485 10
Emmerson (1990) 92 Cr App Rep 284, [1991] Crim LR 194 127
European Parliament v Council [1990] ECR I-2041 28

Factortame Ltd v Secretary of State for Transport (No 1) [1989] 2 All ER 692 26
Fennelley [1989] Crim LR 142 .... 143, 145
Fisher v Bell [1961] 1 QB 394; [1960] 3 All ER 731 77
Fitzpatrick v Sterling Housing Association Ltd [1999] 4 All ER 705 237
Ford [1989] 3 WLR 762 108

Fulling [1987] 2 WLR 923, CA 127

G, Re [2004] EWHC 1474 (Fam) 47
Gallie v Lee [1971] AC 1004 70
Goldenberg (1988) 152 JP 557, CA 124, 126–7
Golder v United Kingdom (1979–80) 1 EHRR 525 50
Greenough v Gaskell (1833) 1 My & K 98; [1824–34] All ER Rep 767 185

Hall (Arthur JS) & Co v Simms and Others [2000] 3 WLR 543 186
Handyside v United Kingdom (1979–80) 1 EHRR 737 50
Harper-Taylor, Baker and Bakker [1991] RTR 76n, [1988] NLJR 80;
  (1988) The Times, 3 March 160
Heaney and McGuiness v Ireland [2001] Crim LR 481 123
Herrington v British Railways Board [1972] AC 877 .... 38, 39–40
Heydon's Case (1584) 3 Co Rep 7a 77
Home Secretary v Wainright [2002] 3 WLR 405 83
Horton v Sadler [2006] UKHL 27 .... 38, 40–1
Hurnam v DPP of Mauritius [2005] UKPC 49; [2007] UKPC 24 151

Inze v Austria (1988) 10 EHRR 394 51
IRC v Frere [1969] 3 WLR 1193, CA 83
IRC v National Federation of Self-Employed and Small Businesses Ltd
  [1982] AC 617; [1981] 2 All ER 93 229
Ireland v United Kingdom (1979–80) 2 EHRR 25 50

Jose da Conceicao Guerreiro v Portugal (2002) App No 00045560/99 (G Ress P),
  31 January 178

Kenlin v Gardiner [1967] 2 QB 510; [1967] 2 WLR 129 .... 143, 144
Kjeldson and others v Denmark (1979–80) 1 EHRR 711 50

Lemsatef [1977] 1 WLR 812, CA 143
Lewis (John) & Co Ltd v Tims [1952] AC 676 .... 147, 149, 150
Linton v Ministry of Defence (1983) 133 NLJ 1103 56
Locabail (UK) Ltd v Bayfield Properties Ltd and Another [2000] 2 WLR 870;
  (1999) 149 NLJ 1793, CA 101, 102
London Tramways Co Ltd v London County Council [1898] AC 375 38
London Transport Executive ex p GLC [1983] QB 484 233

McCay [1991] 1 All ER 232 144

xi

McIlkenny and Others (1991) The Times, 1 April 60
McIvor [1987] Crim LR 409 130
Marks v Beyfus (1890) 25 QBD 494 88
Marshall v Southampton and West Hampshire AHA [1993] 3 WLR 1054, CA 28
Martinez-Tobon [1994] 2 All ER 90 119
Mason [1987] 3 All ER 481; [1988] 1 WLR 139 .... 124, 125
Maynard (1979) 69 Cr App Rep 309 56
Meering v Grahame-White Aviation Co Ltd (1919) 122 LT 44;
  [1918–19] All ER Rep Ext 1490 147
Melluish (Inspector of Taxes) v BMI (No 3) Ltd [1995] 4 All ER 453 82
Mendoza v Ghaidan [2002] EWCA Civ 1533; [2003] 2 WLR 478 .... 75, 79, 237
Miliangos v George Frank (Textiles) Ltd [1975] 3 WLR 758, CA; [1976] AC 443 69
Miller [1986] 1 WLR 1191 .... 88, 124
Moy v Pettmann Smith [2005] UKHL 7 191

North Range Shipping Ltd v Seatrans Shipping Corporation [2002] EWCA Civ 405 212

P [1991] 2 AC 447; [1992] Crim LR 41 84
Paris (1992) 97 Cr App Rep 99, [1994] Crim LR 320 127
Parkes [1976] 3 All ER 380 .... 134, 136
Parris [1989] Crim LR 214, CA 130
Pepper v Hart [1993] 1 All ER 42, CA 78, 80, 81, 82
Pitman [1991] 1 All ER 468, CA 156, 159
Poplar BC (Nos 1 and 2) [1922] 1 KB 72 227
Powell v Kempton Park Racecourse [1899] AC 143 84
Price v Leeds City [2006] UKHL 10 .... 69, 236

R (1991) (Rape: Marital Exemption) [1992] 1 AC 599; [1991] 4 All ER 481 .... 31, 74
R (on the application of Gillan) v (1) Commissioner of Police for the
  Metropolis (2) Secretary of State for the Home Department
  [2004] EWCA Civ 1067; [2005] QB 388 .... 49–50, 51
R (on the application of Greenpeace Ltd) v Secretary of State for
  Trade and Industry [2007] EWHC 311 (Admin) 170–1
R v A [2001] UKHL 25; [2002] 1 AC 45 .... 75, 79
R v (1) Abdroikov (2) Green (3) Williamson [2005] EWCA Crim 1986;
  [2006] 1 Cr App Rep 1 .... 106, 110, 111
R v Argent [1997] 2 Cr App Rep 27 136
R v Beycan [1990] Crim LR 185, CA 132

R v Bow Street Metropolitan Stipendiary Magistrate ex p Pinochet Ugarte
  (No 2) [2000] 1 AC 119; [1999] 1 All ER 577 .... 101–2, 103
R v Camborne Justices ex p Pearce [1955] 1 QB 41; [1954] 2 All ER 850 103
R v Clinton [1993] 1 WLR 1181 190
R v Condron [1997] 1 Cr App Rep 85 136
R v Cooper [1969] 1 QB 267; [1968] 3 WLR 1225 138
R v Cowan [1996] QB 373; [1995] 4 All ER 939, CA 136
R v Cox and Railton (1884) 14 QBD 153; [1881–5] All ER Rep 68 .... 184, 185
R v Gough [1993] AC 646; [1992] 4 All ER 481 .... 101, 103
R v Greenfield (The Angry Brigade) [1973] 1 WLR 1151 109
R v Inhabitants of Sedgley (1831) 2 B & Ad 65 84
R v Inspector of Pollution ex p Greenpeace [1994] 4 All ER 321 229
R v Kansal [2001] All ER (D) 311 (May) 83
R v L (1994) [2004] EWCA Crim 1414 127
R v Lambert [2001] 1 All ER 1014 83
R v Momodou [2005] EWCA Crim 177 .... 162, 163, 164
R v Nottingham Justices ex p Davies [1980] 3 WLR 15 155
R v Rand LR 1 QBD 230 103
R v Secretary of State for Foreign Affairs ex p World Development Movement
  [1995] 1 WLR 386 229
R v Secretary of State for the Home Department ex p Brind [1991] 2 WLR 588, CA 234
R v Sussex Coroner ex p Homberg [1924] 1 KB 256 45
R v Sussex JJ ex p McCarthy [1924] 1 KB 256; [1923] All ER Rep 233 101
R (on the application of Jackson) v Attorney General [2005] 3 WLR 733 16
R (on the Application of Quintavalle) v Secretary of State for Health
  [2003] 2 WLR 692 79
R (on the Application of Rottman) v Commissioner of Police [2002] 2 WLR 1315 82
Ras Behari Lal v King-Emperor (1933) 102 LJPC 144 42
Rice v Connolly [1966] 3 WLR 17 .... 118, 134–5
Ricketts v Cox [1982] Crim LR 184 .... 134, 135
Ridge v Baldwin [1964] AC 40; [1963] 2 WLR 935, CA 227
Rogers (1994) 158 JP 909; [1995] Crim LR 148 .... 84, 87
Rondel v Worsley [1967] 3 WLR 1666, CA; [1969] 1 AC 191 .... 56, 187, 188
Roquette Frères SA v Council (1980) ECR 3333 171
Royal College of Nursing v DHSS [1981] 2 WLR 279, CA 81

S, Re [2002] 2 WLR 720 31

Samuel [1988] 2 WLR 920, CA 88, 130
Sang [1980] AC 402; [1979] 3 WLR 263, CA 124, 125, 127
Secretary of State for the Home Department v JJ and Others
  [2007] All ER (D) 489 (Oct); [2007] UKHL 45 241
Secretary of State for the Home Department v MB and AF
  [2007] All ER (D) 01 (Nov) 241
Self [1992] 1 WLR 657, CA 147, 149
Selvey v DPP [1970] AC 304; [1968] 2 All ER 497 .... 84, 85
Sharp [1988] 1 All ER 65 .... 124, 126
Smith v Eric S Bush [1988] QB 743; [1987] 3 All ER 179 130
Sparks v R [1964] AC 964 86
Spencer [1987] AC 128; [1986] 2 All ER 928 70
Spicer v Holt [1977] Crim LR 364 147
Stafford v DPP [1974] AC 878; [1973] 3 All ER 762 56
Straffen [1952] 2 QB 911 86
Sutcliffe (1981) The Times, 23 May 159
Sweet v Parsley [1969] 2 WLR 470, CA; [1970] AC 132, HL 82–3

Taylor v Chief Constable of Cheshire [1987] 1 All ER 225; [1986] 1 WLR 1479 87
Telford JJ ex p Badham [1991] 2 WLR 866, CA 227
Three Rivers DC v Bank of England (No 2) [1996] 2 All ER 363 82
Townsend [1987] Crim LR 411 87
Turner [1970] 2 WLR 1093, CA 156, 158

Wadman [1996] EWCA Crim 1540 133
Walkley v Precision Forgings Ltd [1979] 2 All ER 548 .... 40, 41, 42
Walsh (1990) 12 Cr App Rep (S) 243 131
Walters v WH Smith & Son Ltd [1914] 1 KB 595 .... 147, 148, 149
Weekes (1993) 97 Cr App Rep 222 88

Young, James and Webster v United Kingdom (1981) 4 EHRR 38 51
Young v Bristol Aeroplane Co Ltd [1944] KB 718 .... 69, 70

Z [1990] 2 QB 355; [1991] Fam Law 137 86
Zavekas [1990] 2 QB 355; [1991] Fam Law 137 .... 124, 126

Table of Statutes

Abortion Act 1967 14
Access to Justice Act 1999 .... 169, 179, 188, 201
Anti-terrorism Crime and Security Act 2001 .... 21, 224, 239, 240
    s 21 .... 239, 240
    s 21(1) 239
    s 23 .... 98, 240
    s 23(1) 240
Arbitration Act 1950 208
Arbitration Act 1975 208
Arbitration Act 1979 208
Arbitration Act 1996 .... 198, 207, 208, 212, 213
    s 1 208
    s 5 209
    s 5(3) 209
    s 6 209
    ss 9–11 210
    s 12 211
    s 15 209
    s 17 209
    s 18 211
    s 20(4) 209
    s 24 211
    ss 28–30 209
    s 32 211
    s 33 .... 210, 211
    s 35 210
    s 39 210
    s 43 211
    s 45 211

s 46	210
ss 48–50	210
s 58	210
s 66	210
ss 67–68	211
s 69	212
Bail Act 1976	**150, 152, 153, 154, 156**
s 3	155
s 4	152
ss 6–7	154
s 9	154
s 154	155
Sched 1	152
Bail (Amendment) Act 1993	**150, 151, 155**
Civil Evidence Act 1968	**56**
s 1	56
s 23(1)	58
s 23(1)(c)	58
s 23(2)	58
Civil Procedure Act 1998	**30, 183, 194**
Companies Act 1985	**17**
ss 431–441	123
Constitutional Reform Act 2005	**91, 92, 93**
s 1	223
s 17(1)	223
s 23	93
s 23(3)	94
s 23(6)	94
ss 24–25	94
s 26	94
s 26(4)	94
s 27	94
s 27(2)–(3)	94
s 27(8)–(9)	94
s 28	94

s 28(1) 94
　　s 29 94
　　s 30 94
　　s 30(1) 96
　　s 30(3) 96
　　s 31 94
　　Sched 8 94
County Courts Act 1984 19
Courts and Legal Services Act 1990
　　s 71 43
Criminal Appeal Act 1968 .... 55, 57
　　s 2 55
Criminal Appeal Act 1995 .... 37, 55, 56, 59, 63, 138
　　ss 1–2 57
　　s 4 58
　　s 12 57
　　s 13 59
　　s 19 59
Criminal Evidence Act 1898
　　s 1 85
Criminal Justice Act 1967
　　s 11 121
Criminal Justice Act 1982
　　ss 43–50 116
　　s 155 155
　　s 321 116
Criminal Justice Act 1987
　　s 2 .... 118, 123
Criminal Justice Act 1988 .... 87, 105, 108
Criminal Justice
　　Act 2003 .... 92, 105, 106, 107, 110, 111, 113, 153, 154
　　Part 2 153
　　Part 9 60
　　s 177 .... 107, 113
　　ss 227–228 .... 107, 113
　　s 321 111

Sched 33
  para 2 .... 106, 111
  para 3 .... 107, 113
Criminal Justice and Immigration Act 2008 115
Criminal Justice and Public Order Act 1994 .... 105, 117, 118, 136, 138, 155
  s 25 .... 150, 151, 152, 153
  s 26 151
  s 27 .... 150, 151, 152
  s 28 151
  s 29 .... 151, 152
  s 30 151
  ss 32–33 116
  s 34 .... 116, 120, 121, 135, 136, 137, 138
  s 34(1) 137
  s 35 .... 116, 118, 120, 121, 136, 138
  s 36 .... 116, 120, 121, 136, 137, 138
  s 37 .... 116, 117, 120, 121, 136, 137, 138
  s 38 .... 136, 138
  s 168 118
Criminal Law Act 1977
  s 62 132

Dangerous Drugs Act 1965
  s 5(b) 83

Employment Rights Act 1996 199
European Communities Act 1972
  s 2(2) 19
  s 3 69
  s 3(1) 70, 236

Gender Recognition Act 2004 31

Human Fertilisation and Embryology Act 1990 79
Human Rights Act 1998 .... 3, 13, 17, 18, 21, 30, 31, 68, 70, 75, 76, 79, 83,
                                       97, 98, 99, 100, 110, 121, 217, 218, 224, 230, 232,
                                       233, 234, 235, 236, 237, 238, 239, 240, 241, 242
  s 2 .... 70, 75, 79, 236, 242
  s 3 .... 75, 79, 83, 237, 239, 242

s 4	237, 238, 239
s 4(6)	242
s 6	237, 242
ss 7–8	237
s 10	242
s 19	236
s 22(4)	83
Sched 1	235
Hunting Act 2004	15–16

Insolvency Act

s 22	123
s 131	123
Interpretation Act 1978	81
Judicature Acts 1873–75	12
Juries Act 1974	105, 109
s 9	107, 113
s 9(1)	107, 113
s 9AA	113
s 12(6)	108
Law Commission Act 1965	31

Licensing Act 1872

s 12	78
Limitation Act 1980	40
s 11	40, 41
s 33	40, 41
Limited Liability Partnership Act 2000	19
ss 14–15	19
Local Government Act 1972	19
Local Government Act 1974	204, 205
Magistrates' Courts Act 1980	19
Merchant Shipping Act 1988	26, 27

Offences Against the Person Act 1861

s 38	149
Offences Against the State Act 1939 (Ireland)	123

Official Secrets Act 1911 .... 77, 109
    s 11 123
Parliament Act 1911 .... 15, 16
Parliament Act 1949 .... 15, 16
Parliamentary Commissioner Act 1967 .... 204, 205
    s 12(3) 205
Partnership Act 1890 17
Police Act 1964
    s 51 142
    s 51(3) 135
Police and Criminal Evidence Act 1984 .... 116, 126, 131, 142, 148
    Codes of Practice 144
        Code A 117, 144, 145, 146
        Code B 141
        Code C 120, 124, 126, 127, 128, 129, 130, 131, 132, 133, 137
        Code D 137
    Part IV 152
    Part VIII 125
    s 1 .... 117, 144, 154
    s 1(7)(b)(i) 144
    s 1(8)(a) 144
    s 2 .... 117, 145, 154
    s 2(3) 145
    s 2(9) 146
    s 8 117
    s 10(1)(a) 140
    ss 15–17 117
    s 18 .... 117, 139, 140, 141, 142
    s 19 .... 139, 141
    s 20 139
    s 24 .... 116, 140, 147, 148
    s 24(1)(b) 129
    s 24(4) 148
    s 24(5) 148, 149
    s 25 .... 117, 148
    s 28(3) 147

s 32	117, 139, 140, 141, 142
s 38	152
s 38(1)(a)	151
s 47	152
s 51	139
s 54	117
s 56	132
s 56(5)	132
s 56(6)	129, 132
s 58	128, 130, 131
s 58(1)	129
s 64	89
s 64(1)	89
s 67	154
s 67(11)	139, 141, 144
s 76	58, 124, 125, 126, 127, 137
s 76(2)	125
s 76(2)(a)	127
s 76(2)(b)	126, 127, 129
s 78	125, 127, 131, 137, 138, 139, 141, 144, 145, 154
s 78(1)	89, 124
s 82	124, 125, 127
s 82(1)	124, 125, 126
s 116	129
s 116(6)(e)–(f)	129
s 117	139, 142
Sched 5	129
Powers of Criminal Courts (Sentencing) Act 2000	
s 91	107, 113
Prevention of Terrorism Act 2005	240, 241
Prevention of Terrorism (Temporary Provisions) Act 1989	
s 18	123
Proceeds of Crime Act 2002	186
Rent Act 1977	237
Royal Assent Act 1967	16

Sale of Goods Act 1893 17
Serious Organised Crime and Police Act 2005 157
Sex Discrimination Act 1975 28
Solicitors Act 1974 19
Statute of Gloucester 1278 8
Sunday Entertainments Act 1932 172
Supreme Court Act 1981 19
    s 42 48

Terrorism Act 2000 .... 49, 186
    s 44 .... 49, 50
    ss 45–47 49
Treasure Act 1996 43
Tribunals and Inquiries Act 1971
    s 12 200
Tribunals, Courts and Enforcement Act 2007 .... 198, 202, 203

War Crimes Act 1991 83
War Damage Act 1965 83

Table of Secondary Legislation

Civil Procedure Rules 1998 .... 30, 168, 169, 173, 176, 178, 179, 180, 183, 195, 214, 226, 227, 228, 229
    r 1.1(1) 168
    r 1.2 168
    r 8.2 228
    r 24.2 188
    r 35.7(3) 195
    r 54.1 228
    r 54.5 228
    r 54.17 229
Criminal Procedure Rules 196

Human Rights Act 1998 (Designated Derogation) Order 2001 240

Limited Liability Partnership Regulations 2001 19

Rules of the Supreme Court
    Ord 53 228

Table of International Instruments

EC Treaty 1957 22
    Arts 85–86 24
    Art 234 .... 25, 26, 27, 28
    Art 249 22
Equal Treatment Directive 76/207/EEC 26
    Art 6 26
European Convention on Human Rights 3, 17, 21, 31, 49, 50, 69, 75, 79, 97, 98, 123,
                                                   153, 217, 232, 233, 234, 238, 239, 240, 241
    Art 1 235
    Arts 2–4 .... 235, 236
    Art 5 .... 49, 235, 240, 241
    Art 6 .... 52, 106, 111, 121, 212, 235
    Art 6(1) 123, 178
    Art 6(2) 123
    Art 7 .... 235, 236
    Art 8 .... 50, 235, 236, 241
    Art 9 .... 235, 236
    Art 10 .... 50, 235, 236, 241
    Art 11 .... 50, 235, 236, 241
    Art 11(2) 236
    Art 12 235
    Art 14 .... 235, 236, 237, 240
    Protocol 1: Arts 1–3 235
    Protocol 6: Arts 1–2 236
Maastricht Treaty 1992 22
Nice Treaty 2001 22
Single European Act 1986 .... 22, 23, 25, 26

CHAPTER 1

SOURCES OF LAW AND LEGAL REFORM

INTRODUCTION

There are different interpretations of the phrase 'source of law'. It can, in jurisprudence, refer to what it is in our nature or society that necessitates law. More generally, however, the expression refers to the procedural origin of the law which is applied in the courts. There are three main sources: Parliamentary legislation, delegated legislation and the common law. Used in this sense, the latter phrase 'common law' connotes all judge made law and therefore includes equity.

If you are covering this theme, you should be very familiar with the origins and modern role of both common law and equity. You should also understand the details of the process of enacting legislation from the stage before the publication of Green Papers to the final stage, the Royal Assent. However, the English legal system cannot be treated as static; it is continuously responding to changes that take place in society as a whole. To deny the relevance of European law in an English legal system course would not only be restrictive, it would be wrong to the extent that it ignored an increasingly important factor in the formation and determination of UK law.

You should also have a good knowledge of the different bodies associated with reform: permanent institutions, that is, the Law Reform Committee, the Criminal Law Revision Committee and the Law Commission, and *ad hoc* bodies, such as Royal Commissions. You should also understand how the system resolves the interplay of several competing interest groups in order to produce legislation. This is a subject area where it is especially useful to have a sound knowledge of recent examples.

Checklist

You should be familiar with:
- the origin and modern operation of the common law;
- the origin and modern operation of equity;
- the stages of promulgation of legislation;
- Parliamentary sovereignty and types of legislation;

- the types of delegated legislation and its advantages and disadvantages;
- the major institutions of the European Union (EU), particularly the European Court of Justice (ECJ);
- the institutions of law reform, the Law Commission, *ad hoc* bodies, etc.

Question 1

What are the main sources of law today?

Answer plan

This is, apparently, a very straightforward question, but the temptation is to ignore the European Community (EU) as a source of law and to overemphasise custom as a source. The following structure does not make these mistakes:

- in the contemporary situation, it would not be improper to start with the EU as a source of UK law;
- then attention should be moved on to domestic sources of law: statute and common law;
- the increased use of delegated legislation should be emphasised;
- custom should be referred to, but its extremely limited operation must be emphasised.

Answer

European law

Since the UK joined the European Economic Community (EEC) (now the EU), it has progressively but effectively passed the power to create laws which are operative in this country to the wider European institutions. The UK is now subject to Community law, not just as a direct consequence of the various treaties of accession passed by the UK Parliament, but increasingly, it is subject to the secondary legislation generated by the various institutions of the EU.

European law takes three distinct forms: regulations, directives and decisions. Regulations are immediately effective without the need for the UK Parliament to produce its own legislation. Directives, on the other hand, require specific legislation to implement their proposals, but the UK Parliament is under an obligation to enact such legislation as will give effect to their implementation. Decisions of the ECJ are binding throughout the EU and take precedence over any domestic law.

Parliamentary legislation

Under UK constitutional law, it is recognised that Parliament has the power to enact, revoke or alter such and any law it sees fit to deal with and no one Parliament can bind its successors. The extent of this sovereignty may be brought into question with respect to the EU for such time as the UK remains a member, but within the UK, Parliament's power is absolute. This absolute power is a consequence of the historical struggle between Parliament and the Stuart monarchy in the seventeenth century. Parliament arrogated to itself absolute law-making power, a power not challenged by the courts, which were in turn granted an independent sphere of operation. It should be remembered, however, that the **Human Rights Act (HRA) 1998** has, for the first time, given the courts the power to question, although not strike down, primary legislation as being incompatible with the rights protected under the **European Convention on Human Rights (ECHR)**. It also allows the courts to declare secondary legislation to be invalid for the same reason.

Parliament makes law in the form of legislation, that is, Acts of Parliament. There are various types of legislation. Whereas public Acts affect the public generally, private Acts only affect a limited sector of the populace, either particular people or people within a particular locality. Within the category of public Acts, a further distinction can be made between government Bills and Private Member's Bills. The former are usually introduced by the Government, whilst the latter are the product of individual initiative on the part of particular MPs.

Before enactment, the future Act is referred to as a Bill and many Bills are the product of independent commissions, such as the Law Commission, or committees, such as the Law Reform Committee and the Criminal Law Revision Committee. Without going into the details of the procedure, Bills have to be considered by both Houses of Parliament and have to receive Royal Assent before they are actually enacted.

Delegated legislation has to be considered as a source of law, in addition, but subordinate, to general Acts of Parliament. Generally speaking, delegated legislation is law made by some person or body to whom Parliament has delegated its general law-making power. In statistical terms, it is arguable that at present, delegated legislation is actually more significant than primary Acts of Parliament. The output of delegated legislation in any year greatly exceeds the output of Acts of Parliament and, each year, there are over 3,000 sets of rules and regulations made in the form of delegated legislation, compared to fewer than 100 public Acts of Parliament. Delegated legislation can take the form of Orders in Council, which permit the

Government to make law through the Privy Council. This power is usually considered in relation to impending emergencies, but perhaps its widest effect is to be found in relation to EU law, for under s 2(2) of the **European Communities Act 1972**, ministers can give effect to provisions of the Community which do not have direct effect. Most delegated legislation, however, takes the form of statutory instruments, through which government ministers exercise the powers given to them by general enabling legislation to make the particular rules which are to apply to any given situation within its ambit. A third type of delegated legislation is the bylaw, through which local authorities and public bodies are able to make legally binding rules within their area of competence or authority.

Delegated legislation has developed for a number of reasons. One such reason is the increased pressure on Parliamentary time, with the consequent hiving off of detailed and time-consuming work to ministers and their specialist departments. Another reason for the growth in the output of delegated legislation is the highly technical nature of the subject matter to which it tends to be addressed and the concomitant need for such rules themselves to be highly technical. Any piece of delegated legislation is only valid if it is within the ambit of the powers actually delegated by Parliament. Any law made outside that restricted ambit of authority is void, as being *ultra vires*, and is open to challenge in the courts under the process of judicial review.

Common law

The next source of law that has to be considered is case law, the effective creation and refinement of law in the course of judicial decisions. It should be remembered that the UK's law is still a common law system and, even if legislation in its various guises is of ever increasing importance, the significance and effectiveness of judicial creativity should not be discounted. Judicial decisions are a source of law, through the operation of the doctrine of judicial precedent. This process depends on the established hierarchy of the courts and operates in such a way that generally, a court is bound by the *ratio decidendi*, or rule of law implicit in the decision of a court above it in the hierarchy and usually by a court of equal standing in that hierarchy. Where statute law does not cover a particular area, or where the law is silent, it will be generally necessary for a court deciding cases relating to such an area to determine what the law is and, in so doing, that court will inescapably and unarguably be creating law. The scope for judicial creativity should not be underestimated and it should be remembered that the task of interpreting the actual meaning of legislation in particular cases also falls to the judiciary and provides it with a further important area of discretionary creativity. As the highest court in the land, the House of Lords has particular scope for creating or extending the common law, and a relatively contemporary example of its adopting such an active stance can be seen in the way in which it overruled the long-standing presumption that a man could not be guilty of the crime of rape against his wife (see *R* (1991)). It should, of course, always be remembered that Parliament remains sovereign as regards the creation of law and any aspect of the judicially created common law is subject to direct alteration by statute.

An extension of the doctrine of judicial precedent leads to a consideration of a further possible source of law, for when the court is unable to locate a precise or analogous precedent, it may refer to legal textbooks for guidance and assistance. Such books are sub-divided, depending on when they were written. In strict terms, only certain venerable works of antiquity are actually treated as authoritative sources of law. Amongst the most important of these works are those by Glanvill from the twelfth century, Bracton from the thirteenth century, Coke from the seventeenth century and Blackstone from the eighteenth century. Legal works produced after *Blackstone's Commentaries of 1765* are considered to be of recent origin, but although they cannot be treated as authoritative sources, the courts on occasion will look at the most eminent works by accepted experts in particular fields in order to help determine what the law is or should be.

Custom

The final source of law that remains to be considered is custom. The romantic view of the common law is that it represented a crystallisation of common customs, distilled by the judiciary in the course of its travels around the land. Although some of the common law may have had its basis in general custom, a large proportion of these so-called customs were invented by the judges themselves and represented what they wanted the law to be, rather than what people generally thought it was.

There is, however, a second possible customary source of law and that is rules derived from specific local customs. Here, there is the possibility that the local custom might differ from the common law and thus limit its operation. Even in this respect, however, reliance on customary law as opposed to common law, although not impossible, is made unlikely by the stringent test that any appeal to it has to satisfy. Amongst these requirements are that the custom must have existed from 'time immemorial' (that is, since 1189) and must have been exercised continuously within that period and without opposition. The custom must also have been felt as obligatory, have been consistent with other customs and, in the final analysis, must be reasonable. Given this list of requirements, it can be seen why local custom does not loom large as an important source of law.

Question 2

How far would you agree with the contention that King Henry II deserves to be called 'the father of the common law'?

Answer plan

A suggested plan for answering this question is as follows:

- introduction – the range of contributory factors;
- 'tradition expressed in action' (Simpson, *Legal Theory and Legal History*, 1987);
- the role of Henry II's clerics – itinerant royal justice;
- royal justice in competition with other sorts of justice;
- Pollock and Maitland's six principles (in *History of English Law*, 1911);
- conclusion – evaluating the role of an individual in legal history.

Answer

Before the Norman conquest in 1066, the English legal system involved a mass of oral customary rules, which varied according to region. Most writers agree with Pollock and Maitland's view that the common law had been largely established by the accession to the throne of Edward I in 1272. Certainly, the three courts of King's Bench, Common Pleas and Exchequer were operational by this time. It is true that Henry II, who reigned 1154–89, did much of significance to enhance the development of the common law, for instance, by popularising the King's court with the introduction of the Petty Assizes. However, we are not really familiar with how the *Curia Regis* acted during the Norman period before Henry II, because the earliest plea rolls date from his reign, so it would perhaps be over-presumptuous to credit too much to Henry II. In any event, the development of the common law was contributed to by many factors of a general historical nature and it might be more meaningful to speak of the various parties which helped nurture the common law from its first green shoots to its full bloom rather than to try and find a 'father'.

Unlike continental civil law, the English system does not originate from any particular set of texts or digests but from what Simpson has called 'tradition expressed in action'. It began as customary law used in the King's court to settle disputes and conflicts which touched the monarch directly. To begin with, these only included the graver crimes which became Pleas of the Crown. After the Norman invasion, there were still many different types of court apart from the royal court: the stannary courts of Devon and Cornwall and the courts of the royal hunting forests but, principally, in potential rivalry with the royal court, were the feudal and manorial courts. It was during Henry II's reign (but clearly not wholly attributable to this one man), that the clerics in his court (that is, his royal entourage) began specialising in legal business and acting in a judicial capacity.

In the jurisdictional expansion considered presently, an important role was played by the clerics who developed a range of writs and establishing procedures which, perhaps very significantly, afforded them greater importance and provided them with a generous income. These practices developed into the common law of England, the law which was available throughout the realm. In Simpson's words: 'It was common as a prostitute is common: available to all.' On this point, perhaps the most convincing of the reasons why Henry should be regarded as the 'father of the common law' is that he was largely responsible for the regional and itinerant royal justice, through which (by sending his judges up and down the country) the law truly became common.

Henry sent officials from the royal household to the counties and the travelling judges formed a nucleus of *iusticiarii totius Angliae* who had no local roots. They were thus much less susceptible to the corruption which had spoilt a similar attempt, earlier in the twelfth century, in which the royal judges had actually been based in the local communities. It was under Henry II that judges were for the first time sent on 'circuits', hearing pleas in the major places they visited and taking over the work of the local courts. In this travelling mode, the royal representatives were *iusticiae errantes* (wandering justices) or *iusticiarii in itinere* (justices in eyre, that is, law French for journey). The judges were periodically sent on a 'general eyre', which included the whole country. Baker has argued, however, that it was the smaller circuit which was to prove 'the essence of the common law system', by bringing royal justice regularly to the counties.

The era running from the Norman invasion to the accession of Edward I saw the important struggle to administer justice between the royal judges and the tribunals of feudal lords, the shires and the hundreds which had survived from Anglo-Saxon times. The efforts of the royal judges were significantly assisted by the works of the text writers Glanvill and Bracton. Glanvill's *Tractatus de Legibus Angliae* (published under Henry II) was the first clear statement of the law, administered throughout the procedure of the royal courts. Glanvill was a senior royal judge. The writer's preface (it was probably not actually written by Glanvill, but by Hubert Walter or by Henry II's Chief Justiciary) divides the pleas into criminal and civil and the body of the work is mostly practical.

With only a few principles of general application before them and by virtue of some particular advantages of the evolving system, the royal judges had established the supremacy of their courts over all competing jurisdictions by the time of Edward's reign. Pollock and Maitland formulated six principles upon which was founded the usurpation of general jurisdiction by the *Curia Regis*. These principles show that while much was done by Henry II to promote the common law, there were several other factors which engendered it, some of which were effective only after Henry II's reign.

First, the King's court was a court to go to in default of justice. Under the Norman kings, the litigant who wished to proceed in the ordinary court obtained the King's 'Writ of Right Patent' which contained the threat *quod nisi feceris vicecomes meus faciet* (if you do not do this, my sheriff will). Complaints and petitions for justice were numerous and these cases formed the basis of the growth of the common law throughout the development of the Register of Writs (added to each time a judge accepted a new writ as suitable to be used again in similar cases).

Secondly, the Writ of Right issued by the Royal Chancery became compulsory for all pleas relating to freehold land, according to an apparently lost ordinance of Henry II. This was so, even where the case was to be tried in the seigniorial court and so gave the King power over manorial courts.

Thirdly was the introduction by Henry II of the Grand Assize as an alternative to trial by battle in the proceedings on the Writ of Right. As these cases were decided by impartial neighbours, it became much more popular than trial by battle and was only available in the royal court.

Fourthly was Henry II's introduction of the Petty Assizes, also only obtainable in the King's court. These assizes were for trying disputes concerning *disseisin* of land. They did not actually infringe the feudal rights of the lord to try actions relating to the title to the freeholds of his tenants. They did, however, become very popular because of their summary nature and were frequently used by dispossessed owners to recover *seisin*, since the opponent rarely took any further action if his claim was weak.

The fifth factor accounting for the usurpation of jurisdiction by the King's court was the expansion of the 'King's Peace' (the monarch's as opposed to a lord's right to deal with any local disorder, crime, etc). Pleas of the Crown increased rapidly at this time and included many claims that would eventually evolve into torts.

Finally, Pollock and Maitland mention the important series of writs which began with the word *praecipe*, where the sheriff was commanded to investigate a matter and give any wrongdoer the right to give satisfaction, or else face the royal judges for their judgment. This was among the Pleas of the Crown and again quickly became quite popular on account of its efficiency.

Kiralfy (in *English Legal History*, 1958) has advanced another factor significant in the acquisition of jurisdiction by the royal courts, namely, the construction given to the **Statute of Gloucester 1278** by the royal judges. This statute provided that no cases involving an amount of less than 40 shillings should be brought in the royal courts, but that they should be tried before local tribunals. The judges interpreted this to mean that no personal actions to recover a sum greater than 40 shillings could be commenced in the local courts, thus reserving all important legislation for themselves. It is relevant here that the judges were anxious to attract litigants because their fees varied with the amount of business done.

Apart from the advantageous nature of the remedy in the recovery of land provided by the Petty Assizes, the growth in popularity of the royal courts is connected with the progressive move towards strong, centralised government and its accompanying ability to compel attendance at court and enforce execution of its judgments. By contrast, we can look at the diminution in power of the feudal lords, their dilatory procedures and the inadequate powers to make defendants appear in their courts and to enforce judgments. Additionally, only the royal courts could give litigants the novel and desirable method of proof, the *recognitio* or jury, as it came to be called.

In conclusion, it can be seen that although Henry II was instrumental in making a number of important innovations which promoted the development of the common law, these policies were part of a wide and complex struggle for the power and revenue to be enjoyed by whoever controlled and administered justice. There were many other important figures involved, such as the clerics, the judges and the writers, whose own behaviour and interests it is important to appreciate in developing a proper understanding of the origins of the common law.

Question 3

Why was the development of equity necessary? Did equity satisfy those needs?

Answer plan

In response to this question, you should:
- define the concept of equity;
- outline the origins of the system of equity;
- examine defects in the common law: expense, delay, corruption, single remedy, etc;
- note trusts;
- note the advantages of equity – no formality, enforceable judgments, mobility of court, varied remedies, etc;
- include some mention of the 1873–75 legislation;
- comment on the irony of modern equity being slow and rule-bound.

Answer

In his *Nicomachean Ethics*, Aristotle argued that law operates through general rules in the pursuit of justice and is thus imperfect because it will fail to deal fairly with all eventualities. It is impossible for those who draft law to anticipate the infinite variety of circumstances which could arise in the future. Thus, if we are to have justice, we must use not simply a system of rules but also a power to depart from the rules in certain cases. Aristotle referred to *epieikia*, 'equity' as it was later known in its English form, as the absolute justice which corrects law in particular cases. In the light of the many problems encountered by litigants at common law, and the concerns of many Chancery personalities, equity developed to 'soften and mollify the extremity of the law': *per* Lord Ellesmere in *The Earl of Oxford's Case* (1615).

The establishment of the common law courts in the early medieval period did not represent the full extent of the Crown's jurisdiction. The monarch as the 'fountain of justice' retained a residuary power 'to do equal and right justice and discretion in mercy and truth' (Coronation Oath). The King received many petitions for justice from dissatisfied litigants and, by the fourteenth century, there were so many that they were being dealt with by the King's Council. By the end of the century, most were being sent directly to the Chancellor, the most senior officer of the Council.

The Chancery originated as the royal secretariat (its name comes from the chancel or latticed screen behind which the clerks worked) and the Chancellor was responsible for authenticating writs in ordinary cases. The earliest judicial work in Chancery was concerned with settling disputes within the department. Petitions to the King for legal redress against the Crown also began here. These proceedings were recorded in Latin, but it was the so-called 'English side' of Chancery, which grew to meet the more mundane needs of litigants, that hatched the Court of Chancery.

By the late fourteenth century, the Chancellor was dealing with a high number of petitions which could not properly be heard on the 'Latin side' of Chancery. By 1460, the Court of Chancery was as established as the common law courts. The ordinary ways of obtaining justice were not feasible options for many prospective litigants because they were too poor to afford the expensive process entailed in an action through the Court of Common Pleas. The claimant had to take care that the writ he chose was the appropriate one and that all the particulars were correct, otherwise the case might be lost as a result of the procedural defect.

A greater problem was that the common law only provided the remedy of damages, whereas a claimant might really wish for the defendant to desist from carrying out some activity (for example, a nuisance) or force him to carry out an obligation (for example, to sell a particular area of land). Additionally, the common law did not recognise simple breaches of common law as actionable. Actions for breaches of agreement could only be brought if they could be framed as writs for debt or detinue (wrongful detention of another's goods). The common law courts did not recognise actions for breaches of contract *per se*.

Local corruption also thwarted many claims. There is even evidence, mentioned by Baker (in *An Introduction to English Legal History*, 1971), that some supplicants complained of witchcraft.

The common law had been quite well developed and was, as Simpson has argued, passed down as an essentially oral tradition amongst a very small legal profession (not many more than 50 judges and important lawyers in about 1450). This group, however, had a very conservative conception of law. The response of the common law to the development of trusts, for example, illustrates how its conservatism led to the need for equity. The practice of making trusts (for example, a father giving property to two trusted friends to hold, on trust, for his son until the son reached a certain age) was becoming more popular by the end of the fourteenth century, especially amongst those who were going off to battle and were uncertain of whether they would return. The common law courts, though, did not recognise such an arrangement. The property had been given to the trustees and it was theirs, thought the common law, to do with as they pleased. The intended beneficiary, the son, could have no legal remedy if the trustees abused their position. The Chancellor could, and did, act in such circumstances to order the trustees to fulfil the trust reposed in them.

The law was no respecter of persons and afforded no justice to those who came a cropper of a technicality. By contrast, equity acts *in personam*, that is, it is concerned with the conscience of the individual. In one fifteenth-century case, Fortescue CJ rebuked counsel for advancing a legal point: 'We are here to argue conscience not the law!'

There were, principally, two theoretical justifications used by the Chancellors who developed the doctrines of equity. The first was that they were administering not law, but *conscience*. Thus, those who abused their position as trustee or who sought to take an unconscionable advantage of another's mistake in a contract were corrected by equity. In the fifteenth century, the Chancellor's court was called a court of conscience. The use of the term 'equity' in this context, and its Aristotelian meaning, became more popular in the sixteenth century.

There were great advantages in the early forms of Chancery action. Unlike the actions at common law, the petition required no formality and the *subpoena* which was issued was much more effective than the common law *capias*. The former commanded the respondent to appear in Chancery and answer the petition under a fixed pain, often £100. There were none of the sort of problems involved at common law, where litigants were defeated by errors on the face of the writ because no cause of *subpoena* was stated on the petition. The hearings were not hampered by rules of evidence like those which required debts to be proven with deeds, and the Chancellor – who acted without a jury – could take evidence from the parties themselves. Unlike the common law courts, Chancery was not in a fixed place and followed the Chancellor. The court could even convene in his private house. A number of discretionary remedies were developed by Chancery. Specific performance was an order to compel a defendant to perform a specified activity, usually involving the sale of land. The injunction was an order used to prevent defendants from taking some specified action.

By the sixteenth century, the distinct approaches and procedures of law and equity had become clear. Law was concerned with a body of rules applicable to certain facts, whereas the Chancellor was concerned with individual cases which were dealt with according to the dictates of 'conscience'. Equity was consolidated during the seventeenth and eighteenth centuries, but difficulties were still experienced by litigants who had to seek legal and equitable remedies in separate courts. This could be problematic (slow and expensive), where a case required consideration from both legal and equitable perspectives. The administration of law and equity was achieved through the **Judicature Acts 1873–75**, after which equity could be obtained in any division of the High Court.

It was a problem for equity that, on the one hand, its justice flowed from its not being a rule-bound system, but one operating on discretion whilst, on the other hand, uncontrolled discretion could itself become oppressive by its unpredictability. Conscience varied from man to man. It was Selden (in *A Brief Discourse Touching the Office of Lord Chancellor of England*, 1617) who remarked that if the measure of equity was the Chancellor's conscience, then one might as well make the standard measure of one foot the Chancellor's foot. Chancellors began to give reasons for their decisions in the seventeenth century and these were reported and gradually formed into a set of rules. Some maxims of equity were published in 1727 by Richard Francis, and have been relied on by courts ever since. They include the propositions 'he who comes to equity must have clean hands'; 'equity is equality'; 'equity does nothing in vain'; and 'equity regards the substance not the form'. However, the improved system of reporting during the eighteenth century helped a system of equity precedents to develop and by then, as Baker puts it, *rigor aequitatis* had set in. It is an irony of legal history that as equity developed, it became less discretionary and was often as rigid as law.

Not long after its emergence, the Court of Chancery, with its cheap, quick and effective procedures, became attractive to the wealthy as well as the poor. Avery (in 'The history of the equitable jurisdiction of the Court of Chancery before 1460' (1969)) has shown that between 1432 and 1450, the total number of petitions to the court increased sixfold and over 90 per cent of the cases were, by this time, disputes about land.

From the seventeenth century, Chancery became notorious for delay and expense, a theme given a wonderfully biting and humorous exposure in Dickens' *Bleak House*. The court was insufficiently staffed with judges and had no effective appeal system. Estimates of cases pending in Chancery at this time went as high as 20,000. Some cases were still pending after 30 years. The court was also plagued with corruption. Gifts of gold or silver to court officials could often expedite proceedings and, by long usage, many of the gifts became 'fees' which could be demanded as of right. Fees could be demanded at each distinct stage of the proceedings, so Masters procured rules of court which extended court cases beyond any reasonable length.

What had begun as a system based on speed, cheapness, informality and a concern to assist the poor had collapsed by the nineteenth century into an incredibly protracted, rule-bound, expensive system for the wealthy.

This irony can, however, be overstated. There were several more positive contributions made by equity to the legal system. Its discretionary remedies of the injunction and specific performance, the law of trusts and the equity of redemption should all be cited in this regard.

Question 4

What is legislation? Where does it come from, how is it produced and what does it do?

Answer plan

This is a wide-ranging question that requires a fairly close knowledge of the workings of Parliament. A suggested structure is as follows:

- distinguish statute law from judge-made common law;
- consider where the actual proposals for legislation come from – for example, government policy, Green Papers, White Papers;
- mention the limited scope for individual MPs to generate legislation;
- set out the actual process that legislation has to pass through to be enacted;
- make reference to the various types of legislation, emphasising the role of delegated legislation; mention should also be made of the potential impact of the **Human Rights Act (HRA) 1998**.

Answer

Although the courts retain an essential function in the interpretation of statutes, it has to be recognised that legislation is the predominant form of law making in contemporary times. The process through which an Act is passed by Parliament is itself a long one, but before concentrating on that process, some attention should be focused on the pre-Parliamentary process through which the substantive content of the Act is generated.

Sources of legislation

There are various sources of legislative proposals.

The majority arise from government departments, in pursuit of their policies in relation to their allocated area of responsibility. Actual policy will, of course, be a consequence of the political persuasion and imperatives of the government of the day and as, by convention, the Government is drawn from the majority party, it can effectively decide what legislation is to be enacted through its control over the day to day procedure of the House of Commons, backed by its majority voting power. The decision as to which Bills are to be placed before Parliament in any session is under the effective control of a cabinet committee known as the Legislation Committee, which draws up the legislative programme announced in the Queen's Speech, delivered at the opening of the Parliamentary session.

In some cases, the Government will set out its tentative plans for legislation in the form of a Green Paper and will invite interested parties to comment on the proposals. After considering any response, the Government may publish a second document, in the form of a White Paper, in which it sets out its firm proposals for legislation.

If the Government is the source of most legislation, the role of the individual MP, acting through the process for the enactment of Private Member's Bills, should not be forgotten. There are, in fact, three ways in which an individual MP can propose legislation. These are through the ballot procedure, by means of which backbench MPs get the right to propose legislation on the 10 or so Fridays specifically set aside to consider such proposals, under Standing Order 39 and under the 10-minute rule procedure. Of these procedures, however, only the first has any great chance of success and, even then, success will depend on securing a high place in the ballot and, in practice, must not incur government disapproval. If such a proposal is looked upon with favour by the Government, it has an especially good chance of being enacted, since the Government may provide additional time to allow it to complete its passage. Perhaps the most famous Private Member's Bills have related to the provision of abortion. The original **Abortion Act 1967** was introduced by the Liberal MP David Steel, and has been subject to numerous attempts to amend it by further Private Member's Bills.

Alternative sources for proposed legislation are the recommendations of independent commissions and committees, such as the Law Commission, or the Law Reform Committee, which considers alterations in the civil law, and the Criminal Law Reform Committee, which performs similar functions in relation to the criminal law.

It is always open to pressure groups to lobby political parties and individual MPs in an attempt to have their particular interests made concrete in legislation. However, some concern has been expressed at the growing number of professional lobbyists who are paid to make sure that their clients' cases are prominently placed before the appropriate people within the legislature.

The legislative process

Before any legislative proposal (known at that stage as a Bill) can become an Act of Parliament, it must proceed through, and be approved by, both Houses of

Parliament and must receive the Royal Assent. A Bill must be given three readings in both the House of Commons and the House of Lords before it can be presented for the Royal Assent. It is possible to commence the procedure in either House, although 'money Bills' (containing only financial provisions) must be placed before the Commons in the first instance.

When a Bill is introduced in the Commons, it undergoes five distinct procedures:

(a) it receives its first reading. This is purely a formal procedure in which its title is read and a date set for its second reading;
(b) after this comes the second reading; this is the time when its general principles are subject to extensive debate. The second reading is the critical point in the process of a Bill. At the end, a vote may be taken on its merits and if it is approved, it is likely that it will eventually find a place in the statute book;
(c) if the Bill passes its second reading, it is sent for consideration by a standing committee which will consider its provisions in detail. The function of the standing committee, which, if it is successfully proposed, may be replaced by a Select Committee or committee of the whole House, is to go through the Bill clause by clause and to amend it to bring it into line with the general approval given by the House at its second reading;
(d) the next stage is the report stage, at which the standing committee reports the Bill back to the House for the consideration of any amendments made by it;
(e) the final stage in the process is the third reading, during which further debate may take place, although on this occasion, it is restricted strictly to matters relating to the content; matters relating to general principles cannot be raised.

When a Bill has passed all these stages, it is passed to the House of Lords for its consideration, which is essentially similar, if less constrained by the pressures of time. After consideration by the Lords, the Bill is passed back, with any amendments, to the Commons, which must then consider such amendments. Where one House refuses to agree to the amendments made by the other, Bills can be repeatedly passed between them, but it should be remembered that Bills must complete their passage within the life of a particular parliamentary session and that a failure to reach agreement within that period might lead to the total loss of the Bill. Given the fact that the House of Lords is a non-elected institution and that the Members of the House of Commons are the democratically elected representatives of the voters, it has been apparent since 1911 that the House of Lords should not be in a position to block the clearly expressed wishes of the Commons. The **Parliament Act** of that year and of 1949 restricted the blocking power of the Lords. The situation now is that a money Bill can be enacted without the approval of the House of Lords after only one month's delay and any other Bill can only be delayed by one year by the House of Lords' recalcitrance.

The most recent use of the **Parliament Acts** occurred in relation to the **Hunting**

Act 2004, which in turn led to the Court of Appeal's determination of the legality of the later **Parliament Act**, which itself was introduced through the earlier **Act of 1911**. In *R (on the application of Jackson) v Attorney-General* (2005) the Court of Appeal concluded that the **1949 Act** was properly introduced and consequently the **Hunting Act** could not be challenged. However, the Court of Appeal also suggested that the **1949 Act** might not be capable of being used to introduce major constitutional reforms, such as completely doing away with the House of Lords, for example.

Subsequently an augmented nine-member panel of the House of Lords unanimously held that the reasoning of the Court of Appeal could not be sustained. In reaching that conclusion the House of Lords rejected the argument that the **Parliament Act of 1911** was an exercise in the *delegation* of powers from Parliament to the House of Commons, which could not later be used to extend those powers. Rather as Lord Bingham stated:

> The overall object of the 1911 **Act** was not to delegate power: it was to restrict, subject to compliance with the specified statutory conditions, the power of the Lords to defeat measures supported by a majority of the Commons . . .

The House of Lords, however, did differ in their assessment of the extent of the power extended to the House of Commons under the **Parliament Acts**. It is clear that a majority of the House of Lords were of the view that the House of Commons could use the powers given to it under the **Parliament Acts** to force through such legislation as it wished, but a number of the judges were of the view that the Commons could not extend its own lifetime through such a procedure, as that would be in direct contradiction to the provisions of the **Parliament Act 1911**.

No statute becomes law unless it has received the Royal Assent and although in the unwritten constitution of the UK, no specific rule expressly states that the monarch has to assent to any Act passed by Parliament, there is, by now, a convention to that effect and any monarch would place their constitutional status in extreme jeopardy by a refusal to grant the Royal Assent to legislation passed by Parliament. The procedural nature of the Royal Assent was highlighted by the **Royal Assent Act 1967**, which reduced the process of acquiring Royal Assent to a formal reading out of the short titles of any Act in both Houses of Parliament.

An Act of Parliament comes into effect on the date of the Royal Assent, unless there is any provision to the contrary in the Act itself. It is quite common for newly enacted statutes to contain commencement clauses which provide for the Act to become operational at some date in the future. Difficulty and an inevitable lack of certainty is produced, however, by the now common occurrence of passing general enabling Acts which delegate powers to a government minister to introduce specific parts of the Acts in question at some later date, through the means of statutory instruments.

Types of legislation

There are two distinct types of legislation: the public Act and the private Act. The former relates to questions which affect the general public, whereas the latter relates to the powers and interests of particular individuals or institutions. Public Bills can be further categorised into government Bills and Private Member's Bills, to which reference has already been made.

Acts of Parliament can also be distinguished on the basis of their function. Some are designed to initiate new legislation to cover new areas of activity, previously not governed by legal rules, but other Acts are aimed at rationalising or amending existing legislative provisions. Examples of the latter type of legislation are the consolidating Act and the codifying Act. The purpose of any consolidating Act is to bring together the various statutory provisions contained in a number of discrete pieces of legislation, without altering them, for the main part. Company law is a classic example of this procedure, in that it has evolved through the enactment of numerous Acts of Parliament which have, every so often, been brought together under one large consolidating Act. The **Companies Act 1985** is just such an Act, although it is arguable that a new consolidation Act is due in the light of the subsequent changes that the **1985 Act** has undergone since it was passed.

Codifying Acts seek not just to bring existing statutory provisions under one Act, but also look to give statutory expression to common law rules. The classic examples of such legislation are to be found in the commercial sector; amongst them are the **Partnership Act 1890** and the **Sale of Goods Act 1893**.

The HRA 1998

Traditionally, by virtue of the operation of the doctrine of Parliamentary sovereignty, Parliament could pass whatever laws it thought proper, without the courts being able to challenge the legality of such legislation. Although the **HRA 1998** has not directly challenged this relationship, it has nonetheless altered it significantly. Even where a court holds that a piece of primary legislation does not comply with the provisions of the **ECHR**, that court cannot declare the legislation invalid: the court has no such power to strike down primary legislation. However, the court can issue a declaration of incompatibility stating that the Act breaches the provisions of the Convention (see, for example, *Bellinger v Bellinger* (2003)). Although changing the incompatible Act remains solely the power of Parliament, it is highly likely that a judicial declaration of incompatibility would lead to an alteration of the Act in question. The **HRA 1998** provides for a fast-track procedure for changing any Act subsequently found to be in breach of the Convention.

Question 5

What do you understand by 'delegated legislation'? Consider its advantages and disadvantages and explain how it is controlled by Parliament and the courts.

Answer plan

This question focuses more closely than the previous one on delegated legislation. It is suggested that the increased importance of delegated legislation makes it a likely question topic. A good answer plan will do the following:

- give an explanation of what is meant by delegated legislation;
- emphasise the large amount of delegated legislation that is produced annually;
- provide examples of the various types of delegated legislation;
- list and consider in some detail the various advantages and disadvantages;
- mention Parliamentary scrutiny of delegated legislation;
- consider the powers of the courts to control delegated legislation, through judicial review and under the **Human Rights Act (HRA) 1998**;
- weigh the advantages and disadvantages and offer a conclusion in favour or against its use.

Answer

Modern legislation tends to be of the enabling type, which simply states the general purpose and aims of the Act and lays down a broad framework, whilst delegating to ministers of the state the power to produce detailed provisions in pursuit of those general aims.

Generally speaking, delegated legislation is law made by some person or body to whom Parliament has delegated its general law-making power. In statistical terms, it is arguable that at present, delegated legislation is actually more significant than primary Acts of Parliament. The output of delegated legislation in any year greatly exceeds the output of Acts of Parliament and each year there are over 3,000 sets of rules and regulations made in the form of delegated legislation, compared to fewer than 100 public Acts of Parliament.

Any piece of delegated legislation has the same legal force and effect as the Act of Parliament under which it is enacted, but equally only has effect to the extent that it is authorised by its enabling Act.

Delegated legislation can take the form of Orders in Council which permit the Government, through the Privy Council, to make law. The Privy Council is nominally a non-party political body of eminent Parliamentarians, but in effect, it is simply a means through which the Government, in the form of a committee of ministers, can introduce legislation without the need to go through the full Parliamentary process. Although legal textbooks tend to use situations of state emergency as exemplifying occasions when the Government will resort to the use of Orders in Council, in actual fact, a great number of Acts are brought into operation through these provisions. Perhaps the widest scope for Orders in Council is to be found in relation to EU law, for under s 2(2) of the **European Communities Act 1972**, ministers can give effect to provisions of the Community which do not have direct effect.

Statutory instruments are the means through which government ministers introduce particular regulations under powers delegated to them by Parliament by enabling legislation. As with Orders in Council, such provisions do not have to undergo the full rigour of Parliamentary procedure involved in the passing of Acts of Parliament. The relative and, indeed, the absolute importance of statutory instruments can be seen by the fact that in 2004, Parliament enacted 3,459 statutory instruments, as compared to only 38 general public Acts. There is such a range of powers delegated to ministers and such a range of Acts of Parliament which are given practical effect by statutory instruments, that it is almost pointless to give examples, but it is certainly worth pointing out that such regulations tend to be of a highly specific and technical nature. One example of the way in which statutory instruments were used, if not abused, may be found in the **Limited Liability Partnership Act 2000**. Although the Act established this new form of legal entity, it stated very little about how it was to operate and be regulated. **Sections 14 and 15 of the Act** simply stated that appropriate regulations would be made in the future and introduced through statutory instruments (the **Limited Liability Partnership Regulations 2001**).

Bylaws are the third type of delegated legislation, by means of which local authorities and public bodies are empowered by Parliament to make legally binding rules within their area of authority. Bylaws may be made by local authorities under such enabling legislation as the **Local Government Act 1972**.

In addition to the foregoing, the various Court Rule Committees are empowered to make the rules which govern procedure in the particular courts over which they have delegated authority, under such Acts as the **Supreme Court Act 1981**, the **County Courts Act 1984** and the **Magistrates' Courts Act 1980**.

The final source of delegated legislation is to be found in the power given to certain professional bodies to regulate the conduct of their members. An example of this type of delegated legislation is the power that the Law Society has been granted under the **Solicitors Act 1974** to control the conduct of practising solicitors.

Parliament delegates its law-making powers for a number of reasons. Amongst these is the fact that it simply does not have the time to consider every detail that might be required to fill out the framework of enabling legislation. A related point is the fact that given the highly specialised and extremely technical nature of many of the regulations that are introduced through delegated legislation, the majority of MPs simply do not have sufficient expertise or the technical knowledge to consider such provisions effectively.

These reasons why there has been an increased reliance on delegated legislation also suggest its potential advantages over the more traditional set-piece public Acts. For example, the fact that Parliament does not have to spend its time considering the minutiae of specific regulations permits it to focus its attention more closely, and at greater length, on the broader but no less important matters of principle in relation to the enactment of general enabling legislation. The use of delegated legislation also permits far greater flexibility in regulation, permitting rules to be changed quickly in response to changes in the situations they are aimed at regulating. It can also be appreciated that the use of delegated legislation not only permits an *ad hoc* response, but also a quicker response to emergencies or unforeseen problems. With regard to bylaws, it practically goes without saying that local and specialist knowledge should give rise to more appropriate rules than reliance on the general enactments of Parliament.

There are, however, distinct disadvantages in the prevalence of delegated legislation as a means of making legal rules. The most important of these relates to a perceived erosion in the constitutional role of Parliament, to the extent that it does not actually consider provisions made in this way. To the extent that Parliament, as a body, is disempowered, other people, notably government ministers and the civil servants who work under them in order to produce the detailed provisions of delegated legislation, are given more power than might be thought constitutionally correct. The foregoing, which inevitably involves the question of general accountability and the need for effective scrutiny, is compounded by the difficulty which ordinary MPs face in keeping abreast of the sheer mass of technically detailed legislation that is enacted in this form. Also, the point must be raised that if Parliamentarians cannot keep up with the flow of delegated legislation, how can the general public be expected to do so?

These difficulties and potential shortcomings in the use of delegated legislation are, at least to a degree, mitigated by the fact that specific controls exist in relation to it. These controls are twofold: Parliamentary and judicial. Parliament exercises general control, to the extent that ministers are always responsible to Parliament for the regulations they actually make within the powers delegated to them by Parliament. Additionally, it is a usual requirement that such regulations be laid before Parliament. This laying before Parliament can take two forms, depending on the provision of the enabling legislation. The majority of Acts simply require that regulations made under their auspices be placed before Parliament and automatically become law after a period of 40 days, *unless a resolution to annul them is passed*. Other regulations, on the other hand, require a positive resolution of one or both of the Houses of Parliament before they become law. Also, since 1973, there has been a Joint Select Committee on Statutory Instruments, whose function is to consider statutory instruments. It has to be remembered, however, that this committee merely scrutinises statutory instruments from a technical point of view as regards drafting, and therefore has no power as regards any question of policy in the regulation.

Previously, judicial control of delegated legislation was limited, but not unimportant. It was always possible for delegated legislation to be challenged, through the procedure of judicial review, on the basis that the person or body to whom Parliament has delegated its authority has acted in a way that exceeds the limited powers delegated to them. Any provision found to be outside this authority was *ultra vires* and consequently void. Additionally, there is a presumption that any power delegated by Parliament is to be used in a reasonable manner and the courts may, on occasion, hold particular delegated legislation to be void on the basis that it is unreasonable. The **HRA 1998** fundamentally alters the courts' power over delegated legislation. As secondary legislation, rather than primary legislation such as Acts of Parliament, delegated legislation may be declared ineffective by the courts where it is found not to comply with the provisions of the **HRA 1998**, so ministers must be extremely careful to ensure that any delegated legislation is in fact compatible with the **ECHR**. An example of the courts quashing secondary legislation can be seen in *A v Secretary of State for the Home Department* (2005), in which the House of Lords quashed a derogation order wrongly made in relation to the **Anti-terrorism Crime and Security Act 2001**.

Question 6

The English legal system can no longer be considered on its own, but has to be understood within the context of the European Union and its institutions.

What are the institutions referred to and what is their impact on the English legal system?

Answer plan

Again, it has to be emphasised that the English legal system can only be understood in the context of the EU. This straightforward question ensures that a candidate is at least aware of that context. Such an awareness can be shown by covering the following points:

- a short history of the EU – consideration of its present status and, perhaps, its future;

- a detailed account of the various types of EU legislation, that is, treaties, regulations and directives, and how they are each brought into effect;
- a description of the essential institutions of the EU and their relationships and particular roles and functions;
- a focus on the relationship between the ECJ and the domestic courts of the UK, with examples where possible.

Answer

The EC was set up by the **EEC Treaty** (later re-named the **EC Treaty**) in 1957, and the UK joined the Community in 1973.

On joining the Community, now called the European Union, the UK and its citizens became subject to EC law. This subjection to European law remains the case, even where the parties to any transaction are themselves both UK subjects. In other words, in areas where it is applicable, European law supersedes any existing UK law to the contrary.

Community law consists primarily of the **EC Treaty** and any amending legislation such as the **Single European Act (SEA)** to which the UK acceded in 1986, the **Maastricht Treaty 1992** and the **Treaty of Nice 2001**.

The **EC Treaty**, as subsequently amended, provides for two types of legislation: regulations and directives:

(a) Regulations under **Art 249** (formerly **Art 189**) of the **EC Treaty** apply to, and within, member states generally without the need for those states to pass their own legislation. They are binding and enforceable, therefore, from the time of their creation within the European context and need no further validation by national Parliaments.

(b) Directives, on the other hand, are in theory supposed to state general goals and leave the precise implementation to individual member states in the form that they consider appropriate. In practice, however, directives tend to state the means, as well as the ends, to which they are aimed and the ECJ will give direct effect to directives which are sufficiently clear and complete.

The major institutions of the EU are: the Council; the European Parliament; the Economic and Social Committee; the Commission; and the ECJ.

The Council

The Council is made up of ministerial representatives of each of the 27 member states of the Union. Thus, when considering economic matters, the various states will be represented by their finance ministers or, if the matter relates to agriculture, the various agricultural ministers will attend. The Council of Ministers is, in essence, the supreme organ of the EU and, as such, it has the final say in deciding upon Community legislation. Although it acts on recommendations and proposals made to it by the Commission, it does have the power to instruct the Commission to undertake particular investigations and to submit detailed proposals for its consideration.

The European Parliament

The European Parliament is the directly elected European institution and, to that extent, it can be seen as the body which exercises democratic control over the operation of the EU. As in national Parliaments, Members are elected to represent constituencies, the elections being held every five years. Membership is divided amongst the 27 member states in proportion to the size of their various populations. The Parliament's general secretariat is based in Luxembourg and although the Parliament sits in plenary session in Strasbourg for one week in each month, its detailed and preparatory work is carried out through 18 permanent committees which usually meet in Brussels.

The powers of the European Parliament, however, should not be confused with those of national Parliaments, for the European Parliament is not a legislative institution and, in that respect, it plays a subsidiary role to the Council of Ministers. Originally, its powers were merely advisory and supervisory.

In pursuance of its advisory function, the Parliament always had the right to comment on the proposals of the Commission and, since 1980, the Council has been required to wait for the Parliament's opinion before adopting any law. In its supervisory role, the Parliament scrutinises the activities of the Commission and has the power to remove the Commission by passing a motion of censure against it by a two-thirds majority.

The legislative powers of the Parliament were substantially enhanced by the **SEA 1986**. Since that enactment, it has had a more influential role to play, particularly in relation to the completion of the internal market. For one thing, it can now negotiate directly with the Council as to any alterations or amendments it wishes to see in proposed legislation. It can also intervene to question and, indeed, to alter any 'joint position' adopted by the Council on proposals put to it by the Commission. If the Council then insists on pursuing its original 'joint position', it can only do so on the basis of unanimity.

The **SEA 1986** also requires the European Parliament's assent to any international agreements to be entered into by the Community. As a consequence, it has ultimate control, not just in relation to trade treaties, but also as regards any future expansion of the Union's membership.

The Commission

The Commission is the executive of the EU, but it also has a vital part to play in the legislative process. To the extent that the Council can only act on proposals put before it by the Commission, the latter institution has a duty to propose to the Council measures that will advance the achievement of the Union's general policies.

Another of the key functions of the Commission is the implementation of the policies of the Union and to that end, it controls the allocation of funds to the various common programmes within the Union. It also acts, under instructions from the Council, as negotiator between the Union and external countries.

A further executive role of the Commission is to be found in the manner in which it operates to ensure that Treaty obligations between states are met and that Community laws relating to individuals are enforced. In order to fulfil these functions, the Commission has been provided with extensive powers, both in relation to the investigation of potential breaches of Community law and the subsequent punishment of offenders. The classic area in which these powers can be seen in operation is competition law. Under **Arts 85** and **86** of the **EC Treaty**, the Commission has substantial powers to investigate and control potential monopolies and anti-competitive behaviour and it has used these powers to levy what, in the case of private individuals, would amount to huge fines where breaches of Community competition law have been discovered. For example, in 2004 Microsoft were fined 497m euro. If the individual against whom a finding has been made objects to either the result of the investigation or the penalty imposed, the course of appeal is to the ECJ.

The Court of Justice

The ECJ is the judicial arm of the EU and, in the field of Community law, its judgments overrule those of national courts. It consists of 27 judges, assisted by eight advocates general, and the Court sits in Luxembourg. The role of the advocates general is to investigate the matter submitted to the Court and to produce a report, together with a recommendation for the consideration of the Court. The actual court is free to accept the report, or not, as it sees fit.

The jurisdiction of the ECJ involves it in two key areas in particular:

(a) determining whether any measures adopted, or rights denied, by the Commission, Council or any national government are compatible with Treaty obligations. Such actions may be raised by any Union institution, government or individual. A member state may fail to comply with its Treaty obligations in a number of ways. It might fail or indeed refuse to comply with a provision of the Treaty or a regulation; alternatively, it might refuse to implement a directive within the allotted time provided. Under such circumstances, the state in question will be brought before the ECJ, either by the Commission or another member state or, indeed, individuals within the state, as being in dereliction of its responsibility;

(b) determining, at the request of national courts, the interpretation of points of Community law. This procedure can take the form of a preliminary ruling where the request precedes the actual determination of a case by the national court. The point that has to be remembered, however, is that it is the ECJ's role to determine such issues and in relation to those issues, it is superior to any national court.

The Court of First Instance

The **SEA 1986** was not without effect on the operation of the justice system in the Union, in that it provided for a new Court of First Instance to be attached to the existing Court of Justice. The jurisdiction of the Court of First Instance is limited mainly to internal claims by employees of the Union and to claims against fines made by the Commission under Community competition law. The aim is to reduce the burden of work on the Court of Justice, but there is a right of appeal, on points of law only, to the full Court of Justice.

Question 7

Explain the powers of the European Court of Justice (ECJ), paying particular regard to its relationship with UK courts.

Answer plan

Particular attention should be paid to the relationship of that court to the domestic courts within the UK. In answering it, students could usefully apply the following structure:

- detail the role and powers of the ECJ;
- describe its structure and how it operates, making some mention of the Court of First Instance;
- explain the way in which references can be made to the ECJ from domestic courts under **Art 234** (formerly **Art 177**);
- provide some examples of cases decided by the ECJ that have had particular impact on the UK.

Answer

The ECJ is the judicial arm of the EU and, in the field of Community law, its judgments overrule those of national courts. It consists of 27 judges, assisted by eight advocates general, and sits in Luxembourg. The role of the advocates general is to investigate the matter submitted to the Court and to produce a report, together with a recommendation for the consideration of the Court. The actual Court is free to accept the report or not, as it sees fit.

The **Single European Act 1986** provided for a new Court of First Instance to be attached to the existing ECJ. The jurisdiction of the Court of First Instance is limited mainly to internal claims by employees of the Community and to claims against fines made by the Commission under Community competition law. The aim is to reduce the burden of work on the ECJ, but there is a right of appeal, on points of law only, to the full ECJ.

The ECJ performs two key functions:

(a) It decides whether any measures adopted, or rights denied, by the Commission, Council or any national government are compatible with Treaty obligations. Such actions may be raised by any EU institution, government or individual. A member state may fail to comply with its Treaty obligations in a number of ways. It might fail or, indeed, refuse to comply with a provision of the Treaty or a regulation; alternatively, it might refuse to implement a directive within the allotted time provided for. Under such circumstances, the state in question will be brought before the ECJ, either by the Commission or another member state or, indeed, individuals within the state concerned.

(b) It provides authoritative rulings, at the request of national courts under **Art 234** (formerly **Art 177**) of the **EC Treaty**, on the interpretation of points of Community law. When an application is made under Art 234, the national proceedings are suspended until such time as the determination of the point in question is delivered by the ECJ. Whilst the case is being decided by the ECJ, the national court is expected to provide appropriate interim relief, even if this involves going against a domestic legal provision, as in *Factortame Ltd v Secretary of State for Transport (No 1)* (1989). The Common Fishing Policy established by the EEC had placed limits on the amount of fish that any member country's fishing fleet was permitted to catch. In order to gain access to British fish stocks and quotas, Spanish fishing boat owners formed British companies and reregistered their boats as British. In order to prevent what it saw as an abuse and an encroachment on the rights of indigenous fishermen, the British government introduced the **Merchant Shipping Act 1988**, which provided that any fishing company seeking to register as British would have to have its principal place of business in the UK and at least 75 per cent of its shareholders would have to be British nationals. This effectively debarred the Spanish boats from taking up any of the British fishing quota. Some 95 Spanish boat owners applied to the British courts for judicial review of the **Merchant Shipping Act 1988**, on the basis that it was contrary to Community law. The case went from the High Court, through the Court of Appeal, to the House of Lords which referred the case to the ECJ. There, it was decided that the **EC Treaty** required domestic courts to give effect to the directly enforceable provisions of Community law and, in doing so, such courts are required to ignore any national law that runs counter to Community law.

This procedure can take the form of a preliminary ruling where the request precedes the actual determination of a case by the national court. **Article 234** (formerly Art 177) provides that:

> The Court of Justice shall have jurisdiction to give preliminary rulings concerning:
> (a) the interpretation of treaties;
> (b) the validity and interpretation of acts of the institutions of the Union and of the European Central Bank;
> (c) the interpretation of the statutes of bodies established by an act of the Council, where those statutes so provide.
>
> Where such a question is raised before any court or tribunal of a member state, that court or tribunal may, if it considers that a decision on the question is necessary to enable it to give judgment, request the Court of Justice to give a ruling thereon.
>
> Where any such question is raised in a case pending before a court or tribunal of a member state against whose decision there is no judicial remedy under national law, that court or tribunal shall bring the matter before the Court of Justice.

It is clear that it is for the national court, and not the individual parties concerned, to make the reference. Where the national court or tribunal is not the 'final' court or tribunal, the reference to the ECJ is discretionary. Where the national court or tribunal is the 'final' court, then reference is obligatory. However, there are circumstances under which a 'final' court need not make a reference under **Art 234** (formerly Art 177). These are:

(a) where the question of Community law is not truly relevant to the decision to be made by the national court;

(b) where there has been a previous interpretation of the provision in question by the ECJ, so that its meaning has been clearly determined;

(c) where the interpretation of the provision is so obvious as to leave no scope for any reasonable doubt as to its meaning. This latter instance has to be used with caution given the nature of Community law; for example, the fact that it is expressed in several languages using legal terms which might have different connotations within different jurisdictions. However, it is apparent that where the meaning is clear, no reference need be made. In undertaking such a task, a purposive and contextual approach is mainly adopted, as against the more restrictive methods of interpretation favoured in relation to UK domestic legislation. The clearest statement of this purposive contextualist approach adopted by the ECJ is contained in its judgment in the *CILFIT* case:

> Every provision of Community law must be placed in its context and interpreted in the light of the provisions of Community law as a whole, regard being had to the objectives thereof and to its state of evolution at the date on which the provision in question is to be applied.
>
> *CILFIT Srl v Minister of Health (No 283/81)* (1982).

Another major difference between the ECJ and courts within the English legal system is that the former is not bound by the doctrine of precedent in the same way as the latter are. It is always open to the ECJ to depart from its previous decisions where it considers it appropriate to do so. Although it will endeavour to maintain consistency, it has on occasion ignored its own previous decisions, as in *European Parliament v Council* (1990), where it recognised the right of the Parliament to institute an action against the Council.

The manner in which European law operates to control sex discrimination, through the Equal Treatment Directive, is of significant interest and in *Marshall v Southampton and West Hampshire AHA* (1993), a number of the points that have been considered above were highlighted. Ms Marshall had originally been required to retire earlier than a man in her situation would have been required to do. She successfully argued before the ECJ that such a practice was discriminatory and contrary to **Council Directive 76/207/EEC** on the equal treatment of men and women.

The present action related to the level of compensation she was entitled to as a consequence of this breach. UK legislation, the **Sex Discrimination Act 1975**, had set limits on the level of compensation that could be recovered for acts of sex discrimination. Marshall argued that the imposition of such limits was contrary to the **Equal Treatment Directive** and that in establishing such limits, the UK had failed to comply with the Directive.

The House of Lords referred the case to the ECJ under **Art 234** (formerly **Art 177**) and the latter determined that the rights set out in relation to compensation under **Art 6** of the Directive were directly effective, and that as the purpose of the Directive was to give effect to the principle of equal treatment, that could only be achieved by either reinstatement or the awarding of adequate compensation. The decision of the ECJ, therefore, overruled the financial limitations placed on sex discrimination awards and effectively overruled the domestic legislation.

Question 8

One of the hallmarks of an advanced society is that its laws should not only be just, but also that they be kept up to date and be readily accessible to all who are affected by them.

Law Commission, Proposals for English and Scottish Law Commissions, Cmnd 2573, 1965.

Consider the mechanisms and procedures for law reform in Britain in the light of the above quotation.

Answer plan

The quotation above refers to the Law Commission and although the question does, indeed, require an examination of the operation of the Law Commission, the temptation must be resisted to launch straight into such a consideration and other means of law reform must also be considered. The following structure avoids this possible error:

- Parliament enacts reforming legislation and this may be in pursuit of party political agendas, or may be the outcome of Private Member's Bills;
- judges may also alter law, especially the common law;
- both of these mechanisms are not unproblematic and the potential problems should be considered;
- reference should be made to Royal Commissions of inquiry, but the major focus of attention should be on the Law Commission;
- the creation, structure and procedure of the Law Commission should be considered in some detail.

Answer

At one level, law reform is either a product of Parliamentary or judicial activity. However, the enactment of new legislation or the statement of a novel *ratio* in a particular case are the end products of a complex process, and to focus on them, and to ignore the various procedures that led up to them, would be to diminish our understanding of the process of law reform.

Legislation is, by definition, the product of Parliament, but perhaps of more interest is the actual source or inspiration for any particular piece of reforming legislation. Any consideration of the legislative process must be placed in the context of the political nature of Parliament. Thus, a great deal of law reform can be seen as the implementation of party political policies. Examples of this type of legal reform include the changes in trade union law, education law and the financing of local services introduced by past Conservative administrations, as well as the present government's introduction of the **Human Rights Act (HRA) 1998** and its constitutional reforms in the areas of devolution and the House of Lords.

If Parliament tends to focus on narrow political issues, it nonetheless does have access to a wider consideration of law reform through various mechanisms. There is, first of all, the issuing of consultative Green Papers in which the government sets out its proposals for legislation and invites contributions from interested parties.

More formal advice may be provided through advisory standing committees such as the Law Reform Committee, established in 1952, which is charged with the task – in relation to the civil law – of considering what changes to such legal doctrines as may be referred to it by the Lord Chancellor are desirable. In relation to criminal law, the Criminal Law Revision Committee was established in 1959 to perform similar functions.

A further mechanism for considering the need for law reform in specific areas is the Royal Commission. Examples of such commissions include the Commission on Criminal Procedure (1980), which led to the enactment of the **Police and Criminal Evidence Act 1984**, and the Royal Commission on Criminal Justice (the Runciman Commission), which examined pre-trial procedure, the conduct of trials and the provision of redress in the case of alleged miscarriages of justice, reporting in 1993. Also, senior judges may be given the remit of investigating particular aspects of the legal system. The most important recent report of this nature was Lord Woolf's *Access to Justice*, which examined the operation of the procedures of the civil law system.

Lord Woolf's recommendations were subsequently given effect by the **Civil Procedure Act 1997** and the **Civil Procedure Rules 1998**. Lord Justice Sir Robin Auld undertook a corresponding examination of the criminal law system and Sir Andrew Leggatt reviewed the operation of the tribunal system.

The weakness in this panoply of committees and commissions is that they are all *ad hoc* bodies. Their remit is limited to the particular areas of concern that are put before them, and they do not have the power either to widen the ambit of their investigation or to initiate proposals for investigation and reform.

In relation to particular reforms, external pressure groups or interested parties may very often be the original driving force behind them; and, when individual MPs are fortunate enough to find themselves at the top of the ballot for Private Member's Bills, they may well also find themselves the focus of attention from such pressure groups proffering pre-packaged law reform proposals in their own particular areas of interest. The weakness, again, lies in the single issue, *ad hoc* nature of such proposals, at the expense of a general consideration of related issues.

Turning attention to the role of the judiciary, it is a matter of little contemporary controversy to recognise that judges have a potential power to create law. Indeed, it is at least arguable that the whole of the common law is a product of judicial creativity.

Given this potential to create law, it would seem equally obvious and uncontroversial to recognise that the judiciary also has a role to play in law reform. An example of this reforming power was evident in the recognition of the possibility of the crime of rape within marriage (see *R* (1991)). Whereas the common law had previously denied the possibility of such a crime being committed when the parties were married, both the Court of Appeal and the House of Lords held that a husband is not immune from prosecution for rape in relation to his wife.

In the above case, the court restricted itself to reforming common law rules and it is in that limited area that some of those who would recognise the power of the judiciary to reform the law would limit its operation. The argument is that as the judges created the common law, they can be left to reform it. There is an important corollary to this, however, that judges have no place in reforming statutory provisions. They may signal the ineffectiveness of such provisions and call for their repeal or reform, but it would be a usurpation of the legislature's function and power for the courts to engage in such general reform. Of course the introduction of the **HRA 1998** has increased the scope of the courts' power to interpret legislation in such a way as to make it compatible with the provisions of the **European Convention on Human Rights**, but there are limits to such powers (see *Re S* (2002)) and the courts are specifically denied the power to declare primary legislation unlawful. The courts can, however, issue a declaration of incompatibility which may well lead to the revision of the law in question by Parliament (see *Bellinger v Bellinger* (2003) and the subsequent **Gender Recognition Act 2004**).

However, if Parliament is overly concerned with particularities of law reform, and the judiciary is constitutionally and practically disbarred from reforming the law in other than an opportunistic and piecemeal basis, there still remains the need for some institution to concern itself generally with the question of law reform. That need is, at present, met by the Law Commission.

The Law Commission was established under the **Law Commission Act 1965**. It was set up under the auspices of Lord Gardiner LC, with the specific aim of improving the previous *ad hoc* consideration of law reform by charging it with the duty of keeping the law *as a whole* under review and making recommendations for its *systematic* reform. Under the **Act of 1965**, the Law Commission was constituted as an independent body with full-time members. It was given duties with regard to the revision and codification of the law, but its prime duty was, and remains, law reform.

The scope of the Commission is limited to those areas set out in its programme of law reform, but its ambit is not unduly restricted, as may be seen from the range of matters covered in its tenth programme, set out in June 2008. The seven new projects listed in the new programme relate to the following issues:

1. *Adult social care.* The stated aim of reviewing the law under which residential care, community care and support for carers is provided, with the ultimate aim of providing a coherent legal structure, preferably in the form of a single statute, for those services.
2. *Intestate succession and the Inheritance (Provision For Family And Dependants) Act 1975.* This project will involve a general review of the law of intestacy, and the legislation under which family members and dependants may apply to court for reasonable financial provision from the estate of a person who has died.
3. *Level crossings legislation.* This project will undertake a general review of the law relating to level crossings with a view to providing a modern legal structure for their regulation.
4. *Marital property agreements (pre-nuptial contracts).* Such agreements are not currently enforceable in the event of the spouses' divorce or the dissolution of the civil partnerships although courts may take them into consideration in deciding ancillary relief. This project will examine the status and enforceability of such agreements.
5. *Private rights of redress under Unfair Commercial Practices Directive.* Currently the regulations enacting the directive provide no private rights to consumers and breaches can only be enforced by administrative measures or through the criminal courts. This project will consider how far a private right of redress for unfair commercial practices would simplify and extend consumer law.
6. *Simplification of criminal law.* This project will look to identify offences which have ceased to perform any real function due to social changes, or which have been rendered redundant by the creation of new criminal offences, with a view to their abolition or repeal. It is recognised that such a simplification of the criminal law is a prerequisite for any attempt to codify the criminal law, which remains one of the essential goals of the Law Commission.
7. *Unfitness to plead and the insanity defence.* As the programme puts it:

> The current law is based on rules formulated in the first half of the nineteenth century when the science of psychiatry was in its infancy. Those rules are in need of reform. There are important unresolved issues which include the scope of a trial of the facts following a finding of unfitness to plead. In addition, there is a need to reconsider the relationship between automatism and insanity and that between diminished responsibility and insanity.

It is estimated that at any one time, there are some 25 law reform projects being actively considered by the Commission, and it only ever recommends reform after it has undertaken an extensive process of consultation with informed and/or interested parties. It is this process of general and disinterested consultation, as the basis for the formulation of a genuinely informed recommendation, which distinguishes the procedure of the Commission from the reforms of the judiciary and the partial reforms advocated by interested parties. Reference has already been made to the way in which the judges altered the common law rule relating to rape within marriage, but it is perhaps worthy of mention that the Law Commission had already issued a working paper, entitled *Rape Within Marriage* in 1990, and its report of the same name was issued in 1992 (Law Com No 205). The Commission continues to consider whether this particular matter, and other important related matters concerning the relationships of married couples, such as the question of compelling a wife to give evidence against her husband, should be subject to legislative reform. The point to be made is that judges can only change the common law with regard to the problem encapsulated in the case that comes before them: the Commission, on the other hand, is at liberty to consider all matters relating to a specific issue.

Annual reports list all Commission publications and, at the conclusion of a project, a report will be submitted to the Lord Chancellor and Parliament for their consideration and action. In its report covering 2005/06, its 40th anniversary year, the then chairman Sir Roger Toulson expressed some regret, not to say frustration, at the limited impact that the Commission could make in the area of law making and reform. As he stated:

> Today, as in 1965, our principal objective is to seek to achieve a body of law that is accessible to those who are affected by it. The task that faced our predecessors in 1965 was great, but the inexorable increase in the pace of legislation and the increasing readiness of government to seek legislative solutions to problems has made it much greater. In a legislative programme hat is so full of priority government measures, it is increasingly difficult for our work to find the time it needs to be made into law. We continue to be told that some reports issued more than 10 years ago will be implemented 'when Parliamentary time becomes available'. This is a source of very real concern to us. Our process is thorough, involving wide consultation and careful analysis.
>
> The public money spent on enabling us to help provide the citizen with laws that are understandable and relevant to the 21st century can only be justified if the government is able to find time to implement those proposals it accepts.

The Ninth Programme of law reform stated that the Commission would be marking its 40th Anniversary by implementing better means of conducting consultation exercises. As part of this drive, the Commission launched a web discussion forum where members of the public had the opportunity to post Tenth Programme consultation responses online and engage in dialogue with one another and the Commission.

During the 2006/07 period, as detailed in its annual report for that period, the Commission published reports on:

- renting homes;
- inchoate liability for assisting and encouraging crime;

- trustee exemption clauses;
- post-legislative scrutiny;
- termination of tenancies for tenant default;
- murder, manslaughter and infanticide.

CHAPTER 2

THE COURTS AND THE APPELLATE PROCESS

THE COURTS

A sound knowledge of the civil and criminal court structure is essential for a proper understanding of many aspects of the English legal system. You should be aware of the jurisdiction of each court (that is, which types of cases each court is competent to deal with), how its workload compares with other courts, how it is organised and what criticisms have been made of these features. The courts in question are the county courts, magistrates' courts, the Crown Court, the High Court, the Court of Appeal, the House of Lords and the Judicial Committee of the Privy Council.

The court system of 2008–9 is significantly different from that of 10 years earlier. It has undergone many changes to fit in more with the interests and conveniences of litigants and less with the interests of lawyers. In January, 2007, HM Courts Service published a new charter for the civil courts. It states that anyone telephoning a court between 9 am and 5 pm on a weekday will get a prompt and helpful answer. It also says that within 10 working days of a court receiving a letter, the sender will get a reply by letter or telephone.

In 1998, as part of a major reform programme, Lord Woolf said that costs were the most serious problem to be addressed, because problems arising from costs 'contaminate the whole civil justice system'. Many people had been deterred from proceeding with cases because of the possible costs, and others had been pressurised into settling their claims for sums lower than they deserve, for fear of costs escalating beyond their means.

The main reform objectives were:

- to encourage parties to explore alternatives to the resolution of a dispute by a court;
- to introduce a single set of rules governing proceedings in the High Court and the county courts;
- to reduce the time taken for cases to reach court, and the length of trials.

The thrust of the revised system is to give more control to judges in litigation and less influence to lawyers. Most litigants will first be directed to alternative dispute resolution, making court actions a last resort. Community Service funding is available for such settlements. There is a three-tier system: small claims (up to £5,000); a fast track for cases at the lower end of the scale; and a multi-track for the remaining cases. All cases where a defence is received will be examined by a procedural judge who will allocate the case to the appropriate track.

The court structure remains essentially the same, but heavier and more complex cases are concentrated at trial centres which have the resources needed, including specialist judges. Judges are now given 'hands on' management of cases, making decisions about the timetabling of the trial and the issues to be resolved. There are incentives to settle cases early and penalties for causing unnecessary delay, including the obligation for a litigant to be liable for interest rates of up to 25 per cent on top of costs. A litigant who makes an offer of settlement which is not accepted, but which is matched or exceeded at trial, is entitled to additional interest on his damages. There is a fast-track procedure, with a £2,500 limit on costs, for claims of between £3,000 and £10,000 (claims below £5,000 going to small claims courts). These fast-track cases are heard within 30 weeks of being brought and the hearings should not last longer than three hours. For claims over £10,000, and also for claims of less, but where the facts or law are especially complex, or where an issue of public importance is raised or oral evidence from experts is necessary, the cases will be managed by judges. These cases will have a standard fee for advocacy and will usually use written expert evidence, in contrast to today's norm of using expert testimony. Judges now also have the power to allocate the burden of costs at the end of a case by reference to the conduct of the parties.

The reforms have required funding in order to support new computer systems (for case management in the courts) and to retrain judges, but much of this money will come from savings achieved over time by the future early settlement of cases. The new civil process is designed to be co-ordinated with the development of the Community Legal Service.

In March 2007, the Government announced that the Home Office responsibilities would be split in two and much of its historic work would go to the Department for Constitutional Affairs. The announcement was made in a written statement to the House of Commons. The change became operative on May 9, 2007.

The Home Office retains its responsibilities for border control and immigration policy but prisons, the probation service, and sentencing policy has been handed to a new Ministry of Justice: the renamed Department for Constitutional Affairs.

With his expanded role, the Lord Chancellor became the Secretary of State for Justice and took charge of the Government's new National Offender Management System (NOMS), which is intended to join up the handling of offenders from the moment they are convicted, through probation to their eventual release and reintegration back into society.

THE COURTS AND THE APPELLATE PROCESS

The Home Office was founded in March 1782 as the Home Department. It was a large department and has been responsible for several serious errors in recent years. In 2002, a large backlog of applications for clearance built up after a poor launch of the Criminal Records Bureau whose establishment had cost £940 million. In 2004–05 the Home Office lost control of its finances and the National Audit Office refused to give it a seal of approval. Then, in 2006, 1,025 foreign prisoners were released without, as required, being considered for deportation. In the same year, the Prison Service ran out of places in jails. In 2007, it was disclosed that there was, waiting to be processed, a 27,500 backlog of files on British citizens convicted abroad.

The new Home Office will have responsibility for the police, the intelligence agency MI5, and the UK's borders. There will be an Immigration and Nationality Directorate with 16,000 employees, and an Identity Cards and Passport Service with 3,000 staff. The idea is to enable the Governmental response to terrorist threats to be better co-ordinated. The new Ministry of Justice will continue to have responsibility for the courts. It will also have responsibility for probation, criminal justice policy, sentencing, drugs and crime reduction. It will have a staff of 47,000 for prisons, and 1,300 for the National Offender Management Service. It remains to be seen, how far, if at all, these reforms will achieve improved efficiency or delivery of justice. There is clearly a danger in separating issues of immigration and terrorism away from the umbrella of the Ministry of Justice.

THE APPELLATE PROCESS

You should be familiar with:

- what rights of appeal exist and what conditions, if any, apply in relation to all courts (civil and criminal);
- the findings and recommendations of the Runciman Commission on Criminal Justice (1993) about criminal appeals;
- appeals procedure: what powers the appellate courts have;
- the systems for references to be made to the Court of Appeal (Criminal Division) by the Home Secretary and the Attorney-General;
- how the **Criminal Appeal Act 1995** changed the system of criminal appeals, and changes made from 1998 to the work of the Court of Appeal (Civil Division) as a result of the Bowman Report;
- the recommendations of the Royal Commission on Criminal Justice, under the chairmanship of Viscount Runciman, which reported in July 1993. Many of its 352 recommendations address matters relating to the courts, juries and the appellate process. Wherever appropriate, the relevant proposals have been incorporated into answers here;

- the findings and recommendations of the Auld Review of the Criminal Courts of England and Wales.

Question 9

State and explain in what circumstances the House of Lords can overrule one of its own previous decisions, and illustrate your answer with an example.

Answer plan

A good answer will:

- Set the historical and legal theory context, and say why the matter is important within the English legal system.
- Explain in some detail the provisions of the 1966 Practice Statement.
- Explain something of the meaning of the 1966 formula as given in subsequent case law like *Herrington v British Railways Board*.
- Illustrate the principle being used to change the law, for example in *Horton v Sadler* (2006).
- Conclude with some evaluation or appraisal of the power being used in this case, perhaps revisiting the essay's opening paragraph's coverage of the finality/flexibility issue, and examining that issue in relation to the case.

Answer

One expected quality of the court at the apex of a pyramidal court structure is finality of judgment. What is laid down as the law by such a court will be certain and reliable because there is no court above it to which a dissatisfied side can appeal for another decision on the law. The House of Lords for a long time would not overrule its earlier decisions even if they later seemed wrong. Since 1966, however, it has been able to overrule its earlier rulings. It seldom does so but did so in 2006, and thereby conduced to greater justice for litigants.

House of Lords' decisions are binding on all other courts in the legal system, except the House of Lords itself. The House of Lords was bound by its own previous decisions until it changed this practice in 1966. The historical practice of always sticking faithfully to whatever it had earlier ruled was the law had been established by the nineteenth century and was reaffirmed in a famous case in 1898 – *London Tramways Co Ltd v London County Council*.

However, this approach did not appear to create certainty and had become very rigid by the end of the nineteenth century. Several areas of law fossilised because rules laid down by the Lords remained fixed, while social developments rendered them archaic and Parliament did nothing to modernise them using legislation. The practice was eventually changed in July 1966 when Lord Gardiner, the Lord Chancellor, made a statement on behalf of himself and his fellow Law Lords. This *Practice Statement* says:

> Their Lordships regard the use of precedent as an indispensable foundation upon which to decide what is the law and its application to individual cases. It provides at least some degree of certainty upon which individuals can rely in the conduct of their affairs as well as a basis for orderly development of legal rules.
>
> Their Lordships nevertheless recognise that too rigid adherence to precedent may lead to injustice in a particular case and also unduly restrict the proper development of the law. They propose, therefore, to modify their present practice and, while treating former decisions of this House as normally binding, to depart from a previous decision when it appears right to do so. In this connection they will bear in mind the danger of disturbing retrospectively the basis on which contracts, settlements of property, and fiscal arrangements have been entered into and also the special need for certainty as to the criminal law. This announcement is not intended to affect the use of precedent elsewhere than in this house.
>
> [1966] 3 All ER 77

The current practice enables the House of Lords to adapt English law to meet changing social conditions. It was also regarded as important at the time that the House of Lords' practice be brought into line with that of superior courts in other countries, like the United States Supreme Court and state supreme courts elsewhere which are not bound by their own previous decisions.

The possibility of the House of Lords changing its previous decisions is a recognition that law, whether expressed in statutes or cases, is a living, and therefore changing, institution which must adapt to the circumstances in which, and to which, it applies if it is to retain practical relevance.

Since 1966, the House has used this power quite sparingly. It will not refuse to follow its earlier decision merely because that decision was wrong. A material change of circumstances will usually have to be shown.

In *Herrington v British Railway Board* (1972), the House of Lords overruled *Addy and Sons v Dumbreck* (1929). In the earlier case, the House of Lords had decided that an occupier of premises was only liable for the injury to a trespassing child if that child was injured by the occupier intentionally or recklessly. In its later decision, the House of Lords changed the law in line with the changed social and physical conditions since 1929. Their Lordships felt that even a trespasser was entitled to some degree of care, which they propounded as a test of 'common humanity'. In imposing a duty of care on occupiers, and arguing for the overruling of the 1929 decision, Lord Pearson said:

> It seems to me the rule in *Addie v Dumbreck* has been rendered obsolete by changes in physical and social conditions and has become an incumbrance impeding the proper development of law. With the increase in population and the larger proportion living in cities and towns and the extensive substitution of blocks of flats for rows of houses with gardens or back yards and quiet streets, there is less playing space for children and so a greater temptation to trespass. There is less supervision of children so they are more likely to trespass ... Also with the progress of technology there are more and greater dangers for them to encounter ...
>
> [1972] 1 All ER 749 at 785–786

The rarely used power of the House of Lords was utilised in *Horton v Sadler* in 2006 (below). Under the **Limitation Act 1980**, certain time-limits are imposed on people who want to bring legal actions for compensation. For actions concerning personal injuries, a claimant must sue within three years of the injury being caused, or whenever the injury or illness became apparent, (s 11). By virtue of **s 33** of the Act, however, that three-year time-limit can be disapplied by the courts (so that the claimant *can* sue) but only if the time-limit would, if applied, 'prejudice' the claimant, and if suspending the three-year rule would be 'equitable' in the all the circumstances. If, for example, the claimant's solicitors make the claim one day late beyond the three-year limit, and the defendant does not really suffer any disadvantage by virtue of that very slight rule violation, the courts will probably use **s 33** to disapply the three-year limit.

Horton v Sadler (2006) was a case about a traffic accident in Salford. The claimant was seriously injured, and the driver at fault was not insured.

The claimant had initially issued proceedings before the three-year time-limit had expired. That claim was not properly made by the claimant's lawyers, so new proceedings were issued, but after the end of the original three-year period. It was ultimately held by the Lords that the court *could* use its discretion under the **Limitation Act 1980 s 33** to disapply the three-year time-limit. In reaching that decision, it overruled its earlier decision in *Walkley v Precision Forgings Limited* (1979). The 1979 decision had deprived many claimants of a right that Parliament had intended them to have, and had given rise to much unsatisfactory jurisprudence.

In the 2006 case, the appellant, Mr Horton (H) appealed against a decision applying the ordinary three-year time-limit under the **Limitation Act 1980 s 33** in his road traffic claim against the respondents (S). The Motor Insurers' Bureau (MIB), which is liable to make payments where the defendant is uninsured, nominated insurers and made an interim payment to H.

H issued proceedings two days before expiry of the three-year limitation period, but failed to comply with a condition precedent of the MIB's liability, namely the requirement to give them notice.

When it was later sued, the MIB served a defence that denied its liability because of the claimant's failure to comply with the notice condition, and counterclaimed for the return of its interim payment to the injured man. H then issued duplicate proceedings against S, giving the correct notice to the MIB who were again joined as a party to the second action. The MIB had defended the claim arguing that it was now statute-barred under the **Limitation Act 1980 s 11**. H responded seeking an order disapplying the ordinary three-year time-limit under **s 33** of the Act.

The judge indicated that had it been permissible for him to disapply the time-limit under **s 33** then he would have exercised his discretion in favour of H. H's subsequent appeal had been dismissed based on binding authority, in particular *Walkley v Precision Forgings Ltd* (1979). H submitted that the reasoning in *Walkley* could not be supported; the Court of Appeal had in various subsequent cases sought to rely on 'fine distinctions' (that is minutely nuanced differences) to enable it to disapply *Walkley* in any case where it was not strictly constrained to apply it. The law was unfair and judges had to try to find ways around it. H also argued that the decision was inconsistent with the wide and unfettered discretion which the legislation had intended to give the court.

The House of Lords held that the appeal by Mr Horton would be allowed. It reasoned in this way:

The true question for the court under **s 33** of the Act was always whether it was equitable or inequitable as between the parties to override the time bar, which, if relied on by the defendant and unless disapplied by order of the court, would defeat the action that a claimant (here H) had brought out of time. That analysis could not be reconciled with *Walkley* which had held that **s 11** could not prejudice a claimant who had commenced proceedings within the three-year period, and so it was only in exceptional circumstances that such a claimant could have the time bar disapplied. *Walkley* was therefore overruled.

While the House of Lords had exercised its power to depart from its own precedent rarely and sparingly, and it had never been thought enough to justify doing so that a later generation of Law Lords would have resolved an issue or formulated a principle differently from their predecessors, too rigid an adherence to precedent might lead to injustice in a particular case and unduly restrict the development of the law. The House would depart from a previous decision where it appeared right to do so. The instant case was not one in which contracts, settlements of property or fiscal arrangements had been entered into on the faith of a settled legal rule. The criminal law, where certainty was particularly important, would be unaffected if the House departed from *Walkley*. There would be no detriment to public administration. While injustice might bear more hardly on individuals, that concept was not to be regarded as inapplicable to judgments affecting corporations with competing interests. In the result, *Walkley* should be departed from as it unfairly deprived claimants of a right Parliament intended them to have; it had driven the Court of Appeal to draw distinctions which were so fine as to reflect no credit on the instant area of law; and it subverted the clear intention of Parliament.

It held that the case would be remitted to the county court for the judge to resolve the application under **s 33**.

One of the main reasons that the House of Lords decided to overrule the legal analysis it had given in the 1979 case was that the decision had caused great unfairness ever since. Every so often, car accident victims whose lawyers issued claims within the three-year period were barred from suing when there was something wrong with the claim, and then another claim issued after the three years was struck down as time-barred. When such defeated litigants tried to get the courts to utilise the discretion to override the three-year rule, the courts refused because they said the litigant had 'not been prejudiced by the *three-year* rule', he had not been dilatory, as he *had* issued claim within the time, albeit an ineffective one.

That is an odd argument because when the same claimant came to issue a second claim in respect of the same harm, the reason he would *then* fail was precisely because of the three-year rule (because he usually issued the second claim more than three years after the accident) so he *was* being prejudiced by it! To give justice to injured claimants who would otherwise fall foul of the 1979 House of Lords' decision, subsequent courts had to make all sorts of dubious distinctions. The House of Lords was right to change its mind. The authority and 'finality' of the 1979 decision created many human difficulties, and as Lord Atkin one observed (*Ras Behari Lal v King-Emperor* (1933)): 'Finality is a good thing, but justice is a better.'

Question 10

Describe the work of the coroners' courts and explain what social role this part of the legal system is expected to perform.

Answer plan

You should:
- explain the historical setting of coroners' courts;
- note current numbers and duties of coroners;
- consider verdicts and purpose of classifications;
- consider patterns of death;

- discuss the problems posed by the meaning of the word 'how' in the requirement for inquests to decide 'how' someone died.

Answer

The coroners' courts are one of the most ancient parts of the English legal system, dating back to at least 1194. They are not, in modern function, part of the criminal courts, although, for historical reasons, they have an association with that branch of the justice system.

Coroners were originally appointed as *custos placitorum coronae*, keepers of the pleas of the Crown. They had responsibility for criminal cases in which the Crown had an interest, particularly if this interest was financial. By development of their role, however, and particularly through the pioneering work of the nineteenth-century coroner Dr Thomas Wakley, the coroner became, in Wakley's phrase, 'the people's judge'. The coroner is the ultimate public safeguard in an area of unmatched importance: the official documenting of how people die. Marilyn Lannigan, an authority on the history of the coroner, has pointed to the fact that it was Wakley who originally campaigned for all suspicious deaths, deaths in police custody or prison, and deaths attributable to neglect, to be brought within the jurisdiction of the coroner. He was an energetic reformer, who was also an MP and the founder of the medical journal *The Lancet*.

Today, there are 157 coroners' courts, of which 21 sit full-time. Coroners are usually lawyers (with at least a five-year qualification within **s 71** of the **Courts and Legal Services Act 1990**), although about 25 per cent are medical doctors with a legal qualification. The main jurisdiction of the coroner today concerns unnatural and violent deaths, although treasure troves are also something occasionally dealt with in these courts. However, the **Treasure Act 1996** which came into effect in 1997 introduced new rules relating to the reporting of finds and how they should be dealt with. The number of inquests into treasure troves will eventually fall away to zero.

The classifying of types of death, of which there are about 500,000 each year in England and Wales, is clearly of critical importance, not just to the state, politicians and policy makers, but also to the sort of campaign groups that exist in a constitutional democracy to monitor suicides, drug-related deaths, deaths in police custody and prison, accidental deaths, deaths in hospitals and through industrial diseases. About 40 per cent of deaths each year are reported to coroners as unnatural, or violent, or as reportable from certain industries, or are from an unknown cause.

In 2004, there were 514,300 registered deaths in England and Wales. Of all deaths, those that must be reported to a coroner are those of which there is evidence that they occurred in an unnatural or violent way. The coroner will order a post-mortem and this may reveal a natural cause of death which can be duly registered. If not, or in certain other circumstances, such as where the death occurred in prison or police custody, or if the cause is unknown, there will be an inquest. There were 234,000 deaths reported to coroners in 2007 resulting in 110,400 post-mortem examinations and 30,800 inquests.

Having a reliable system for charting who is dying, and in what circumstances, is of considerable social value. It is important for us to know, for example, that there were 3,000 suicides in England and Wales in 2007, as this should inform public policy related to the health service, community services, custodial policy and the emergency services.

Most inquests (96 per cent) are held without juries, but the state has been insistent that certain types of case must be heard by a jury in order to promote public faith in government. When in 1926, legislation, for the first time, permitted inquests to be held without juries, certain types of death were deliberately marked off as still requiring jury scrutiny and these included deaths in police custody, deaths resulting from the actions of a police officer on duty and deaths in prison. This was seen as a very important way of fostering public trust in potentially oppressive aspects of the state. In 1971, the Brodrick Committee Report (Cmnd 4810) on the coronial system saw the coroner's jury as having a symbolic significance and thought that it was a useful way to legitimate the decision of the coroner.

The coroner's court is unique in using an inquisitorial process. There are no 'sides' in an inquest. There may be representation for people like the relatives of the deceased, insurance companies, prison officers, car drivers, companies (whose policies are possibly implicated in the death) and train drivers, etc, but all the witnesses are the coroner's witnesses. It is the coroner who decides who shall be summoned as witnesses and in what order they shall be called.

Historically, an inquest jury could decide that a deceased had been unlawfully killed and then commit a suspect for trial at the local assizes. When this power was taken away in 1926, the main bridge over to the criminal justice system was removed. There then followed, in stages, an attempt to prevent inquest verdicts from impinging on the jurisdictions of the ordinary civil and criminal courts. Now, an inquest jury is exclusively concerned with determining who the deceased was and 'how, when and where he came by his death'. The court is forbidden to make any wider comment on the death, and must not determine or appear to determine criminal liability 'on the part of a named person'. Nevertheless, the jury may still now properly decide that a death was unlawful (that is, a crime). The verdict of 'unlawful killing' is on a list of options (including 'suicide', 'accidental death' and 'open verdict') made under legislation and approved by the Home Office.

Some of the legal questions vexing the coronial process are quite significant when one considers the general role of the coroner system to plot national patterns of death. It is, as noted above, the purpose of an inquest to determine, among other things, how the deceased died, and 'how' in this context means, according to one view, simply by what physical cause and in what immediate circumstances. According to another proposition however, one needs to take a much broader interpretation of the word 'how', in order to give a sufficiently thorough investigation to the issue (in some cases) of whether there was an unlawful killing.

Among the possible scenarios covered by the phrase 'unlawfully killed' is manslaughter through gross negligence committed by a company. The problem here is that in a case involving a member of the public, or an employee who has been killed in an event arising from a company's operations, one often cannot properly tell whether the death has resulted from 'gross negligence' on the company's part, unless and until one has found out the answers to all sorts of questions about how the company ran its business prior to the death. But to ask such questions can be objected to, on the basis that such an explorative exercise involves an excursus into matters beyond the proper scope of the inquest, according to the Divisional Court in *R v Sussex Coroner ex p Homberg* (1994).

The meaning of the word 'how' in a coroner's court was addressed in *Homberg*. Simon Brown LJ stated that although the word 'how' is to be widely interpreted, it means 'by what means' the death came about, rather than 'in what broad circumstances'. Thus, a coroner or counsel at an inquest can object to any line of inquiry which seeks to find out about 'the broad circumstances of the death'. On the other hand, unless the court knows something about the broad circumstances of a company's operations, it is impossible to determine whether there has been 'gross negligence'. Questions from counsel designed to elicit information from witnesses about the past practices of a company, its record on safety, or who in the company knew what and at what time, could thus be objected to on the basis of *Homberg*, while being perfectly defensible on the basis of testing whether the principle of 'gross negligence' manslaughter is applicable.

It is not always possible to identify suspicious deaths, and the recent case of Dr Harold Shipman highlighted the need to have a system which generally identifies cases which require further investigation, before the cause of death is officially certified and the matter closed. In 2002, it became apparent, following the report of Dame Janet Smith, that Dr Shipman was able, while practising as a GP, to kill over 215 people without the system detecting this homicidal conduct.

Not all of the work of coroners is as riddled with intrigue as a day in the life of the American medical examiner, as portrayed in contemporary fiction and television. Nonetheless, the importance of the system in maintaining an open society and acting as a buttress against sinister conduct is immense.

NOTES

If governmental legislative plans are implemented, coroners will be given stronger powers to respond to the wishes of bereaved relatives to ensure that lessons are learned from a sudden death, helping to prevent the same thing from happening in the future.

Coroners can already make reports to public or private sector organisations about what preventative actions could help avoid repeat incidents. New powers to be included in the draft **Coroners Bill 2007** will build on the existing law in four ways:

Coroners will be able to require organisations to respond to their reports and to say what action they will take to prevent future deaths.

The coroner will be able to request a written response to his or her report within a specified time and there will be a legal obligation for agencies and organisations to respond.

The Chief Coroner, to be appointed under the Bill, will monitor the reports made and responses received. An annual report of these responses will be made to the Lord Chancellor and laid before the House of Commons, to ensure accountability.

A similar system has been successful in Australia where the State Coroner in Victoria believes it has saved lives and claims that recommendations have led to legislative and policy changes in cases involving pedestrian safety in the workplace, tractor roll-overs, drowning of children in swimming pools, accidental child hangings from blind and curtain cords, and prison cell design.

Question 11

In what ways does the English legal system seek to balance interests? Using examples, discuss the challenges faced by the system in doing this effectively.

Answer plan

A good answer will:

- give some general examples (like freedom of speech) to put the question in a context;
- give an example of the English legal system itself having to balance interests, as where, even before arguments about balancing interests over freedom of speech, it has to decide questions like who to let into court and how long litigants get to put their cases;
- look at an example from beyond the formal legal system (like the NHS) where the same considerations apply;
- show considerations of time and resources;

- explore a concrete case example, *Re G* (2004);
- put the question into a political context.

Answer

One of the important functions of the legal system is to balance interests. This it does in hundreds of different ways. One person's right to 'free speech' must be balanced against another person's right to be protected against being defamed by lies, or being attacked because of incitements to racial hatred. One person's right to play loud music or operate an airport near a residential area needs to be balanced against the rights of others not to be badly disturbed. People have the right to bring legal actions in the civil courts but it is in the interests of society that we are protected against being bothered by serial litigants who want to use the legal system in an obsessive way and, therefore, such people can be barred from the courts as 'vexatious litigants'.

These issues often raise questions of fundamental social and political importance. For example, consider the question of at exactly what point we should exclude an intending litigant from the courts. Someone might have a genuine case against a part of the central or local governmental machinery. He or she might have been the real victim of repeated unfairness, or of a miscarriage of justice, or malice or prejudice. History shows that such things can happen. Such victims might then find themselves in an awful legal battle, like the case in Franz Kafka's novel *The Trial*, trying to use the law to fight parts of some huge organisation (like a governmental department, or a large telecom company, or financial institution) only to then be branded as a 'vexatious litigant' and excluded from the very processes of justice that exist to examine alleged wrongs.

Like the legal system, the health system also has to balance interests. It must be disposed to treat all sorts of patients because you do not cease to be entitled to civilised care just because you are an irritating person, or an eccentric, or have incurred ill health or injury in the course of some reproachable conduct. In 2006, for example, over 3,000 people under 16 years old were treated in hospital accident and emergency departments for excessive alcohol intake or alcohol-related injuries. Their folly did not debar them from treatment. There is, though, a limit to those who will be given the provision of health care. In May 2004, Norman Hutchens, 53, from York, became the first person to be banned by a magistrates' anti-social behaviour order, from entering or calling any National Health Service premises in the country. The court had been told Hutchens, who has a fetish for surgical masks, had verbally and physically abused NHS staff 47 times in the previous five months. In the juridical weighing scales, the interests of NHS staff eventually tip the balance against the interest of the man who was hassling staff.

The legal system can also exclude from all its own law courts a litigant who has 'habitually and persistently and without reasonable cause' instituted vexatious proceedings. In 1897, it was ruled that a court can consider the number and general character of a serial litigators' cases, and can make an exclusion order even if there may have been reasonable grounds for the proceedings in each case considered separately: *Re Chaffers, ex parte A-G* (1897). The **Supreme Court Act 1981** s 42 prevents a vexatious litigant from commencing any further proceedings without the permission of the High Court.

Similarly, the time taken in court by litigants and their lawyers needs to be controlled. It might well be that given an extra few weeks in court, a claimant or defendant might (in his or her own view) be able to make their case much more persuasively through their lawyer. If, however, they have been afforded a reasonable time, and time in line with general practice, it will commonly be seen as fair that their period for argument is curtailed. Their right to talk at inordinate length must be balanced with other considerations like that of allowing a good flow of cases through the courts. With limited resources (judges, courtrooms, court staff), a court will usually be doing better to hear, say, 10 cases in a month in a time-managed way as opposed to one case in an unlimited way. Sometimes, the exceptional nature of a case will warrant the court being generous with its time. On 30 June 2004. Gordon Pollock QC finished his opening speech in the unprecedented litigation taken against the Bank of England by the liquidators of the Bank of Credit and Commerce International (BCCI). He had begun his introduction, the longest opening courtroom speech in English legal history, on 13 January. In 2005, that record was broken again, in the same case, by Nicholas Stadlen QC, the barrister for the other side. This, though, was a case in which 80,000 investors lost money, and where a body as august as the Bank of England is alleged to have acted wrongly – so, in allowing this unusually long speech, the balancing scales were tipped in favour of the interests of the numerous creditors, and the huge sums of money involved, as against the other smaller and less momentous cases that might otherwise be before the court.

Another recent example of the courts balancing interests can be found in a recent case from the Civil Division of the Court of Appeal. In times of heightened awareness of terrorist threats, a balance must be made between civil liberty and public safety. The scales could be weighted entirely in favour of public safety by giving the police the unlimited authority to do anything they saw fit in order to counter possible terrorist threats: to arrest anyone and question him for months or years without having to give a reason for the suspect having been arrested. Tens of thousands of people could be imprisoned on the basis of suspicion as evidenced by their clothes or ethnicity or religion; traffic could be outlawed from whole sections of cities; and the population could be put under an 8.00 pm curfew. That might reduce the risk of terrorist acts but there would be a high price to pay in the dimension of civil liberty.

By contrast, the police could be asked to prevent and detect terrorism without being given any extra powers. That would allow a high degree of civil liberty but would arguably make life easier for terrorists. These issues were considered in the following case. The Court of Appeal decided that the disadvantage of the intrusion imposed on individuals by being stopped and searched by police officers under the **Terrorism Act 2000 s 44** was outweighed by the advantage of the possibility of a terrorist attack being avoided or deterred by use of that power.

In *R (On the application of Gillan) v (1) Commissioner Of Police For The Metropolis (2) Secretary Of State For The Home Department* (2004), the Court of Appeal addressed these issues. The applicants (G and Q) appealed against the dismissal of their claim for judicial review of the lawfulness of their being stopped and searched by police officers. In September 2003, G, a student, was on his way to demonstrate at an arms fair in London when he was stopped and searched under the **Terrorism Act 2000 s 44** for articles concerned in terrorism. G was allowed to go after 20 minutes. Q was stopped and searched under the same provisions at the same event. She was at the fair to film the protests. She felt distressed by the search. Nothing incriminating was found on G or Q and they later complained. The police officers relied on an authorisation made under **s 44** of the **2000 Act** by the Assistant Commissioner and its subsequent confirmation by the secretary of state to justify their actions.

The authorisation ran for 28 days and had then been further authorised twice for two further periods of 28 days. G and Q stated that the evidence showed that the rolling programme of authorisations had become part of day-to-day policing, contrary to the intention of the 2000 Act. G and Q argued that the court erred in: (a) concluding that the authorisation under **s 44** was lawful; (b) concluding that the use of stop and search powers under the authorisation against G and Q did not frustrate the legislative purpose of the **2000 Act**; (c) failing to construe **ss 44 to 47** of the **2000 Act** in accordance with the principle of legality or in accordance with the requirements of the **Human Rights Act 1998 s 3** so that it would be compatible with rights under the **European Convention on Human Rights 1950**; and (d) concluding that the authorisation and the use of the powers there under were prescribed by law. They argued that the use of the powers was not a proportionate means of achieving the legislative purpose of preventing acts of terrorism.

The Court of Appeal held that:

(1) The **2000 Act** was to be given its ordinary meaning. It was entirely consistent with the framework of the legislation that a power to stop and search should be exercised when a senior police officer considered it advantageous for the prevention of terrorism. Interpreted as such, **ss 44 and 45** could not conflict with the provisions of the European Convention. The courts would respect the authorities' view on matters of security but the court did have a role as to proportionality. The ultimate determination of what was proportionate rested with the court.

(2) The stop and search powers did not constitute an infringement of **Art 5** (right to

liberty and security) as the search was usually of a limited nature and its aim was not to deprive an individual of his liberty but to effect a verification. **Article 8** did apply to the stop and search process. However **Arts 10** and **11** could not be invoked as the powers were limited to searching for articles of a kind used in connection with terrorism.

(3) The procedure complained of was prescribed by law. The law that was under criticism was the statute and not the authorisation. Further, the statute contained controls on the powers.

(4) As to the authorisations, the disadvantage of the intrusion imposed on individuals by being stopped and searched was outweighed by the advantage of the possibility of a terrorist attack being avoided or deterred by use of the power. The rolling programme was justified in the current situation and there was nothing to support the suggestion that the powers were used for day to day policing.

(5) The police commander had been entitled to decide to use the s 44 powers at the arms fair, given the nature of the fair, its location close to an airport and the site of a previous terrorist incident. However, the respondents had not provided sufficient evidence that police officers had received careful instruction on the use of the powers. It was important that, when the police were given exceptional powers, they were prepared to demonstrate that they were being used with appropriate circumspection. The onus was on the first respondent to show that the interference with G's and Q's rights was lawful. On the evidence, it was not possible to say that that onus had been discharged.

(6) The court's provisional view was the judgment was best left to speak for itself and there be no order on the appeal as to the merits.

This case is a good illustration of the way a law court can be engaged in the evaluation of social or political issues in the process in deciding what is the appropriate balancing (or imbalance) of oppositional interests. Several cases have sought to balance the interests of the individual and those of the state, especially in respect of issues, as in the *Gillan* case above, arising from the **European Convention on Human Rights**.

In *Human Rights and Criminal Justice* (Ben Emmerson QC and Andrew Ashworth QC, 2001), the authors note (p. 60, para 2–03), that the principal object and purpose of the **European Convention on Human Rights** is the protection of individual rights from infringement by the contracting states (*Ireland v United Kingdom* (1979–80) 2 EHRR 25 at para 239). The convention seeks to achieve this objective through the maintenance and promotion of 'the ideals and values of a democratic society' (*Kjeldsen and others v Denmark* (1979–80) 1 EHRR 711 at para 53). The authors observe that particularly important features of a democratic society in the context of criminal cases are 'pluralism, tolerance and broadmindedness' (*Handyside v United Kingdom* (1979–80) 1 EHRR 737 at para 49) and 'the rule of law' (*Golder v United Kingdom* (1979–80) 1 EHRR 525 at para 34). The authors note (2–05) that it is important to distinguish between 'democratic values' and the protection of majority sentiment. The duty to protect inalienable rights sometimes requires the Court to set standards, even where these do not meet with majority approval. They then cite *Inze v Austria* (1988) 10 EHRR 394 at para 44, where the Court considered that support amongst the local population for measures discriminating against illegitimate children merely reflected 'the traditional outlook'. The authors conclude this point with an apposite quotation from the Court that ruled that 'although the interests of the individual must on occasion be subordinated to those of a group, democracy does not simply mean that the views of the majority must always prevail: a balance must be achieved which ensures the fair and proper treatment of minorities and avoids any abuse of a dominant position' (*Young, James and Webster v United Kingdom* (1981) 4 EHRR 38 at para 63).

In *Gillan*, the Court of Appeal makes a comparably 'political' point when it ruled that the disadvantage of individuals by being stopped and searched by police officers was outweighed by the advantage of the possibility of a terrorist attack being avoided or deterred by use of that power.

One thing that this case illustrates, along with the other issues examined in this essay, is that, ultimately, the balancing of interests is an exercise that must be carried out according to large political or social principles that are above and beyond clinical legal questions.

Question 12

Explain and assess the effectiveness of cross-examination as a method of getting to the truth in court.

Answer plan

The court case – the civil and criminal trial – is at the heart of the English legal system. Within such trials, the process of cross-examination is a key mechanism for producing the truth, or at least of producing a just result. The answer should make it clear how, in general terms, the system works and why it is used.

- Introduce the procedure.
- Explain its basic purpose.
- Explain the balance of power between advocate and witness.
- Illustrate effective use of questioning: Isaacs and Seddon.

- The use of sustained questioning: e.g. Cadbury's case.
- Conclusion – effective unless one too many questions are asked.

Answer

Cross-examination is an important feature of criminal and civil trials. It has been recognised by the Court of Appeal that an unwarranted restriction of an advocate's opportunity to cross-examine a witness can render a trial unfair under Art 6 of the **European Convention on Human Rights**, and therefore be a reason for ordering a re-trial: *R v John K* (2007). The simple point of significance decided in this case in the context of the English legal system is the indispensable value of cross-examination.

In court, cross-examination is where an advocate questions a witness who is part of the other side of the case. The questions cross from one side's lawyer to the other side's witness.

The aim of the exercise is to weaken the opponent's case, and to help establish facts which are favourable to the side of the cross-examiner. It is an opportunity to expose any unreliability in an opposing witness's testimony. Cross-examination can be done politely and without hostility. Sir John Mortimer QC notes (*Clinging to the Wreckage*, 1982, p. 106) that his late father (also a distinguished barrister) used to say 'the art of cross-examination is not the art of examining crossly'.

When a prosecuting advocate has finished questioning (called 'examining') a witness called by the prosecution, defence counsel can cross-examine that witness. Later the prosecution has the same chance to discredit the evidence of defence witnesses. In a civil case, similarly, the claimant and the defendant (usually through advocates) can cross-examine each other, and each other's witnesses. The procedure has a long history. The noun 'cross-examination' was first recorded in a case in 1729, although the technique itself is much older, appearing in one case involving a will in Norwich at the beginning of the thirteenth century. Cross-examination is an excellent method of clarifying the facts of a disputed matter. It is a serious intellectual contest fought in the threat of grave consequences. It is people at the peek of rational truth-finding.

The advocate has many advantages over the witness, such as knowing the rules of evidence, and choosing the line of inquiry in cross-examination. But the advocate does not always get the upper hand. A barrister in Ireland once began a cross-examination of an Irish Prelate with the words: 'Am I wrong in thinking you are the most influential man, and decidedly the most influential Prelate or Potentate, in the Province of Connaught?' The witness replied: 'Well, you know, they say these things, but it is in the sense that they would say that you are the very light of the Bar of Ireland: these are children's compliments'.

Cross-examination can involve counsel taking a witness through a sequence of propositions he will have to agree with until he is eventually cornered into agreeing with one final deadly point. But, equally, advocates sometimes pivot quickly to a riveting question. In opening the cross-examination of Frederick Seddon (who was on trial for the murder of his lodger, Miss Eliza Barrow), Sir Rufus Isaacs, Attorney General, began thus:

ISAACS: Miss Barrow lived with you from July 26, 1910, to September 14, 1911?

SEDDON: Yes.

ISAACS: Did you like her?

This flummoxed Seddon and he did not regain his composure. He could see that if he said he had liked her he would be asked why he had put her in a pauper's grave, whereas if he said he had not liked her he would tilt the case further against himself. Decidedly, this was a killer question. Seddon was eventually executed for the murder.

One masterful cross-examination was that in 1909 by Sir Edward Carson KC of the witness William Cadbury, director of the chocolate company (see Richard Du Cann, *The Art of the Advocate*, 1964, ch. 7). Between 1901 and 1908, Cadbury's chocolate obtained half their cocoa from islands off Angola which exploited forced slave labour. Cadburys knew about the slavery, and profited hugely from it for years but did not reveal it to the public. Instead, it traded on its reputation as a model employer, and the benevolent treatment of its workers at Bourneville in England. Meanwhile, people were snatched as slaves and forced to march up to a thousand miles to the plantations, and killed if they did not keep up. *The Evening Standard* published an article critical of Cadburys, and the firm sued saying it made them look like 'a bunch of canting hypocrites'. In a brilliant cross-examination lasting five hours, Carson dismantled the case of William Cadbury and the firm. The final exchange was a dramatic dénouement. After hours of quizzing about how much slave blood and suffering was involved in the production of the chocolate, and the complicity of Cadbury, there was this question:

CARSON: Have you formed any estimate of the number of slaves who lost their lives in preparing your cocoa from 1901 to 1908?

That is a bit like asking 'have you stopped beating your wife?' – a question which, answered either way, condemns the quizzed person. In answer to the question whether he had quantified the suffering on which he had sold chocolate, the director replied meekly:

CADBURY: No, no, no.

The jury found Cadburys had been libelled but awarded damages of one farthing.

Sir Henry Curtis-Bennett KC (1879–1936) was famous for maintaining that in cross-questioning an advocate should never ask a question if he did not already know the answer. A modern case in point was recounted by Sir Oliver Popplewell (*Benchmark*, 2003, p. 130). As a young barrister defending a man charged with careless driving, Mr Popplewell was cross-examining a prosecution witness who had testified that the defendant had been speeding. The witness was repeatedly pressed to estimate the speed of the car but declined. Having satisfactorily established the witness's incompetence in car-speed estimation, Mr Popplewell did not sit down but asked one final fatal question: 'Why are you telling the court you cannot estimate the speed of my client's car?' The witness's response was calm and clear: 'Because I have never seen a car go as fast as that in all my life!'

Question 13

What general principles (if any) can be deduced from the existing appeal structure in England and Wales? Is any extension or limitation on existing rights of appeal desirable?

Answer plan

You should include:

- changes in criminal appeals;
- recommendations from the Runciman Commission and the Auld Report;
- changes in civil appeals;
- the *Practice Direction on Civil Appeals* (2000).

Answer

Several general principles emerge from a study of the current appeal structure, principles which relate to the evolved purposes of the appeal process. These purposes include:

(a) the opportunity for a litigant to have more than one occasion to put his case – an idea based upon the premise that people and processes are fallible;

(b) the opportunity to reconsider a problem in the light of new evidence; and

(c) the need for an appellate body to standardise the legal response to particular sorts of problem.

Research undertaken for the Royal Commission on Criminal Justice (1993) revealed that of 300 appeals in 1990, just over one-third were successful. Almost two-thirds of defendants appealed against conviction on the ground that the trial judge had made a critical mistake and of these, 43 per cent succeeded in having their convictions quashed. In about 80 per cent of cases where convictions were quashed, there had been an error at the trial, usually by the judge.

In general, the Anglo-Welsh system of appeals avoids 'finality' after just one appeal hearing. There is for most cases (subject to the approval of the first appeal court or the next intended forum) more than one possible appeal hearing. An appeal from the civil jurisdiction of the magistrates' court, for example, could be taken to the Divisional Court of the Family Division and thence to the Court of Appeal Civil Division and finally, within the UK, to the House of Lords. Additionally, both the Civil and Criminal Divisions of the Court of Appeal can order retrials where the interests of justice so require.

The appeal structure puts great emphasis on the principle of extempore judicial wisdom. In the USA, the appeal system relies more upon reserved, written judgments, and most appellate judges enjoy the services of 'law clerks' (accomplished graduates from law school, paid from public funds), who assist the judges with research work and discussion of complex and contentious points of law. The English system makes much use of unreserved judgments in the Court of Appeal, after listening to oral argument, again in contrast to the American preference for appellate judges considering long, written submissions in respect of the appeals. This principle of orality was reaffirmed by Sir John Donaldson MR (as he then was) in an article in 1982; he said that 'the conduct of appeals by way of oral hearing lies at the heart of the English tradition' ((1982) 132 NLJ 959).

Another principle clearly governing the operation of the appeal system is that of carefully controlled accessibility. Probably as a deterrent against what might be regarded as overuse of the system by all convicted defendants, there are several obstacles placed in front of anyone contemplating an appeal. Leave must be obtained in all appeals, for example, from the Crown Court to the Court of Appeal (Criminal Division), unless the matter is concerned only with a point of law. The Court of Appeal also has a power to order that time spent appealing will not count towards the sentence. Shortly after this policy was introduced in 1970, the number of applications for leave to appeal in such cases was reduced by about half.

Accessibility to the appeal courts is also restricted by the poor record of trial proceedings in magistrates' and county courts. Additionally, appeals can be based upon fresh evidence, but the courts have sometimes taken a very narrow view of what is within this term. In criminal cases, the Court of Appeal has discretion whether to admit new evidence if it thinks it 'necessary or expedient in the interests of justice' (**Criminal Appeal Act 1968**). The court 'shall' admit the new evidence, that is, it *must*, where it: (a) affords a ground for appeal; (b) looks credible; (c) would have been admissible at the trial; and (d) the court is satisfied of a reasonable explanation as to why the evidence was not adduced at the trial.

Similar rules apply in respect of civil appeals. If the new evidence is something that could, with 'reasonable diligence', have been obtained for use in the trial, then it will not be permitted as the foundation of an appeal. In *Linton v Ministry of Defence* (1983), the House of Lords upheld this principle and denied a fresh trial to the appellant in circumstances where it was clear that his case would be very much stronger than in the original trial. This principle also applies to points taken by counsel; if they could have been put at trial, then they cannot form the basis of an appeal. In *Maynard* (1979), Roskill LJ said that if the rule were otherwise, it would enable counsel to keep a point up their sleeve at trial and then, if the case went against them, try to raise the point for the first time on appeal, thus having a second bite at the 'forensic cherry'.

If an appellant has not succeeded in the ordinary appeal process, he cannot get around the problem indirectly by taking an action for negligence against his lawyers (*Rondel v Worsley* (1969)). Neither may a convicted person re-open the trial by suing for defamation anyone who says he was rightly convicted (**Civil Evidence Act 1968**).

Access to the final appellate court, the House of Lords, is very limited, since it will only hear cases with leave, and in criminal appeals, there must also be a certificate from the Court of Appeal that the case involves a point of law of general public importance.

Even when access to the appeal process has been granted to the appellant, a constellation of rules is set to prevent technical abuse of the system. Thus, the 'proviso' to **s 2** of the **Criminal Appeal Act 1968** allows the court to agree with the ground for the appeal, but to keep the conviction if no substantial miscarriage of justice has occurred.

Suggested extensions and limitations

Criminal appeals

It was argued by Lord Devlin that it is wrong whenever judges, rather than juries, try to decide whether a defendant/appellant is guilty. There are still cases, however, where this happens. In cases involving new evidence, Viscount Dilhorne said (*Stafford v DPP* (1974)) that even if there was a chance that a jury might have come to a different view had it heard the new evidence, the conviction should not be quashed if the appeal court was satisfied that there was no reasonable doubt about the guilt of the accused.

An abandonment of this policy would bring appeal practice more in line with the theoretical constitution.

The **Criminal Appeal Act 1995** introduced significant changes to the law.

Section 1 amends the **Criminal Appeal Act 1968** so as to bring an appeal against conviction, an appeal against a verdict of not guilty by reason of insanity and an appeal against a finding of disability, on a question of law alone, in line with other appeals against conviction and sentence (that is, those involving questions of fact, or mixtures of law and fact). Now, all appeals against conviction and sentence must first have leave from the Court of Appeal, or a certificate of fitness for appeal from the trial judge, before the appeal can be taken. Before the new Act came into force, it was possible to appeal without the consent of the trial judge or the Court of Appeal on a point of law alone. In Parliament, the reason for this change was given as the need to 'provide a filter mechanism for appeals on a ground of law alone which are wholly without merit' (HC Official Report, *SCB (Criminal Appeal Bill)*, 1995, 21 March, col 6).

Section 2 changes the grounds for allowing an appeal under the 1968 Act. Under the old law, the Court of Appeal was required to allow an appeal where:

(a) the conviction, verdict or finding should have been set aside, on the ground that, under all the circumstances, it was unsafe or unsatisfactory; or
(b) the judgment of the court of trial or the order of the court giving effect to the verdict or finding should be set aside, on the ground of a wrong decision of law; or
(c) there was a material irregularity in the course of the trial.

In all three situations, the Court of Appeal was allowed to dismiss the appeal if it considered that no miscarriage of justice had actually occurred. The new law requires the Court of Appeal to allow an appeal against conviction under s 1 of the **1968 Act**, an appeal against a verdict under s 12 (insanity) or an appeal against a finding (disability) if it thinks that the conviction, verdict or finding is 'unsafe' (as opposed to the old law, which used the 'unsafe or unsatisfactory' formula).

During the Parliamentary passage of the Act, there was much heated debate about whether the new provisions were designed to narrow the grounds of appeal. That would amount to a tilt in favour of the state, in that it would make it harder for (wrongly) convicted people to appeal. Government ministers insisted that the effect of the new law was simply to restate or consolidate the practice of the Court of Appeal. One government spokesman said that:

> In dispensing with the word 'unsatisfactory', we agree with the Royal Commission on Criminal Justice that there is no real difference between 'unsafe' and 'unsatisfactory'; the Court of Appeal does not distinguish between the two. Retaining the word 'unsatisfactory' would imply that we thought there was a real difference and would only lead to confusion.

There were many attempts during the legislation's passage to insert the words 'or may be unsafe' after the word 'unsafe'. The Law Society, the Bar, Liberty and Justice called on the Government to make such a change. Also opposed to the use of the single word 'unsafe' was the eminent criminal law expert Professor JC Smith. He has argued cogently that there are many cases where a conviction has been seen as 'unsatisfactory' rather than 'unsafe', so that there is a need for both words. Sometimes, the Court of Appeal might be convinced that the defendant is guilty (so the conviction is 'safe'), but still wish to allow the appeal because fair play according to the rules must be seen to be done. Accepting improperly extracted confessions (violating s 76 of the **Police and Criminal Evidence Act 1984**) simply because it might seem obvious that the confessor is guilty will promote undesirable interrogation practices, because police officers will think that even if they break the rules, any resulting confession will nevertheless be allowed as evidence.

Professor Smith has given an example (see (1995) 145 NLJ 534) of where there has been a serious breach of the rules of evidence: see *Algar* (1954). In that case, the former wife of the defendant testified against him regarding matters during the marriage. The Court of Appeal allowed his appeal against conviction, but Lord Goddard said: 'Do not think that we are doing this because we think that you are an innocent man. We do not. We think that you are a scoundrel.' The idea underpinning such remarks is that rules are rules, and the rules of evidence must be obeyed in order to ensure justice. Once you start to accept breaches of the rules as being justified by outcome (ends justifying means), then the whole law of evidence could begin to collapse.

The proposal to include 'or might be unsafe' was rejected for the reason probably best summarised by the former Lord Chief Justice, Lord Taylor, who argued in the Lords that there was no merit in including the words 'or may be unsafe', as the implication of such doubt is already inherent in the word 'unsafe'.

Section 4 provides a unified test for the receipt of fresh evidence in the Court of Appeal. Under the old law, the Court of Appeal had a discretion, under **s 23(1)(c) of the 1968 Act**, to receive fresh evidence of any witness if it was thought necessary or expedient in the interests of justice. **Section 23(2)** added a duty to receive new evidence which was relevant, credible and admissible, and which could not reasonably have been adduced at the original trial. There was often much argument about whether new evidence should be received under the court's discretion or its duty. Gradually, the 'duty' principles came to be merged into the 'discretion' principles. The aim of the latest amendment is to reflect the current practice of the court. The general discretion under **s 23(1)** has been retained, but the 'duty' principle has been replaced with a set of criteria which the court must consider. These are:

(a) whether the evidence appears to the court to be capable of belief;

(b) whether it appears to the court that the evidence may afford any ground for allowing the appeal;

(c) whether the evidence would have been admissible at the trial on the issue under appeal; and

(d) whether there is a reasonable explanation for the failure to adduce the evidence at trial.

The 1995 Act also legislated for the new Criminal Cases Review Commission (CCRC). The CCRC has taken over the Home Secretary's power to reinvestigate already unsuccessfully appealed cases, and refer back to Court of Appeal cases of suspected miscarriages of justice. The wide power to reinvestigate cases where there appears to be a 'real possibility' (s 13) of miscarriage has been generally greeted with approval, but it is a matter of regret in some quarters that those reinvestigating cases will not be CCRC investigators but, usually, police officers (s 19). As many allegations of injustice involve accusations against the police, there is a school of thought suggesting that a manifestly impartial, outside body should be responsible for the reinvestigation. In order to establish that there is a real possibility of an appeal succeeding regarding a conviction, there has to be:

- an argument or evidence which has not been raised during the trial or at appeal; or
- exceptional circumstances.

In order to establish that there is a real possibility of an appeal succeeding against a sentence, there has to be:

- a legal argument or information about the individual, or the offence, which was not raised in court during the trial or at appeal.

Other than in exceptional circumstances, the Commission can only:

> ... consider cases in which an appeal through the ordinary judicial appeal process has failed, and once a decision is taken to refer a case to the relevant court of appeal, the Commission has no other involvement.
> Criminal Cases Review Commission, *Annual Report*, 2000

The Commission cannot overturn a conviction or change a sentence. In those cases where the criteria above are met, the Commission can refer a case to the Court of Appeal (in the case of Crown Court convictions) or the Crown Court (in the case of magistrates' court convictions). Only about 5 per cent of new cases received by the Commission since 1997 have been against summary convictions.

Since its inception, the CCRC has had some notable, high profile 'successes', in the sense that important cases it has referred have resulted in the Court of Appeal allowing appeals.

In 1997, for example, in one of its first referrals, the Commission referred the case of Derek Bentley to the Court of Appeal. Mr Bentley, although hanged for murder in 1953, eventually had his conviction quashed in August 1998 by the Court of Appeal.

The Auld Report (2001) recommended some changes in this area. It argued (para 18) that there should be the same tests for appeal against conviction and sentence at all levels of appeal, and suggested there should be a single line of appeal from the magistrates' courts and above to the Court of Appeal in all criminal matters. That would involve the abolition of the appeal from the magistrates' courts to the Crown Courts by way of rehearing, and its replacement with an appeal to a single judge in the Crown Court. It would also involve the abolition of the appeal from the magistrates' courts and the Crown Court to the High Court by way of 'case stated', or a claim for judicial review, and their replacement by an appeal to the Court of Appeal. The Report also suggested (para 19) that there should be provision for appeal by the defence or the prosecution against a special verdict of a jury which is 'perverse'. Other suggestions included the idea that procedures in the Court of Appeal should be improved to enable it to deal more efficiently with appeals touching on matters of general public importance or of great complexity. **Part 9** of the **2003 Criminal Justice Act** institutes an interlocutory prosecution right of appeal with leave, against rulings that would terminate a trial.

Civil appeals

The civil work of the Court of Appeal continues to increase. Figures available in 1995 show that whereas 1,338 appeals were set down in 1989, this had risen to 3,006 being set down in 2007. The House of Lords, however, has seen a fall in the number of appeals, from 72 to 62, over the same period. There is less clamour for the machinery and rules here to be revised. In part, this follows from the fact that civil appeals are different in nature from criminal appeals. This difference was highlighted by the Court of Appeal in quashing the convictions of the Birmingham Six (*McIlkenny and Others* (1991)). It said that in a civil appeal, there is a rehearing of the whole case and the appeal court is concerned with fact as well as law, so that it may take a different view of the facts from the court below. In a criminal case, on the other hand, primacy is enjoyed by the jury, so that the appellate court is really just a 'court of review'. It is thus easier for the Court of Appeal (Civil Division) to reverse the decision of a civil trial court than for the criminal courts to do the same.

The Report of the Review of the Court of Appeal (Civil Division), undertaken by Sir Jeffrey Bowman (1997), contains important recommendations for reducing the number of cases coming to the Court of Appeal and for improving practice and procedure in the Civil Appeals Office and in the Court of Appeal itself.

Based on averages, the time between setting down and final disposal of 70 per cent of appeals in 1996 had increased to 14 months. The corollary is that 30 per cent of appeals took over 14 months and at the end of 1996, some appeals had been outstanding for over five years. The Review's major recommendations include:

(a) that certain appeals which now reach the Court of Appeal (Civil Division) should be heard at a lower level – the largest category of such cases being appeals against decisions in fast-track cases;

(b) it should still be possible for appeals which would normally be heard in a lower court to reach the Court of Appeal (Civil Division) in certain circumstances. In particular, an appeal could be considered if it raises an important point of principle or practice, or one which, for some other special reason, should be considered by the Court of Appeal (Civil Division);

(c) the requirement for leave to appeal should be extended to all cases coming to the Court of Appeal (Civil Division), except for adoption cases and child abduction cases;

(d) an increasing role for appropriate judicial case management;

(e) more focused procedures – cases should be better prepared, at a much earlier stage in the process, and realistic timetables should be set, which must be strictly observed;

(f) the Court of Appeal (Civil Division) should impose appropriate time-limits on oral argument – on appeal, the balance of judicial time should lean more towards reading and less towards sitting in court;

(g) the greater use of IT to support the other recommendations of the review;

(h) information for litigants in person about the appeal process and what it can deliver must be available at an early stage. The information must be easily understandable and delivered in a range of different ways.

Some of the Report's more controversial recommendations include the following:

(a) there should be a power to appoint lawyers of outstanding distinction as academics or practitioners to sit as members of the Court of Appeal on occasions;

(b) there should be a discretion to list cases before a single member of the Court of Appeal;

(c) where specialist knowledge of law, procedure or subject matter is an advantage, the constitution of the Court of Appeal (Civil Division) should usually include one or two members with the appropriate specialist knowledge, but the constitution should not usually consist solely of specialist members.

One problem still remaining, however, with the civil appeal process is whether or not the Court of Appeal should 'correct' the discretionary decision of a trial court which it believes has made an error of judgment. As this matter is unsettled, advice to prospective appellants can be very difficult to give. The traditional rule, expressed by the Court of Appeal in *Culver v Beard* (1937), is that the appeal court should not interfere with a discretionary decision, unless it can be shown to be 'wrong in principle'. A decision can, therefore, be reversed if it has been based on a mistake of law or of fact or took into account legally irrelevant matters. This approach has been affirmed by the Court of Appeal in *Eagil Trust Co Ltd* (1985), where it was said that lawyers should not use the discretionary decision of a High Court judge as a mere 'conduit pipe' to the Court of Appeal. This is quite clear, but there are other decisions of the Court of Appeal (for example, *D v M* (1982)) which interpret its role as being to arrive at the correct, proper, just decision, even if this means contradicting the discretion of the trial judge – not to do so would be to perpetuate injustice. Legislation, perhaps, should settle this matter.

Finally, it is important to note evidence given by Adrian Zuckerman to the Woolf inquiry in 1995. Sometimes, it was pointed out, if a claim or defence is amended, the fate of the amendment may take two appeal hearings to decide. In one case, the issue of whether a writ had been properly served on the opposing side had to be considered by a Master and, on appeal, by a judge, and then by the Court of Appeal. The process is so protracted that the pre-trial dispute can take on a life of its own.

An attempt has recently been made to try to streamline and rationalise the civil appeals system in the wake of the new Civil Procedure Rules. The contents of a Practice Direction from Lord Woolf (*Court of Appeal (Civil Division): Leave to Appeal and Skeleton Arguments*, November 1998) have now been digested in a consolidating Practice Direction about civil appeals (*Practice Direction for the Court of Appeal (Civil Division)*, 16 May 2000). The Direction states (para 2.1.3) that:

> The experience of the Court of Appeal is that many appeals and applications for permission to appeal are made which are quite hopeless. They demonstrate basic misconceptions as to the purpose of the civil appeal system and the different roles played by appellate courts and courts below. The court below has a crucial role in determining applications for permission to appeal. This guidance indicates how applicants, and courts, should approach the matter.

In answer to the following question 'From which court should permission to appeal be sought?', the Direction articulates the following two key propositions. First (para 2.2.1), it notes that:

> The court which has just reached a decision is often in the best position to judge whether there should be an appeal. It should not leave the decision to the Court of Appeal. Courts below can help to minimise the delay and expense which an appeal involves. Where the parties are present for delivery of the judgment, it should be routine for the judge below to ask whether either party wants permission to appeal and to deal with the matter then and there. However, if the court below is in doubt whether an appeal would have a realistic prospect of success or involves a point of general principle, the safe course is to refuse permission to appeal. It is always open to the Court of Appeal to grant it.

The Direction then states (para 2.2.2) that:

> The advantages which flow from permission being considered by the court of first instance are lost if the application cannot be listed before the judge who made the decision which is the subject of the application.

It states that where it is not possible for the application for permission to be listed before the same judge, or where undue delay would be caused by so listing it, the Court of Appeal will be sympathetic to applicants who claim that it was impracticable for them to make their application to the court below, and will not require such an application to be made. The new directions will clearly assist in the introduction of a more nationally uniform response to appeals and to greater expedition in their processing, factors which will, arguably, improve the experience of all those using the system.

Question 14

Explain the role of the Criminal Cases Review Commission (CCRC) in the English legal system, and evaluate how effective it has been in its work.

Answer plan

Your answer should incorporate the following:
- discussion of what led to the establishment of the CCRC;
- description of who is on the CCRC and how it works;
- an explanation of the legal criteria for referring cases;
- some illustration, with an example of a case being processed by the CCRC;
- data to evaluate the CCRC's performance.

Answer

The CCRC is an independent body set up under the **Criminal Appeal Act 1995**. Its establishment followed a recommendation by the Runciman Royal Commission on Criminal Justice (1993) for an independent body to consider alleged cases of miscarriages of justice. The Runciman Commission itself resulted from the successful appeal of several notorious 'miscarriage of justice' cases in the 1980s and early 1990s, culminating in the release of the 'Birmingham Six' in 1991, after they had spent 16 years in jail for crimes they did not commit.

The CCRC came into being on 1 January 1997. Over 250 cases were transferred from the Home Office around 31 March 1997, when the Commission took over responsibility for casework. It is responsible for investigating suspected miscarriages of criminal justice in England, Wales and Northern Ireland.

There are 14 Commission members from a wide variety of backgrounds, including industrialists, senior lawyers with organisational experience, accountants and academic lawyers. Any decision to refer a case to the relevant court of appeal has to be taken by a committee of at least three members. The CCRC considers whether or not there is a real possibility that the conviction, finding, verdict or sentence would not be upheld were a reference to be made. Under the old system, the Criminal Cases Unit in the Home Office (known as C3) would make a recommendation to the Home Secretary as to whether a case should be referred back to the Court of Appeal. In the CCRC, the decision-making role of the Home Office Minister is taken by members of the Commission.

In order to establish that there is a real possibility of an appeal succeeding regarding a conviction, there has to be:

- an argument or evidence which has not been raised during the trial or at appeal; or
- exceptional circumstances.

In order to establish that there is a real possibility of an appeal succeeding against a sentence, there has to be:

- a legal argument or information about the individual or the offence which was not raised in court during the trial or at appeal.

Other than in exceptional circumstances, the CCRC can only consider cases in which an appeal through the ordinary judicial appeal process has failed and, once a decision is taken to refer a case to the relevant court of appeal, the CCRC has no other involvement.

The CCRC cannot overturn a conviction or change a sentence. In those cases where the criteria above are met, the Commission can refer a case to the Court of Appeal (in the case of Crown Court convictions) or the Crown Court (in the case of magistrates' court convictions). Only about 5 per cent of new cases received by the CCRC since 1997 have been against summary convictions.

Since its inception, the CCRC has had some notable, high-profile 'successes', in the sense that important cases it has referred have resulted in the Court of Appeal allowing appeals. In 1997, for example, in one of its first referrals, the Commission referred the case of Derek William Bentley to the Court of Appeal. Mr Bentley was convicted of the murder of PC Sidney Miles at the Central Criminal Court on 11 December 1952. Mr Bentley did not actually shoot the officer: the gun was fired by his accomplice during the course of a failed burglary attempt, but Mr Bentley was convicted under the principles of joint enterprise. An appeal against conviction was heard by the Court of Criminal Appeal on 13 January 1953 and was dismissed. Mr Bentley was hanged on 28 January 1953.

Bentley's conviction and sentence were the subject of numerous representations to the Home Office. The trial was seen as unfair in a number of respects. For example, although aged 18, the fact that Bentley had a mental age of 11 was kept a secret from the jury, and the judge's summing-up to the jury was astonishingly biased in favour of the police. In July 1993, on the recommendation of the Home Secretary, Her Majesty the Queen, in the exercise of the Royal Prerogative of Mercy, granted to Mr Bentley a posthumous pardon limited to sentence.

Following submissions from the applicants' solicitors and the completion of its own inquiries, the CCRC concluded that Mr Bentley's conviction should be reconsidered by the Court of Appeal. In August 1998, on a momentous day in legal history, the Court of Appeal cleared Bentley of the murder for which he was hanged 46 years earlier. In giving judgment, the Lord Chief Justice, Lord Bingham, said: 'The summing-up in this case was such as to deny the appellant that fair trial which is the birthright of every British citizen.'

Assessing the success of the CCRC more generally is difficult. The volume of documents it has to deal with (albeit electronically) is formidable, averaging around 2,000 pages per case. This is a considerable workload, as the CCRC is currently dealing with about 1,000 cases per year.

In a report to the House of Commons Home Affairs Committee at the end of 1997, the Chairman of the CCRC, Sir Frederick Crawford, stated that at that time, it had received 892 applications for review of cases. Of that total, 738 had had CCRC files opened on them, with 251 being actively worked on. One hundred and thirty-one had been closed for reasons of ineligibility (for example, they were at that time still being appealed in the court system or no appeal had been made through the court system).

From 1997 to February 2007, the Commission received 9,469 applications to review convictions and sentences. It has completed 8,653 case investigations and referred 356 cases to the Court of Appeal. Of these 310 have already been heard, and, of those, 218 resulted in convictions being quashed and 92 resulted in convictions being upheld.

Professor Graham Zellick, chairman of the CCRC, has made observations about the commission's work during its first 10 years (Frances Gibb, *The Times*, 17 February 2007). He said 'Widespread dishonesty, impropriety, corruption within whole sections of police forces . . . I think are a thing of the past.' However, failings or dishonesty of individuals – whether police, lawyers, or witnesses – can never be eliminated. Critics have said that the low rate of referral shows the commission is too cautious. There is a view the test should be lowered to 'an arguable case'. Professor Zellick disagrees.

> We are an extra-ordinary remedy. It's not as if people had no appeal or right to apply to appeal. So our test should be different. We were also appointed to exercise judgment in these matters, not just interfere and dump on the Court of Appeal.
>
> Cited by Gibb, as above.

And, he adds,

> If 90 to 100 per cent of referrals were being quashed, then critics would say that the commission was being too restrictive, usurping the courts' role and not applying the test fairly and properly. But with one third of cases that go

through the commission and the court being upheld, it seems we get the balance right.

Delays, though, are problematic. Most cases are dealt with within a year, but in the 20 per cent of more complex cases the delay is up to 20 months for those in custody and 32 months for people at liberty.

Ultimately, however, the test of success for the CCRC will be the same one as that which was apparently failed by its predecessor – carrying the confidence of the general public and of politicians – that it represents a safe, quick and impartial method of dealing with cases not given justice in the ordinary courts.

CHAPTER 3

JUDICIAL REASONING

INTRODUCTION

This chapter examines the way in which judges reach decisions in particular cases. Central to the common law is the doctrine of judicial precedent. This means that, depending on the level of the court in the hierarchy, previous 'decisions' of one court are supposed to be binding on later courts. The implication of the traditional approach to precedent is that it is a strictly applied, highly rational and almost scientific process. However, as will be demonstrated, the mechanisms deployed by judges in deciding cases allow them a large degree of discretion in reaching decisions. This introduction of the possibility of discretion necessarily opens the question of the accountability of the judges, which will be addressed directly in the following chapter.

Whilst the common law is, by definition, judge made, the extent to which judges can influence the operation of statute law through interpreting it in particular ways should not be underestimated.

It is obvious, but no less important for that, that the outcome of cases to a large extent depends upon what evidence the parties to the action can put before the court. That in turn is dependent upon the rules of evidence which apply in the courts.

Checklist

You should be familiar with:

- the nature of legal reasoning, as opposed to reasoning in general;
- the hierarchy of the courts;
- the doctrine of binding precedent;
- how judges avoid the strict operation of precedent;
- the rules of, and presumptions relating to, statutory interpretation;
- the rules of evidence.

Question 15

Consider how the doctrine of binding precedent operates in the English courts, having particular regard to its advantages and disadvantages.

> ### Answer plan
>
> This is a very straightforward, traditional question. It requires the following:
>
> - define what binding precedent is in such a way as to explain how it is supposed to operate, with appropriate reference to *ratio decidendi* and *obiter dictum/dicta*;
> - emphasise the authoritative hierarchy of the court structure in the UK legal system, although mention should be made of the European Court of Justice (ECJ) and the European Court of Human Rights (ECtHR);
> - consider the relationship between the various courts within the hierarchy, and also the extent to which they are governed by their own previous decisions;
> - establish the difference in status between decisions of the European Court of Justice and the European Court of Human Rights;
> - consider the difference between the criminal and civil law at the level of the Court of Appeal;
> - refer to the process of distinguishing cases on the basis of their facts;
> - consider advantages and disadvantages – it is essential to note that some of the supposed advantages are, in fact, problematic, not to say contradictory.

Answer

The doctrine of binding precedent, or *stare decisis*, lies at the heart of the English legal system. In essence, the doctrine refers to the fact that within the hierarchical structure of the English courts, a decision of a higher court will be binding on a court below.

The House of Lords stands at the summit of the English court structure and its decisions are binding on all courts below it in the hierarchy. It always has to be borne in mind, as regards European Community (EC) law, that the ECJ is superior to the House of Lords, and its decisions are binding on all UK courts. Also, as a consequence of the **Human Rights Act (HRA) 1998**, the decisions of the ECtHR are now part of the jurisprudence of the UK courts. This latter factor means that it is possible that the superior courts will find it necessary to alter previous precedents where they have been generated without reference to the **European Convention on Human Rights (ECHR)**. Those issues apart, as regards its own previous decisions, up until 1966, the House of Lords regarded itself as bound by its previous decisions. In the *Practice Statement (Judicial Precedent)* of that year, however, Lord Gardiner indicated that the House of Lords would in future regard itself as free to depart from its previous decisions where it appeared right so to do. It should be noted that, given the potentially destabilising effect on existing legal practice based on previous decisions of the House of Lords, this is not a discretion that the House of Lords exercises lightly. However, there have been a number of cases in which it has elected to exercise this discretion (for example, *Miliangos v George Frank (Textiles) Ltd* (1976), in which it decided that damages in English court cases did not have to be awarded in sterling).

The next court in the hierarchical structure is the Court of Appeal, but in order to consider its place within the doctrine of binding precedent, it is necessary to consider its civil and criminal jurisdiction separately.

In a civil case, the situation is that, as an inferior court, the Court of Appeal is generally bound by previous decisions of the House of Lords. Although the Court of Appeal, notably under the aegis of Lord Denning, attempted on a number of occasions to escape from what it saw as the constraints of *stare decisis*, the House of Lords repeatedly reasserted the binding nature of its decisions on the Court of Appeal in such cases as *Broome v Cassell* (1972) and *Miliangos v George Frank (Textiles) Ltd* (1976).

The Court of Appeal is generally also bound by its own previous decisions. As explained, however, by Lord Greene MR in *Young v Bristol Aeroplane Co Ltd* (1944), there are a limited number of exceptions to this general rule. These exceptions arise where:

(a) there is a conflict between two previous decisions of the Court of Appeal, in which case, the later court must decide which decision to follow and, as a corollary, which to overrule;

(b) a previous decision of the Court of Appeal has been overruled, either expressly or impliedly, by the House of Lords, in which case, the Court of Appeal is required to follow the decision of the House of Lords;

(c) one of its previous decisions has been given *per incuriam* or, in other words, that previous decision was taken in ignorance of some authority that would have led to a different conclusion, in which case, the later court can ignore the previous decision in question.

In addition to the above, there is also the possibility that as a consequence of **s 3** of the **European Communities Act 1972**, the Court of Appeal can ignore a previous decision of its own which is inconsistent with EC law or with a later decision of the ECJ. In *Price v Leeds City* (2006) the House of Lords distinguished between decisions of the European Court of Justice and those of the European Court of Human Rights: the former are binding, while the latter are not. As Lord Bingham put it:

> The mandatory duty imposed on domestic courts by **s 2** of the **1998 Act** is to take into account any judgment of the Strasbourg Court and any opinion of the Commission. Thus they are not strictly required to follow Strasbourg rulings, as they are bound by **s 3(1)** of the **European Communities Act 1972** and as they are bound by the rulings of superior courts in the domestic curial hierarchy.

As a consequence the House of Lords decided that the normal rules of precedent should apply, and lower courts should follow the House of Lords, even when their decisions have been overturned by the ECtHR. This does not apply, however, where the previous authority had been set without reference to the **Human Rights Act 1998**.

Once again, there was an attempt by the Court of Appeal under Lord Denning to widen these exceptions in *Gallie v Lee* (1971), but again, the House of Lords reaffirmed the limited nature of these exceptions and reasserted the strict operation of the doctrine of *stare decisis*.

Although, on the basis of *Spencer* (1987), it would appear that there is no difference in principle between the operation of the doctrine of *stare decisis* between the criminal and civil divisions of the Court of Appeal, it is generally accepted that in practice, precedent is not followed as strictly in the former as it is in the latter. Courts in the criminal division are not bound to follow their own previous decisions which they subsequently consider to have been based on either a misunderstanding or a misapplication of the law. The reason for this increased measure of apparent laxity is the fact that the criminal courts deal with matters involving individual liberty and therefore require a wider ambit of discretion to prevent injustice.

Further down the hierarchy, the Divisional Court is bound by the doctrine of *stare decisis* in the normal way and must follow decisions of the House of Lords and of the Court of Appeal. It is also normally bound by its own previous decisions, although in civil cases, it may avail itself of the exceptions open to the Court of Appeal (in *Young v Bristol Aeroplane Co Ltd* (1944)), and in criminal appeal cases, the Queen's Bench Divisional Court may refuse to follow its own earlier decisions where it feels the earlier decision to have been wrongly made.

As regards the High Court, decisions by individual High Court judges are binding on courts inferior in the hierarchy. Such decisions are not binding on other High Court judges, although they are of strong persuasive authority and tend to be followed in practice. Although subject to binding precedent from superior courts, Crown Courts cannot create precedent and their decisions can never amount to more than persuasive authority. The decisions of county courts and magistrates' courts are never binding.

The operation of the doctrine of binding precedent is, of course, dependent on the existence of an extensive reporting service to provide access to judicial decisions. However, it should not be thought that the doctrine is as hard and fast as it originally appears. The technique of 'distinguishing' cases on their facts provides judges with scope for declining to follow precedents by which they would otherwise be bound. The legal decision in any case is an abstraction from the immediate facts of the case. If a judge decides, for some reason, that the facts in the case before him are so different from those of a case setting a precedent, he is at liberty to ignore the precedent and treat the case in question as not being covered by it. He can then decide the case as he thinks fit, without being bound by the otherwise binding precedent.

Scope for further uncertainty is introduced by the necessary distinction between *ratio decidendi* and *obiter dicta*. The only part that is binding in any judgment previously decided is the *ratio* of the case: the actual legal reason for the decision. Anything else in the judgment is by the way, or *obiter*. Difficulty arises from the fact that judges do not label their judgments in this way. They do not actually nominate the *ratio* of the case. Additionally, their judgments may be of great length, or there may be as many as five judges delivering individual judgments on the case, and there is no requirement that all the judgments should agree on the principle of law governing the decision in the case. In any event, it is later judges who, in effect, determine what the particular *ratio* of any case was. The problem in relation to binding precedent is that it is open to later judges to avoid precedents by declaring them to be no more than *obiter* statements.

There are numerous *advantages* to the doctrine of *stare decisis*. Amongst these are the following:

(a) it saves the time of the judiciary, lawyers and their clients, since cases do not have to be re-argued – this also has the benefit of saving the money of potential litigants;

(b) it provides a measure of certainty to law – thus, lawyers and their clients are able to predict what the outcome of a particular legal question is likely to be in the light of previous judicial decisions;

(c) it provides for a measure of formal justice, to the extent that like cases are decided on a like basis;

(d) it provides an opportunity for judges to develop the common law in particular areas without waiting for Parliament to enact legislation.

There are, however, corresponding *disadvantages* in the doctrine. Amongst these are the following:

(a) the degree of certainty provided by the doctrine is undermined by the absolute number of cases that have been reported and can therefore be cited as authorities – this uncertainty is compounded by the ability of the judiciary to select which authority to follow, through use of the mechanism of distinguishing cases on their facts;

(b) law may become ossified on the basis of an unjust precedent, with the consequence that previous injustices are perpetuated – an example of this is the long delay in the recognition of the possibility of rape within marriage, which has only recently been recognised;
(c) in developing law, it might be claimed that the judiciary is, in fact, overstepping its constitutional role by making law rather than simply deciding its application.

Question 16

How can the common law progress if judges are bound by precedent?

Answer plan

A question of this type requires the following approach:
- consider what is meant by the common law;
- explain what is involved in the declaratory view of the role of the judiciary;
- analyse the operation of the system of *stare decisis* as it is supposed to operate;
- highlight some of the loopholes in the traditional version of *stare decisis*, for example, *Curry v DPP* (1994);
- provide some examples where the judges have continued to create new law;
- consider the constitutional role of the judiciary in the UK, and whether it should or should not be allowed to go on making new law.

Answer

This question requires a consideration of the scope of judges to avoid the consequences of *stare decisis* in order to reach their own subjective decisions, and the dangers inherent in so doing. In answering the question, it is necessary to consider the place and function of the judiciary within the constitution of the UK and to consider its role in the creation and development of the common law.

Within the constitutional division of powers in the UK, it is the function of the legislature to make law and it is merely the function of the courts to apply that law. The declaratory view of the function of the English judiciary accepts this constitutional division of power and portrays it as not making law, but merely deciding cases in accordance with existing legal rules. The doctrine of binding precedent operates in such a way that judges, in deciding particular cases, are not merely referred to earlier decisions for guidance, but are actually bound to apply the rules of law contained in those decisions. The operation of this principle depends on the established hierarchy of the court structure: all courts standing in a definite relationship of superiority/inferiority to every other court. Usually, a court is bound by decisions of a court of equal standing, or of higher authority than itself in the court structure. Allowing for the fact that the doctrine of *stare decisis* is supposed to have binding force within this hierarchical framework, two questions still arise.

First, it is axiomatic that legal rules cannot be subject to infinite regression; every rule of the common law must have had an origin. If one rejects as untenable the proposition of natural law – that it is possible for law to exist as an entity outside of, and distinct from, social practice – then it follows that if a particular law was not created by statute, it must have been created by a judge; even if this creative activity is no more than recognising the legitimacy, or otherwise, of the practice in question. As a matter of course, it follows that where there is no established precedent, the doctrine of *stare decisis* breaks down and the courts are faced with the alternatives of either refusing to decide a case, or stating what the law should be. Even in modern times, courts are still required on occasions to consider situations for the very first time without access to precedent. These cases, described as cases of first impression, inevitably involve judges in the establishment of new law.

Second, the question arises as to how the law is to develop and change to cater for changed circumstances if cases are always to be decided according to ageless precedent. In practice, flexibility is achieved through the possibility of previous decisions being either overruled or distinguished, or the possibility of a later court extending or modifying the effective ambit of a precedent. At this stage, it must be emphasised that, strictly speaking, it is wrong to speak of a decision being binding, just as it is technically incorrect to refer to a decision being overruled. It is not the actual decision in a case that sets the precedent, but the rule of law on which that decision is founded. This rule, which is an abstraction from the facts of the case, is known as the *ratio decidendi* of the case. Thus, the *ratio decidendi* of a case may be understood as the statement of the law applied in deciding the legal problem raised by the concrete facts of the case. Moreover, not every statement of law in a judgment is binding; only those which are based on the particular facts of the case, as found and upon which the decision was based, are binding. Any other statement of law is, strictly speaking, superfluous and any such statement is termed *obiter dictum*, that is, said by the way. It is significant that although *obiter dicta* do not form part of the binding precedent of the case in which they occur, and therefore do not have to be followed by judges deciding later similar cases, they do amount to persuasive authority and can be taken into consideration in later cases if the judge in the later case considers it appropriate to do so. This apparently small measure of discretion, in relationship to whether later judges are minded to accept the validity of *obiter* statements in precedent cases, opens up the possibility that judges in later cases have a much wider degree of discretion than is originally apparent in the traditional view of *stare decisis*, when it is realised that it is the judges in the later cases who actually determine the *ratio decidendi* of previous cases. In delivering judgments in cases, judges do not separate and highlight the *ratio decidendi* from the rest of their judgment, and this can lead to a lack of certainty in determining the *ratio decidendi*. This uncertainty is compounded by the fact that reports of decisions in cases may run to considerable length and where there are a number of separate judgments, although the judges involved may agree on the decision of a case, they may not agree on the legal basis of the decision reached. This difficulty is further compounded where there are a number of dissenting judgments. In the final analysis, it is for the judge deciding the case in which a precedent has been cited to determine the *ratio* of the authority and thus to determine whether he is bound by the precedent or not. This factor provides the courts with a considerable degree of discretion in electing whether to be bound or not by a particular authority.

It is somewhat anomalous that within the system of *stare decisis*, precedents gain increased authority with the passage of time. As a consequence, courts tend to be reluctant to overrule long-standing authorities, even though they may no longer accurately reflect contemporary practices or morals. Allied to the wish to maintain a high degree of certainty in the law, the main reason for judicial reluctance to overrule old decisions would appear to be the fact that overruling operates retrospectively. Overruling a precedent might therefore have the consequence of disturbing important financial arrangements previously settled in line with what were thought to be settled rules of law. It might also in certain circumstances lead to the imposition of criminal liability on previously lawful behaviour. It has to be emphasised, however, that the courts will not shrink from overruling authorities where they see them as no longer representing an appropriate statement of law. The legal recognition of the possibility of rape within marriage is simply one example of this process (see *R* (1991)).

In comparison to the mechanism of overruling, which is rarely used, the main device for avoiding binding precedents is that of distinguishing. As has been previously stated, the *ratio decidendi* of any case is an abstraction from, and is based upon, the material facts of the case. This opens up the possibility that a court may regard the facts of the case before it as significantly different from the facts of a cited precedent and thus not binding. The cases have been distinguished on their facts and the court is at liberty to ignore the precedent in the prior case.

Judges use the device of distinguishing where, for some reason, they are unwilling to follow a particular precedent. The law reports provide many examples of strained distinctions, where a court has quite evidently not wanted to follow an authority that it would otherwise have been bound by. An example is *Curry v DPP* (1994), in which the Court of Appeal attempted to remove the previous presumption that children between the ages of 10 and 14 charged with a criminal offence do not know that their actions are seriously wrong and the requirement that the prosecution provide evidence to rebut the presumption. Mann LJ justified reversing the presumption by stating that although it had often been assumed to be the law, it had never actually been specifically considered by earlier courts. On such reasoning, he felt justified in departing from previous decisions of the Court of Appeal which otherwise would have bound him. The House of Lords subsequently restored the original presumption. Although their Lordships recognised the problem, they thought it was a matter more for Parliamentary action than judicial intervention.

A further way in which judges have a creative impact on the law is in the way in which they adapt and extend precedent in instant cases. Judicial reasoning tends to be carried out on the basis of analogy, and judges have a large degree of discretion in selecting what are to be considered as analogous cases. They also have a tendency continuously to extend existing precedents to fit new situations, as the historical evolution of the tort of negligence will show.

The **Human Rights Act 1998**, which incorporated the **European Convention on Human Rights** into United Kingdom law, has had profound implications for the operation of the English legal system. For example **s 2** of the Act requires courts to take into account any previous decision of the European Court of Human Rights. This provision impacts on the operation of the doctrine of precedent within the English legal system, as it effectively sanctions the overruling of any previous English authority that was in conflict with a decision of the ECtHR. In addition, **s 3** requires all legislation to be read, so far as possible, to give effect to the rights provided under the Convention. This power has the potential to permit the courts to overrule previous precedents that were made without reference to the **ECHR** (see *Mendoza v Ghaidan* (2003)). Moreover, **s 3** extends this power to previously accepted interpretations of statutes, which were made, by necessity, without recourse to the Convention (*R v A* (2001) is a case in point).

Question 17

To what extent and why has there been a shift away from the traditional judicial approach to statutory interpretation?

Answer plan

This question recognises the change that has taken place in the way judges interpret, or perhaps more correctly, justify their interpretations of, statutes. Students must know the traditional rules of statutory interpretation, but they must also show that they are fully aware that there has been a shift from the literal to the purposive approach to statutory interpretation. They are not all

> compatible, nor do they form a clear hierarchy. Judges therefore have a measure of freedom to select which ones they wish to follow. Answers should:
> - address the point that interpretation is creative by its very nature;
> - note that statutes may partake of the general uncertainty inherent in language;
> - set out the three rules of statutory interpretation and highlight the use of each with reference to cases;
> - refer to the cases which indicate a shift towards the purposive approach to statutory interpretation;
> - refer to the **Human Rights Act (HRA) 1998**, citing cases in support of the analysis.

Answer

According to the traditional theory of the division of powers, the role of the judiciary is simply to apply the law that Parliament has created. This view is, however, simplistic in so far as it denies, or at least ignores, the extent to which the judiciary has a measure of discretion and creative power in the manner in which it interprets the legislation that comes before it.

Contrary to common-sense views, communication is not a passive, receptive process. Language necessarily involves the listener in a process of active interpretation, in order to determine the content and meaning of what is actually being communicated to him. Legislation can be seen as a form of communication. It represents and passes on to the judiciary and society at large what Parliament has determined should be the law governing a particular situation. To that extent, legislation shares the general problem of uncertainty inherent in any mode of communication. The conflicting aims of legislation, however, give rise to particular problems of interpretation; these conflicting aims are the need to be clear whilst at the same time being general. Clarity and precision tend to be achieved only in inverse proportion to generality, but legislation must, by and large, endeavour to be of general applicability. There is therefore in all legislation a penumbra of uncertainty that can only be illuminated and made certain by judicial interpretation. That interpretation is a creative process and inevitably involves the judiciary in the process of creating law.

The question arises, therefore, as to how judges actually interpret legislation that comes before them and the traditional answer was that in determining the actual meaning of legislation, they make use of the three primary rules of statutory interpretation and a variety of other secondary aids to construction.

The three rules of statutory interpretation are: (a) the literal rule; (b) the golden rule; and (c) the mischief rule. Before any detailed consideration of these rules of interpretation is undertaken, however, it must be emphasised that they are not really rules, but, as will be shown, they may best be considered as *post hoc* justifications for decisions taken in line with judicial preference.

The literal rule

Under this rule, the judge is required to consider what the legislation *actually* says, rather than considering what it *might mean*. In order to achieve this end, the judge should give words in legislation their literal meaning, that is, their plain, ordinary, everyday meaning, even if the effect of this is to produce what might be considered as an otherwise unjust or undesirable outcome. A classic example of this approach from the area of contract law is *Fisher v Bell* (1961). In this case, a shopkeeper who had put a flick-knife in his shop window, together with a price tag, was charged under a particular statute with 'offering the knife for sale'. The charge was dismissed on the basis that in line with the general contract law principles, the placing of an article in a window did not amount to an offer, but was merely an invitation to treat and, therefore, the charge was inaccurate. There was no doubt that the flick-knife was an offensive weapon and that the legislation was aimed at controlling the sale of such weapons, nor was there any doubt that the shopkeeper would have sold the knife, but the court stood by the literal interpretation of the Act in question and refused to extend the usual legal interpretation of the word 'offer'.

The golden rule

This rule is used when application of the literal rule will result in what appears to the court to be an obviously absurd result. An example of the application of the golden rule is *Adler v George* (1964). Under the **Official Secrets Act 1911** in operation at the time, it was an offence to obstruct HM Forces *in the vicinity of* a prohibited place. George had in fact been arrested whilst obstructing such forces *within* such a prohibited place. The court found no difficulty in applying the golden rule to extend the literal wording of the statute to cover the action committed by the defendant.

The mischief rule

This rule is of venerable age, being clearly established in *Heydon's Case* (1584). It gives the court a justification for going behind the actual wording of a statute in order to consider the problem that the particular statute was aimed at remedying. At one level, the mischief rule is clearly the most flexible rule of interpretation, but it is limited by being restricted to using previous common law to determine the particular mischief the statute in question was designed to remedy. In *Heydon's Case*, it was stated that in making use of the mischief rule, the court should consider the following four matters:

(a) What was the common law before the passing of the statute?
(b) What was the mischief in the law with which the common law did not adequately deal?
(c) What remedy for that mischief had Parliament intended to provide?
(d) What was the reason for Parliament adopting that remedy?

An example of the use of the mischief rule is clearly found in *Corkery v Carpenter* (1951), where a person was arrested for being drunk in charge of a bicycle. He was subsequently charged under **s 12** of the **Licensing Act 1872** with being drunk in charge of a carriage, as the legislation made no actual reference to cycles. It is certainly arguable that a cycle is not a carriage, but in any case, the court elected to use the mischief rule to decide the matter. The purpose of the Act was to prevent people from using any form of transport on the public highways whilst in a state of intoxication. The cycle was clearly a form of transport and therefore its user was correctly charged.

It is usually suggested that the above three rules are ranked in a hierarchical order, the first being the preferred rule only giving way to the second in certain circumstances, and the third rule only being brought into use in a perceived failure of the other two to deliver an appropriate result. On consideration, however, it becomes obvious that there is no such hierarchy. The literal rule is to be used unless it leads to a manifest absurdity, in which case, it will give way to the golden rule; but what determines whether any particular result is an absurdity, other than the view of the judge deciding the case? The rules are contradictory, at least to a degree, and there is no way in which the outsider can determine in advance which of them the courts will mobilise to decide the meaning of a particular statute. In reality, it may be seen that the three rules are simply different rules which are no more than devices, by means of which the judges justify their particular decisions.

The foregoing represents the tradition approach to judicial interpretation, however, it has to be recognised that for some time there has been a move away from the over-reliance on the literal approach to statutory interpretation to a more purposive approach. As Lord Griffiths put it in *Pepper v Hart*:

> The days have long passed when the court adopted a strict constructionist view of interpretation which required them to adopt the literal meaning of the language. The courts now adopt a purposive approach which seeks to give effect to the true purpose of legislation and are prepared to look at much extraneous material that bears on the background against which the legislation was enacted.

Such a shift has been necessitated, to no little degree, by the need for the courts to consider matters that were not within the original contemplation of Parliament at the time when the legislation was passed, but which have since been brought into play by the effect of technological advances.

Thus in *Quintavalle v Secretary of State for Health* (2003) the House of Lords held that embryos created by cell nuclear replacement (CNR), a form of human cloning involving a human egg and a cell from a donor's body, were regulated under the **Human Fertilisation and Embryology Act (HFE) 1990**, which had been passed at a time when embryos were only ever created by fertilisation of an egg by a sperm. The House of Lords held that CNR organisms were, in essence, sufficiently like other embryos to be considered as belonging to the same 'genus of facts'. Parliament could not rationally have been assumed to have intended to exclude such embryos from the regulation.

In reaching his decision, Lord Bingham considered the purpose and procedure of statutory interpretation and concluded that:

> The basic task of the court is to ascertain and give effect to the true meaning of what Parliament has said in the enactment to be construed. But that is not to say that attention should be confined and a literal interpretation given to the particular provisions which give rise to difficulty. Such an approach not only encourages immense prolixity in drafting, since the draftsman will feel obliged to provide expressly for every contingency which may possibly arise. It may also (under the banner of loyalty to the will of Parliament) lead to the frustration of that will, because undue concentration on the minutiae of the enactment may lead the court to neglect the purpose which Parliament intended to achieve when it enacted the statute ... The court's task, within the permissible bounds of interpretation, is to give effect to Parliament's purpose. So the controversial provisions should be read in the context of the statute as a whole, and the statute as a whole *should be read in the historical context of the situation which led to its enactment*.

The **Human Rights Act 1998** has also had profound implications for the operation of the English legal system. **Section 2** of the Act requires courts to take into account any previous decision of the European Court of Human Rights. This provision impacts on the operation of the doctrine of precedent within the English legal system, as it effectively sanctions the overruling of any previous English authority that was in conflict with a decision of the ECHR. This has implications for precedents relating to cases in which statutes were interpreted without reference to the ECtHR jurisprudence.

More immediately for this question, however, **s 3** requires all legislation to be read so far as possible to give effect to the rights provided under the Convention. This power has the more obvious potential to invalidate previously accepted interpretations of statutes, which were made, by necessity, without recourse to the Convention (*R v A* (2001) and *Mendoza v Gaihddan* are cases in point).

Question 18

Explain the resources and presumptions that judges may use in their interpretation of legislation.

> ### Answer plan
>
> This fairly narrow, knowledge-based, question asks students to explain the sources, other than the statute itself, to which judges can make reference in search of the actual meaning of legislation. It also requires a consideration of the presumptions that the judges will operate under. As usual, case authorities should be cited in support of all the references made.
>
> In addition to the three main rules of interpretation, there are a number of secondary aids to construction. These can be categorised as either intrinsic or extrinsic in nature:
>
> In particular:
>
> - Candidates should explain the distinction between *intrinsic* and *extrinsic* assistance.
> - Reference should be made to the decision in *Pepper v Hart*, which is important for the fact that it replaced the long-standing rule denying judges the right to use Parliamentary debates to decide the meaning of legislation.
> - The presumptions that the judges will normally apply should then be dealt with in some detail.

Answer

In addition to the three main rules of interpretation, there are a number of secondary aids to construction to which the judges will refer in an endeavour to find the meaning of particular pieces of legislation. These specifically relate to sources to which the judges may make reference, but in addition to these there are a number of presumptions that the judges will accept as normally operating. These latter *may* be overturned by legislation, but in order to do so the legislation in question must be specific to that intent.

As regards to the sources to which judges may resort, these may be divided into intrinsic and extrinsic sources of assistance as below.

Intrinsic assistance

Intrinsic assistance is derived from the statute which is the object of interpretation; the judge uses the full statute to understand the meaning of a particular part of it. The *title*, either long or short, of the Act under consideration may be referred to for guidance (*Royal College of Nursing v DHSS* (1981)). It should be noted, however, that a general intention derived from the title cannot overrule a clear statement to the contrary in the text of the Act.

It was a feature of older statutes that they contained a *preamble*, which was a statement, preceding the actual provisions of the Act, setting out its purposes in some detail and to which reference could be made for purposes of interpretation. Again, however, any general intention derived from the preamble could not stand in the face of express provision to the contrary within the Act.

Whereas preambles preceded the main body of an Act, schedules appear as additions at the end of the main body of the legislation. They are, however, an essential part of the Act and may be referred to in order to make sense of the main text.

Some statutes contain section headings and yet others contain marginal notes relating to particular sections. The extent to which either of these may be used is uncertain, although *DPP v Schildkamp* (1969) does provide authority for the use of the former as an aid to interpretation.

Finally, in regard to intrinsic aids to interpretation, it is now recognised that punctuation has an effect on the meaning of words and can be taken into account in determining the meaning of a provision.

Extrinsic assistance

Extrinsic assistance, that is, reference to sources outside of the Act itself, may on occasion be resorted to in determining the meaning of legislation; but which sources? Some external sources are unproblematic. For example, judges have always been entitled to refer to *dictionaries* in order to find the meaning of non-legal words. They also have been able to look into *textbooks* for guidance in relation to particular points of law, and in using the mischief rule, they have been able to refer to *earlier statutes* to determine the precise mischief at which the statute they are trying to construe is aimed. The **Interpretation Act 1978** is also available for consultation with regard to particular difficulties. Unfortunately, its title is somewhat misleading in that it does not give general instructions for interpreting legislation, but simply defines particular terms that are found in various statutes.

Until fairly recently, however, *Hansard*, the verbatim record of Parliamentary procedure, literally remained a closed book to the courts, but in the landmark decision in *Pepper v Hart* (1993), the House of Lords held that where the precise meaning of legislation was uncertain or ambiguous, or where the literal meaning of an Act would lead to a manifest absurdity, the courts could refer to *Hansard*'s reports of Parliamentary debates and proceedings as an aid to construing the meaning of the legislation.

The operation of the principle in *Pepper v Hart* was extended in *Three Rivers DC v Bank of England (No 2)* (1996) to cover situations where the legislation under question was not in itself ambiguous, but might be ineffective in its intention to give effect to some particular EC directive. Applying the wider purposive powers of interpretation open to it in such circumstances the court held that it was permissible to refer to *Hansard* in order to determine the actual purpose of the statute.

The *Pepper v Hart* principle only applies to statements made by ministers at the time of the passage of legislation, and the courts have declined to extend it to cover situations where ministers subsequently make some statement as to what they consider the effect of a particular Act to be (*Melluish (Inspector of Taxes) v BMI (No 3) Ltd* (1995)).

Presumptions

In addition to the rules of interpretation, the courts may also make use of certain presumptions. As with all presumptions, they are rebuttable. The following presumptions operate:

- *Against the alteration of the common law.* Parliament is sovereign and can alter the common law whenever it decides to do so. In order to do this, however, Parliament must expressly enact legislation to that end. If there is no express intention to that effect, it is assumed that statute does not make any fundamental change to the common law. With regard to particular provisions, if there are alternative interpretations, one of which will maintain the existing common law situation, then that interpretation will be preferred (See *R (Rottman) v Commissioner of Police* (2002)).

- *That a mental element is required for criminal offences.* It is a general requirement of the criminal law that, in order for a person to be convicted of a crime, he is proved not only to have committed the relevant act or conduct but also to have done this with a blameworthy state of mind known as *mens rea*. However, in some areas of social concern, such as traffic offences or underage drinking, Parliament has seen fit to pass what are known as 'strict liability' offences. These are criminal offences for which it is *not* necessary for the prosecution to prove that the defendant had a particular attitude towards the crime in question, for example, that he intended to commit it, but merely that the relevant conduct took place. When, someone comes before the criminal law courts accused of an offence created by statute the courts must decide whether the words of the statute imply that it is necessary for the prosecution to prove the defendant had a mental element. The general rule is that Parliament will be presumed not to have wanted to create a strict liability criminal offence unless it has been explicit about wanting to do so. In *Sweet v Parsley* (1970), the accused had a house which she rented out and visited only occasionally. She was convicted of being concerned in the management of premises used for the purpose of smoking cannabis, contrary to **s 5(b)** of the **Dangerous Drugs Act 1965**; however, she had had no knowledge that the house was being used in this way. The House of Lords held that her conviction should be quashed, since it had to be proved that it was the accused's 'purpose' that the premises were used for smoking cannabis. In the case, Lord Reid said that:

> ... whenever a section is silent as to *mens rea* there is a presumption that ... we must read in words appropriate to require *mens rea*.

- *Against retrospective effect of new law.* The courts operate a presumption of interpretation that statutes will not operate retrospectively. The presumption against retrospective effect was considered by the Court of Appeal in *Home Secretary v Wainwright* (2002). Two relatives visiting a prisoner were strip-searched as a condition of entry to the prison, and subsequently claimed a violation of their right to respect for private life. The court held that since the events in question had happened before the **HRA 1998** came into force, **s 3** of that Act could not be relied on. As Parliament had expressly made **s 22(4)** of the Act retroactive, its failure to do the same for **s 3** must be taken to have been intentional. See also *R v Lambert* (2001) and *R v Kansal* (2001).

  As Parliament is supreme, it can pass retrospective legislation if it wishes, but it must do so using express words to achieve this end. The **War Damage Act 1965** was passed specifically to overrule the decision of the House of Lords in *Burmah Oil Co Ltd v The Lord Advocate* (1965), and to deprive Burmah Oil of the results of having won that case. An example of modern legislation which has been made expressly retrospective is the **War Crimes Act 1991**.

- *Presumption against deprivation of liberty.* The law courts work on the assumption that Parliament does not intend to deprive a person of his liberty unless it is explicitly making provision for such a punishment.

- *Against application to the Crown.* Unless the legislation contains a clear statement to the contrary, it is presumed not to apply to the Crown.

- *Against breaking international law.* Where possible, legislation should be interpreted in such a way as to give effect to existing international legal obligations.

- *In favour of words taking their meaning from the context in which they are used.* This presumption appears as three distinct sub-rules, each of which carries a Latin tag:

  o The *noscitur a sociis* rule is applied where statutory provisions include a list of examples of what is covered by the legislation. It is presumed that the words used have a related meaning and are to be interpreted in relation to each other. (See *IRC v Frere* (1969), in which the House of Lords decided which of two possible meanings of the word 'interest' was to be preferred by reference to the word's location within a statute.)

  o The *ejusdem generis* rule applies in situations where general words are appended to the end of a list of specific examples. The presumption is that the general words have to be interpreted in line with the prior restrictive examples. Thus, a provision which referred to a list that included 'horses, cattle, sheep and other animals' would be unlikely to apply to domestic animals such as cats and dogs. (See *Powell v Kempton Park Racecourse* (1899), in which it was held that, because a statute prohibited betting in a specified number of *indoor* places, it could not cover an *outdoor* location.)

- The *expressio unius exclusio alterius* rule simply means that where a statute seeks to establish a list of what is covered by its provisions, then anything not expressly included in that list is specifically excluded. (See *R v Inhabitants of Sedgley* (1831), where rates expressly stated to be payable on *coal* mines were held not to be payable in relation to *limestone* mines.)

Question 19

Evidence must be sufficiently relevant to be admissible, but sufficiently relevant evidence is only admissible in so far as it is not excluded by any rule of the law of evidence. The consequence . . . is that some relevant evidence is excluded.

> Keane, A, *The Law of Evidence*, 4th edn, 1996

Explain the exclusionary rules of evidence and assess how far they are successful in promoting a fair trial.

Answer plan

A good approach to this discussion and assessment would be to:

- introduce the different types of excluded evidence;
- consider evidence unduly prejudicial to the defendant – **Criminal Evidence Act 1898**, *Selvey v DPP* (1968), *Boardman v DPP* (1974), *P* (1991);
- include discussion of inherently unreliable evidence – children's evidence, hearsay evidence (with exceptions; discuss *Rogers* (1994));
- deal with evidence against the public interest – legal professional privilege, confessions obtained by oppression;
- conclude with some discussion of the need to balance the interests in question.

Answer

The exclusionary rules of evidence are a characteristic of the common law tradition and are not favoured by continental jurisdictions. There are three main types of evidence which can be excluded from a trial, even though containing information relevant to the case: (a) evidence which might be unduly prejudicial to the defendant; (b) evidence which is inherently unreliable; and (c) evidence which it would be against the public interest to admit into the hearing.

It is generally unduly prejudicial to the defendant for the court to learn, during the trial, of his previous convictions. He must be judged according to the evidence relating to the crime in question (*Coombes* (1960)). This exclusionary rule, however, does not apply if the defendant asserts his own good character. Here, the prosecution can rebut the assertion with the defendant's criminal record. A defendant's past misconduct can also be disclosed if he attacks a co-accused, even a co-accused not charged with the same offence. The defendant who is attacked may cross-examine the attacker about his criminal record.

There are two further exceptions to the 'unduly prejudicial' exclusion rule. The defendant's record can be admitted if he attacks a prosecution witness, or where there is a marked similarity of facts between the crimes under consideration and earlier ones for which the defendant has been convicted. Both these exceptions have proved problematic in practice.

Section 1 of the **Criminal Evidence Act 1898** states that a defendant's record can be admitted where the 'nature or conduct of the defence is such as to involve imputations on the character of the prosecutor or the witnesses for the prosecution'. The rationale of the rule is that in circumstances of a simple quarrel on evidence between the sides, where the defence explains the prosecution's story by alleging that the prosecution witness is lying, it is proper for the court to know of any evidence that the defendant is a liar, so as best to judge which side is telling the truth. The problem here is for an innocent defendant who does have a criminal record and against whom there is being put some dishonest evidence. He cannot attack the prosecution's improper case without exposing his criminal record and thus probably damaging his defence. Additionally, as Zander has argued, if it is regarded as generally correct to withhold evidence of past misconduct from the court because it is unduly prejudicial, it does not become any the less prejudicial simply because the accused has impugned a prosecution witness (*Cases and Materials on the English Legal System*, 7th edn, 1996).

In *Selvey v DPP* (1968), the House of Lords ruled that where previous convictions of a defendant are admitted, they are to be treated by the court only as evidence of the defendant's creditworthiness, not of his propensity to commit the offence in question. This, however, is a rather pious hope. Once jury members learn of the defendant's convictions, they are likely to draw unfavourable conclusions about the person and probably do just what the House of Lords have declared should not be done.

As to the 'similar fact' exception, it was held in *Straffen* (1952) that previous convictions can be admitted where the facts in a case are so strikingly similar to the facts in previous cases for which the defendant has been convicted as virtually to rule out coincidence. The test for when the exception can be used was relaxed by the House of Lords in *Boardman v DPP* (1974), where it was suggested that the similarity did not need to be 'striking'. In *P* (1991), the House of Lords held that the real test was whether the 'probative force' of the evidence to be admitted was great enough to justify the prejudice given to the accused. Thus, in a charge of rape and incest against P, it was acceptable for the evidence of one of two victimised daughters to be used in the same hearing as her sister's evidence. Both girls had testified about prolonged misconduct and the probative value of each girl's evidence outweighed the prejudice to the father in using one allegation to fortify another.

Another category of evidence which English law excludes from the trial is that which is inherently unreliable. Thus, a judge can exclude the evidence of a proposed witness who does not have the mental capacity to testify. Two more problematic types of evidence in this class are children's evidence and hearsay evidence.

Traditionally, there was an assumption that young children were not reliable witnesses. Children could give sworn testimony if the judge believed that they appreciated the solemnity of the occasion and understood the importance of the oath. There was a more relaxed rule in criminal cases, where unsworn evidence could be taken from a child who was sufficiently intelligent. Evidence has been heard from children as young as six (*Z* (1990)). Psychological research (for example, Davies, Tarrant and Flin, 'Close encounters of the witness kind' (1989) 80 British Journal of Psychology 415) has now shown, however, that children are more reliable witnesses than was earlier thought. Now, **s 52** of the **Criminal Justice Act 1991** requires that all witnesses under 14 years of age are to give unsworn evidence, unless a judge rules that such a person is incompetent. Another reform was made by **s 34** of the Act, which abolished the requirement for the unsworn evidence of children to be corroborated and provided that the unsworn evidence of children could corroborate any other witness' testimony. The law, prior to these reforms, had made it extremely difficult to get convictions in serious cases of sexual abuse.

Hearsay evidence – that of someone not actually present in court – is regarded as inherently unreliable because the person who actually saw or heard something relevant cannot be tested by cross-examination in court. A document is hearsay unless its author is also present to testify. In *Sparks v R* (1964), a white man was convicted for sexual assault on a three-year-old girl. When asked just after the event by her mother who had assaulted her, the girl allegedly said 'It was a coloured boy', but the Privy Council ruled that the mother could not give this as part of her evidence, as it would be hearsay. There are now so many exceptions to this exclusionary rule that it has been described by Zander as being in 'an advanced state of disintegration'.

The hearsay rule only applies if the statement is to be introduced in order to establish the truth of its contents. It is not counted as hearsay if it is to be introduced as 'direct evidence'. The law on this is somewhat erratic, for example, it was held in *Taylor v Chief Constable of Cheshire* (1987) that a video recording was not hearsay but direct evidence, whereas in *Townsend* (1987), a robbery victim had scribbled down the registration number of the defendant's car. The pen was defective and made only indentations which the police had managed to boost, but they lost the original note. The technical evidence was ruled to be hearsay. Hearsay evidence is admissible where the original statement was made as a dying declaration, or as part of the *res gestae* (a statement made so close to the incident in question that it can be regarded as part of the event).

An interesting decision is *Rogers* (1994). The appellant had been convicted of possession of heroin with intent to supply. He had sought to have admitted as evidence a statement made by the wife of an old associate of his who had died before the trial. The wife's statement was a report of what she said her husband, L, had told her before he died. The statement began: 'L said there were a number of guys after him for the money for the heroin that the police had found.' It continued to the effect that L had been supplying the appellant with heroin for his personal use only and that the appellant knew nothing of the larger stock (which the prosecution alleged he did control). The appellant submitted that Mrs L's evidence fell within an exception to the hearsay rule – that statements made by a deceased were admissible if they were against his pecuniary interest (the rationale being that no one would acknowledge an obligation against his pecuniary interests unless it was true) – in that, the first sentence was such a statement as the deceased was acknowledging that he owed money and the remainder of the statement was admissible as collateral evidence. The appeal was dismissed. It was held that on the facts, the first sentence was not against the deceased's pecuniary interests, since he was not saying that he actually owed anyone any money and so was not acknowledging any obligation. Furthermore, even if that sentence was admissible, the rest of the statement, which was the part on which the defence wished to rely, was not admissible as collateral evidence as it would only be so admissible if further information was needed to explain the nature of the transaction in question, which was not the case.

Documentary hearsay evidence has been admissible in civil cases since 1938 and, in 1968, the rule was widened to include oral evidence with the consent of the other side. In 1991, the Law Commission recommended that the hearsay rule should be abolished in civil proceedings to bring the rules of evidence in line with the recent changes facilitating pre-trial exchange of witness statements. Many erosions of the hearsay rule in criminal cases have also been made, for example, statements of the dead, people who have (since they made the statement) become unfit, the untraceable, business documents and expert evidence are all admissible under the **Criminal Justice Act 1988**. Zuckerman (in *The Principles of Criminal Evidence*, 1989) has argued that these examples of 'non-hearsay' are just convenient ways of avoiding the rule, where it is thought that a certain type of statement will be reliable.

The third category of relevant evidence excluded from trial is that which it would be against the public interest to admit. There are several types of evidence which fall under this heading. Legal professional privilege means that any communications between a client and his legal adviser (arising from an existing or contemplated case, or to enable advice to be given) generally cannot be adduced in evidence by the lawyer without the permission of the client. The privilege is afforded to promote openness between the client and the lawyer. The privilege is not absolute, however, where the material sought to be produced in court would help to establish someone's innocence. This has arisen in cases with several co-accused and the judge must decide whether the legitimate interest of the defendant, who wants to keep the privilege, outweighs that of the client, who wants to breach it.

Since *Marks v Beyfus* (1890), it has been accepted by the courts that it is in the public interest that the identity of police informers should be kept secret. Nonetheless, this principle can be superseded by the principle that the defendant should not be unfairly impeded from establishing his innocence. In *Brown* (1988), convictions were quashed where the trial judge had refused to allow police officers to be questioned about their surveillance operation.

Section 76 of the **Police and Criminal Evidence Act (PACE) 1984** allows for the exclusion of evidence of a confession which has or might have been obtained by 'oppression' or in consequence of anything said or done which was likely to render it unreliable. 'Oppression' is defined as including torture, inhuman or degrading treatment and the use or threat of violence. There have been very few successful appeals using this section and the courts appear to have taken the contentious view that whether police questioning is oppressive or not depends upon the intention of the interrogating officers, rather than the actual effect the questions have on the defendant. This reasoning was adopted in *Miller* (1986).

Much more effectively used has been **s 78** of **PACE**. Under this, the court can refuse to admit evidence if it appears to the court that in all the circumstances, the evidence would have such an adverse effect on the fairness of proceedings that the court ought not to admit it. The majority of cases where the section has been successfully used have concerned breaches of **PACE** or its Codes of Practice with facts involving wrongful refusal to provide legal advice or the failure to record interviews (see, for example, *Samuel* (1988) – defendant denied access to solicitor; *Doolan* (1988) – defendant not cautioned; *Weekes* (1993) – defendant not provided with appropriate adult).

In *AG's Reference (No 3 of 1999)* (2000), the House of Lords gave a ruling which shows how subtle in their reasoning the courts should be when balancing: (a) the interests of the accused not to have prejudicial evidence used against him; and (b) the interests of the public in convicting offenders. In this case, a man was accused of burglary and rape. He was alleged to have broken into the house of a 66-year-old woman and raped her anally. He was arrested and prosecuted after a DNA sample taken from the victim was found to match his DNA taken from a sample he had provided in the investigation of an earlier unconnected burglary. According to s 64(1) of **PACE**, the sample he gave at the time of the first burglary should have been destroyed because he was tried for, but acquitted of, that crime. If that sample had been destroyed, then the police would not have had it, so, when the DNA sample was taken from the woman in the later burglary, it would not have matched any sample in the police records. In the second case, the police had, once they apprehended the defendant, taken a new sample from him to match with that found on the victim. But, they would not have done that had they not identified him as a suspect in the first place, which they only did because of the first, improperly held, sample. The Lords held that in future cases, where there were exceptional circumstances, the courts could, by analogy with **s 78(1)**, admit evidence apparently rendered inadmissible by **s 64** (which deals with the destruction of fingerprints and other samples if a person is cleared of an offence or is told that no prosecution will take place).

In conclusion, it can be noted that the real difficulty in this area is the familiar legal problem of balancing the interests of two sides. English law has taken the view that the judge should be the gatekeeper of much evidence brought to court by lawyers, deciding whether the jury can hear it and make up their own minds. The judge is given guidance by the law on how to decide these matters but ultimately, many of his decisions are matters of personal opinion, for example, whether a child is fit to give evidence, or whether the defendant is imputing the character of a prosecution witness or simply asserting his own innocence.

Chapter 4

Judges and Juries

JUDGES

Judges obviously occupy a central role in the legal system with regard to both civil and criminal law and, for that reason, questions about the judiciary are found in most examination papers on English legal system courses. It is frequently claimed that judges represent the views of a highly limited section of society, being mainly white, middle-aged men. The point to consider, however, is whether this social placement has a deleterious effect on the decisions that the judges make. If judges are simply the mouthpieces of the law and their decisions represent no more than the automatic outcome of a strictly logical process of reasoning, then the actual social situation and background of the judge is immaterial, for the decisions are contained in the law itself. If, on the other hand, legal reasoning is not as prescriptive as outsiders generally consider it to be and judges actually have a substantial measure of discretion in the way in which they reach their decisions, then the social placement of the judiciary does become a matter to be critically analysed with regard to the decisions that they reach. Law becomes not the expression of some imminent authority, but the expression of individual and, perhaps more importantly, group prejudice.

For the above reasons, it is important to avoid reliance on superficial and anecdotal assertions as to the lack of awareness of judges, in favour of a reasoned and well supported critique of the nature of legal reasoning, before attention is focused on the social background of the judiciary. The answers offered in this chapter locate weaknesses in the process of legal reasoning as of central importance and, indeed, as prior to any critical understanding of how judges operate.

Reference should be made to the provision of the **Constitutional Reform Act 2005** in relation to appointment of judges.

JURIES

The role of the jury in the English legal system is the subject of contentious debate. You should be familiar with recent research on this theme and some particular questions which have been addressed by researchers; for instance, how often do juries return 'perverse' verdicts and are such practices desirable? Are juries capable of properly following the details of complex trials? Be careful to observe how much the question you are answering requires a factual account or explanation of procedure, as opposed to evaluative, argumentative material. In any event, you will need a good knowledge of the legal and historical aspects of the jury in order to be able to rehearse the controversial parts of this topic.

Consideration should be given to the provision to further reduce jury trial under the **Criminal Justice Act 2003**.

Checklist

You should be familiar with:

- the way in which judges are appointed and the role of the Lord Chancellor in their appointment;
- how judges can avoid the strict operation of precedent and their powers in relation to the interpretation of statutes;
- the difference between individual and corporate prejudice;
- the social background of the judiciary;
- possible ways of diminishing perceptions of judicial bias;
- the historical justification for trial by jury;
- the rules concerning eligibility (including disqualification and excusal);
- the powers of the prosecution and defence to alter the composition of the jury;
- the practice of jury vetting and issues of selection procedure and impartiality;
- the arguments for and against retaining the jury for criminal trials.

Question 20

Examine the need for a new Supreme Court and evaluate the procedure for appointing members of the Supreme Court under the **Constitutional Reform Act 2005**.

Answer plan

This question requires candidates to evaluate the provisions in the **Constitutional Reform Act 2005** in relation to the appointment of judges to the new Supreme Court. It consequently requires candidates to show some knowledge and understanding of the nature of that new court and why it was introduced, before they go on to describe the procedure for appointing its members. However, it should be noted that the key requirement in the question is 'evaluation'. It is not therefore simply a matter of describing the appointments procedure, some assessment of how it might function is also required, which in turn necessitates some critique of the system that is being replaced.

A possible structure for dealing with the issues might be as follows:

- explain why it was thought necessary to introduce a new Supreme Court, and how it differs from the House of Lords;
- set out what were the perceived problems in the previous appointments procedure;
- describe the structure of the new Supreme Court;
- detail the appointments procedure of the new system, focusing in particular upon the role of the Lord Chancellor;
- offer some evaluation, even if limited, of the new system.

Answer

It has long been considered an anomaly, and contrary to the doctrine of the separation of powers, that the highest court within the United Kingdom has been located within the upper legislative body, the House of Lords. In summer 2004 the Government, somewhat surprisingly, announced its intention to bring the United Kingdom constitution into line with a more clearly delineated separation of powers. To that end the **Constitutional Reform Act (CRA) 2005** provides for the establishment of a new, independent Supreme Court, separate from the House of Lords.

In the past, criticism has also been made of the way in which judges were appointed to the House of Lords, and indeed at any level in the judicial hierarchy. It was suggested that the appointments were, to say the least, lacking in transparency and subject to the control of the judiciary and the senior members of the legal profession. As a consequence of the secret nature of the 'soundings' that were taken on candidates and their perceived right of veto, it was sometimes suggested that the senior judiciary constituted a self-selecting oligarchy. In response to such criticism, the newly constituted Supreme Court will have its own independent appointments system. The new court will also have its own staff and budget and it will eventually have its own building. For the present, however, it is likely that the new court will continue to occupy its present place within the House of Lords, until its own building can be refurbished as required.

Section 23 of the **CRA 2005** establishes the Supreme Court of the United Kingdom, and sets out its composition as being made up of 12 judges, appointed by the Queen. One of the judges is to be President and one Deputy President of the court. **Subsection 23(3)** provides a power to increase the number of judges. This may only be done, however, if, as set out in **subs (4)**, a draft of the Order has been laid before and approved by each House of Parliament (that is, by affirmative resolution procedure). **Subsection 23(6)** provides that the judges of the Supreme Court, apart from the President of the Supreme Court and the Deputy President of the Supreme Court, will be called 'Justices of the Supreme Court'.

Section 24 provides for the first judges of the Supreme Court to be the Lords of Appeal in Ordinary holding office at the date of commencement. The senior Lord of Appeal in Ordinary prior to commencement will become the President and the second senior Lord of Appeal in Ordinary prior to commencement will become the Deputy President of the Court. Thus there will be continuity, as the members of what is currently the House of Lords will become the first justices of the new Supreme Court.

Appointment of judges to the Supreme Court

As regards future appointments to the Supreme Court, **s 25** sets out two possible routes to qualification. These are:

1. having held high judicial office, for at least two years;
2. having been a qualifying practitioner for at least 15 years.

Although appointment to office is by the Crown, **ss 26, 27, 28, 29, 30** and **31** and **Sched 8**, set out the procedure for appointing a member of the Supreme Court.

The Lord Chancellor must convene an *ad hoc* selection commission if there is, or is likely to be a vacancy. Subsequently, the Lord Chancellor will notify the Prime Minister of the identity of the person selected by that commission, and under **s 26(4)**, the Prime Minister *must* recommend the appointment of that person to the Queen.

Schedule 8 contains the rules governing the composition and operation of the selection commission, which will consist of the President of the Supreme Court, who will chair the commission, the Deputy President of the Supreme Court and one member from each of the territorial judicial appointment commissions (see below), one of whom must be a person who is not legally qualified. The next most senior ordinary judge in the Supreme Court will take the unfilled position on the selection commission if either the President or Deputy President is unable to sit.

Section 27 sets out the process which must be followed in the selection of a justice of the Supreme Court. The commission decides the particular selection process to be applied, the criteria or competences against which candidates will be assessed, but in any event the requirement is that any selection must be made solely on merit. However, **subs 27(8)** does require that the commission must take into account the need for the Court to have among its judges, generally at least two Scottish judges and usually one from Northern Ireland. The Lord Chancellor, as provided for by **subs 27(9)**, may issue non-binding guidance to the commission about the vacancy that has arisen, for example on the jurisdictional requirements of the Court, to which the commission must have regard.

Under **subss 27(2)** and **(3)** the commission is required to consult:

- senior judges who are neither on the commission nor willing to be considered for selection;
- the Lord Chancellor;
- the First Minister in Scotland;
- the Assembly First Secretary in Wales;
- the Secretary of State for Northern Ireland.

Subsection 28(1) provides that after a selection has been made the commission must submit a report nominating one candidate to the Lord Chancellor, who then must also consult the senior judges (or other judges) who were consulted by the commission, the First Minister in Scotland, the Assembly First Secretary in Wales and the Secretary of State for Northern Ireland.

Section 29 sets out the Lord Chancellor's options after he has received a name from the commission and carried out the further consultation under **s 28**.

The procedure may be divided into three possible stages:

Stage 1: where a person has been selected and recommended by the appointments commission. At this stage the Lord Chancellor may:

- accept the nomination and notify the Prime Minister;
- reject the selection;
- require the commission to reconsider its selection.

Stage 2: where a person has been selected following a rejection or reconsideration at stage 1. In this event the Lord Chancellor can:

- accept the nomination and notify the Prime Minister;
- reject the selection but only if it was made following a reconsideration at stage 1;
- require the commission to reconsider the selection but only if it was made following a rejection at stage 1.

Stage 3: where a person has been selected following a rejection or reconsideration at stage 2. At this point, the Lord Chancellor *must* accept the nomination unless he prefers to accept a candidate who had previously been reconsidered but not subsequently recommended for a second time.

In effect this means that the Lord Chancellor's options are as follows. He can:

- accept the recommendation of the commission;

- ask the commission to reconsider; or
- reject the recommendation.

Where the Lord Chancellor requires the commission to *reconsider* its original selection, the commission can still put forward the same name with additional justifications for its selection. In such circumstance the Lord Chancellor will either accept the recommendation or reject it. Alternatively the commission can recommend another candidate, whom the Lord Chancellor can accept, reject or require reconsideration of.

However, if the Lord Chancellor *rejects* the original name provided by the selection commission, it must submit an alternative candidate giving reasons for their choice. At this point the Lord Chancellor can either:

- accept the second candidate; or
- ask the selection commission to reconsider.

On reconsideration the commission can either resubmit the second candidate or propose an alternative candidate. At this point the Lord Chancellor must make a choice. He can either accept the alternative candidate or he can then choose the reconsidered candidate.

Under **subs** 30(1), the Lord Chancellor's right of rejection is only exercisable where in his opinion the person selected is not suitable for the office concerned. The right to require reconsideration is exercisable under three conditions:

- where he feels there is not enough evidence that the person is suitable for office;
- where he feels there is not enough evidence that person is the best candidate on merit; or
- where there is not enough evidence that the judges of the Court will between them have enough knowledge of, and experience in, the laws of each parts of the United Kingdom, following the new appointment.

Should the Lord Chancellor exercise either of these options he must provide the commission with his reasons in writing (**s 30(3)**).

Whilst it can be seen that the appointment commission for the Supreme Court will be specifically convened for its purpose, all other judicial appointments will be made under the auspices of a new independent judicial appointments commission, which it is hoped will remove the criticisms levelled at the previous appointments process, that it too lacked openness. In conclusion, whilst the proposed system of appointment certainly appears more open than the system that preceded it, how it operates in practice remains to be seen.

Question 21

Why does the social composition of the judiciary matter?

Answer plan

This question appears to be of the type that asks candidates to consider whether the particular class/race/gender background of the judges leads to a bias in their decisions. It has assumed a contemporary importance, however, given the continued increase in judicial review and the incorporation of the **European Convention on Human Rights (ECHR)** into UK law, in the form of the **Human Rights Act (HRA) 1998**. This question still requires a reference to Professor Griffith's views in *The Politics of the Judiciary*, 5th edn, 1997. A good answer might take the following form:

- examine the actual constitution of the judiciary, referring to any available statistics;
- consider why the composition of the judiciary matters, paying particular regard to judicial review and the **HRA 1998**;
- refer to Professor Griffith's claim as to the biased nature of the judiciary;
- adduce an argument to the contrary;
- offer some proposals as to how the perceived problems might be remedied.

Answer

Central to the general idea of the rule of law is the specific proposition that it involves the rule of *law*, rather than the rule of *people*. From this perspective, judges are seen as subservient to, and merely the instruments of, the law; and the outcome of the judicial process is understood as being determined through the straightforward application of legal rules, both statute and precedent, to particular factual situations. In applying those rules, the judge is expected to act in a completely impartial manner, without allowing his personal preferences to affect his decision in any way. A further assumption is that in reaching a decision, the judge is only concerned with matters of law and refuses to permit politics, economics or other non-legal matters to influence his decision. The law is assumed to be distinct from, and superior to, those non-legal issues and the assumption is that the judge operates, in the words of Professor JAG Griffith, as a 'political, economic and social eunuch'. In reality, however, judges have a large measure of discretion in determining which laws to apply, what those laws actually mean and how to apply them. Equally, judges are by necessity involved in political issues when they are called upon to provide judicial review of the actions of the state and its functionaries. Although some judges have denied the political nature of such decisions, others have actually welcomed and justified the growth in judicial review, on the grounds that it permits the judiciary to protect individuals from the abuse of the power by what they perceive as an over-mighty state and an otherwise uncontrolled executive. This overtly political role, which sets the courts up against the state, cannot but be increased by the enactment of the **HRA 1998**. This Act, which incorporates the **ECHR** into UK law, places the courts in the position of acting as the protectors of individual rights from incursions by the state. Although the Act expressly declines to challenge the supremacy of Parliament by denying the courts the power to strike down particular legislation as being unconstitutional, it does permit them to make declarations to the effect that such legislation is incompatible with the human rights protected under the Act. Such declarations, and there are bound to be some, if not many, will inevitably place the judiciary in a political, not to say confrontational, relationship with Parliament.

The potential for conflict between the judiciary and the executive arising from the **Human Rights Act** can most clearly be seen in relation to the House of Lords' decision in the *Belmarsh* case (*A v Secretary of State for the Home Department* (2004)) in which the House of Lords, by a majority of eight to one, held that the detention powers under **s 23** of the **Anti-terrorism Crime and Security Act 2001** were not compatible with the rights provided under the **European Convention on Human Rights**. Some of the speeches delivered by the judges in the case were extremely, if not excessively, critical of the action taken by the Government in introducing the Act.

In the light of this potential creative power, it is essential to ensure that the judiciary satisfactorily represents society at large, in relation to which it has so much power, and to ensure further that it does not merely represent the views and attitudes of a self-perpetuating elite. This desideratum could be reformulated in the form of a stark question: are judges biased, and do they use their judicial positions in such a way as to give expression to that bias?

Bias can operate at two levels. The first is personal bias and occurs where individual judges permit their own prejudices to influence their understanding and implementation of the law. Such bias is a serious matter and reprehensible, but the very fact that it is individual makes it more open to control and, in the long run, less serious than the accusation of corporate bias that some observers, such as Professor Griffith, level against the judiciary. Corporate prejudice involves the assertion that the judiciary, as a body, do not decide certain types of cases in a fair and unbiased way; rather that as a consequence of their shared educational experience, shared training and practical experience at the Bar, along with shared social status, they have developed a common ideology comprising a homogeneous collection of values, attitudes and beliefs as to how the law should operate and be administered. The claim is that because, as individuals, they share the same prejudices, this leads to the emergence of an in-built group prejudice which precludes the possibility of some cases being decided in a neutral way.

The essence of Griffith's argument is that judges in the UK are in the position of being required to make political choices in the many cases that come before them which require a determination of public interest. This situation will necessarily become more frequent as the judges are required, under the **HRA 1998**, to weigh individual rights against public interest. His further point is that in determining what constitutes the public interest, the judges give expression to their own values, which are in turn a product of their position in society as part of the Establishment, the group in society which is the location of established authority. The argument runs that as the judiciary are part of the machinery of authority within the state, they cannot exercise their functions in a truly neutral way, but must, whether consciously or not – and Griffith himself suggests that it is unconscious – further the interests of that state. The consequence of this is that they decide cases in a fundamentally conservative manner, operating in such a way as to maintain the status quo and resist challenges to the established authority.

It is claimed that the most obvious examples of the judiciary's overzealous solicitude for the state's interests occur when those interests come into conflict with individual interests or the right to public information. Griffith claims that in such cases, the courts will tend to give undue preference to the state and cites various examples – such as the unilateral withdrawal of rights of trade union representation at the GCHQ – the total ban on publication of extracts from the *Spycatcher* book being simply the most recent of a number of notorious cases demonstrating the courts' readiness to promote the interests of the state and the Government above those of the individual.

With regard to the maintenance of law and order generally, but with particular reference to direct challenges to the state, Griffith cites the way in which the courts have reacted to alleged terrorists. It cannot but be admitted that the history of the trials and appeals of the Guildford Four, the Maguire Seven, the Birmingham Six and the solitary Judith Ward has resounded to the extreme discredit of the British courts, the British appeal system and British justice in general. The question has to be asked, however, do these cases reflect an inherently and inescapably conservative judiciary or are they simply unfortunate instances of errors which can occur within any system? Indeed, it could be argued that as the accused were all ultimately released, these cases actually demonstrate the neutrality and long-term validity of the British legal system. But, at the culmination of his attack on the judiciary, Griffith accuses them of actually promoting Conservative Party political views in their attitudes towards race relations, immigration and trade unions.

It is hardly surprising to find that Professor Griffith's attack on the judiciary has met with opposition. One notable response (and presumed rebuttal) was provided by Lord Devlin in a review article on Griffith's book, *The Politics of the Judiciary* (1978)

41 MLR 51. Lord Devlin pointed out that in most cases, and on most issues, there tended to be plurality rather than unanimity of opinion and decision amongst judges. He also explained any apparent Conservative bias on the part of judges as a product of age rather than class and that in any case, even if the judiciary were biased, its bias was well known and allowances could be made for it. It has to be stated that Lord Devlin's response is extremely complacent and, in the light of the alleged terrorist cases mentioned previously, worryingly so.

It is apparent that senior judges are still being appointed from the same limited social and educational elite as they always have been and that this gives rise to the accusation, if not necessarily the reality, that the decisions made by this elite merely represent the interest of a limited and privileged segment of society, rather than society as a whole. It is arguable that even if the accusations of those commentators such as Professor Griffith are inaccurate, it remains appropriate and, indeed, essential that in order to remove even the possibility of those accusations, the present structure of the judiciary be examined and altered. It is to be hoped that the establishment of the Judicial Appointments Commission, with its control over the appointment of judiciary, will open up the whole process to much welcome scrutiny in the future. There is one further point that has to be considered in relation to Griffith's attack on the judiciary, and that is the fact that, with the advent of the **Human Rights Act 1998** and the New Labour government of 1997, many on the political left appear to see the judges as the stalwart defenders of human rights in the face of an onslaught by the authoritarian state. This is particularly the case in relation to anti-terrorist legislation, which many see as draconian in its operation and effects.

Question 22

Critically examine the law governing the circumstances in which judges should excuse themselves from presiding in a case because of a possible partiality.

Answer plan

This question involves a consideration of the circumstances under which judges should decline to sit in a particular case. It is one of the rules of natural justice that a person should not be the judge in an action in which they have a personal interest, and the Latin expression of this rule, *nemo judex in causa sua*, goes back a long way. Answers should be able to provide an explanation of the historical context in which the question is set, but the question really demands an examination of the contemporary situation, starting with the various actions relating to the application to extradite the former Chilean dictator Augusto Pinochet and going on to consider the *Locabail* (2000) action. A good answer might adopt the following structure:

- an explanation of the *nemo judex* rule citing cases that show how it has been applied in the past;
- an explanation of how the law understands bias as it affects the judiciary considering *R v Gough* (1993);
- a fairly detailed explanation of the facts and law in the *Pinochet case* (1999);
- a consideration of the post-*Pinochet* applications and the Court of Appeal's ruling in the *Locabail* case.

Answer

The law in this area was, until recently, quite meagre. Judges related to parties before them, or judges with a pecuniary interest in one side of a case, were clearly required to stand down. Beyond that, in the areas of social interest, things were much less clear. However, in 1999, in *R v Bow Street Metropolitan Stipendiary Magistrate ex p Pinochet Ugarte (No 2)*, the House of Lords set aside one of its earlier decisions on the grounds that one of the Lords who delivered an opinion in the first case had a connection with Amnesty International – a body which had issued an opinion on the case.

The English legal system has a rule that no one may be a judge in their own cause, that is, they cannot judge a case in which they have an interest. This is sometimes known by the phrase *nemo judex in causa sua*. Thus, a judge who is a shareholder in a company appearing before him as a litigant must decline to hear the case: *Dimes v Grand Junction Canal* (1852). Even if a judge is unaffected by his interest in coming to a decision, it would still be wrong to preside in such a case because it might look as if the judge was improperly swayed. Thus, in the famous *dictum* of Lord Hewart, it is of fundamental importance that 'Justice must not only be done but should manifestly and undoubtedly be seen to be done' (*R v Sussex JJ ex p McCarthy* (1924), at p 259).

This rule was given another dimension in *Re Pinochet Ugarte*. General Pinochet, a former ruler of Chile, was in England on a visit when he was arrested for crimes of torture and mass killing allegedly orchestrated by him in Chile during the 1970s. His extradition had been requested by Spain. The legal question for the English courts was whether General Pinochet enjoyed a diplomatic immunity.

His case was eventually rejected by the House of Lords (by a 3:2 majority) in November 1998. Pinochet's lawyers then alleged that the Lords' decision was invalid as one of the majority Law Lords, Lord Hoffmann, could not be seen to be impartial, because he had a connection with the organisation Amnesty International, which had been granted leave to intervene in the proceedings and had made representations to the Lords through counsel. Lord Hoffmann, at this time, was an unpaid director of the Amnesty International Charitable Trust. Amnesty International was in favour of General Pinochet being brought to trial. In January 1999, on an appeal brought by Pinochet, another panel of Law Lords set aside the decision of the earlier hearing on the basis that no one should be a judge in his own cause.

Whereas previously, only pecuniary or proprietary interests had led to automatic disqualification, the House of Lords held that if the absolute impartiality of the judiciary was to be maintained, there had to be a rule which automatically disqualified a judge who was involved, whether personally or as a director of a company, in promoting the same causes in the same organisation as was a party to the suit.

Whatever one's views about the merits, sagacity or neutrality of the current judiciary, there is considerable evidence to support the proposition that historically, judges have often been biased towards certain causes and social classes. Griffith's book, *The Politics of the Judiciary*, for example, is brimming with concrete examples of judges who have shown a noted leaning towards one side of debate in cases involving workers, trade unions, civil liberties, Northern Ireland, police powers, religion and other matters. The inclusion of Lord Hoffmann on the panel was wrong because he was a director of an organisation which was represented in the case before him. Nonetheless, it is ironic that while for centuries judges have been permitted to preside in cases where their highly contentious political views have quite evidently affected their decisions (sexist, racist, anti-union, etc), the first senior judge actually to be acted against successfully for bias was someone whose agenda was nothing more than being against torture and governmental killings.

Following a number of other cases in which lawyers sought to challenge a judgment on the grounds that, through a social interest or remote financial connection, the judge was potentially biased, the Court of Appeal gave authoritative guidance on this area. The extraordinary judgment was delivered by Lord Bingham of Cornhill, Lord Chief Justice, Lord Woolf, Master of the Rolls and Sir Richard Scott, Vice Chancellor (*Locabail (UK) Ltd v Bayfield Properties Ltd and Another* (2000)). In respect of five decisions in which the judge's impartiality was questioned, the Court of Appeal ruled on general principles as follows:

(a) a judge who allowed his judicial decision to be influenced by partiality or prejudice deprived a litigant of the right to a fair trial by an impartial tribunal, and violated a most fundamental principle on which the administration of justice rested;

(b) the most effective protection of his right was, in practice, afforded by disqualification and setting aside a decision where real danger of bias was established;

(c) every such case depended on its particular facts, real doubt being resolved in favour of disqualification. It would, however, be as wrong for a judge to accede to a tenuous objection as it would be for him to ignore one of substance;

(d) in determination of their rights and liabilities, civil or criminal, everyone was entitled to a fair hearing by an impartial tribunal.

The Court of Appeal ruled that all legal arbiters were bound to apply the law, as they understood it, to the facts of individual cases, as they found them, without fear or favour, affection or ill will; that is, without partiality or prejudice. Any judge, that term embracing every judicial decision maker whether judge, lay justice or juror, who allowed any judicial decision to be influenced by partiality or prejudice deprived the litigant of his important right and violated one of the most fundamental principles underlying the administration of justice.

There was one situation where, on proof of the requisite facts, the existence of bias was effectively presumed and, in such cases, it gave rise to automatic disqualification, namely, where the judge was shown to have an interest in the outcome of the case which he was to decide or had decided: see *Dimes v Proprietors of the Grand Junction Canal* (1852), *R v Rand* (1866) and *R v Camborne Justices ex p Pearce* (1955).

In any case where the judge's interest was said to derive from the interest of a spouse, partner or other family member, the link had to be so close and direct as to render the interest of that other person, for all practical purposes, indistinguishable from an interest of the judge.

The automatic disqualification rule until recently had widely, if wrongly, been thought to apply only in cases of a judge's pecuniary or proprietary interest in the outcome of the litigation. However, *R v Bow Street Metropolitan Stipendiary Magistrate ex p Pinochet Ugarte (No 2)* (1999) made it plain that the rule extended to a limited class of non-financial interests, such as an interest in the subject matter in issue arising from the judge's promotion of some particular cause.

The law was settled in England and Wales by the House of Lords in *R v Gough* (1993) and in consequence, the relevant test was whether there was, in relation to any given judge, a real danger or possibility of bias. When applying the real danger test, it would often be appropriate to inquire whether the judge knew of the matter relied on as appearing to undermine his impartiality. If it were shown that he did not, the danger of its having influenced his judgment was eliminated and the appearance of possible bias dispelled. It was for the reviewing court, not the judge concerned, to assess the risk that some illegitimate extraneous consideration might have influenced his decision.

While it would be dangerous and futile to attempt to define or list factors which might, or might not, give rise to a real danger of bias, since everything would depend on the particular facts, the court could not conceive of circumstances in which an objection could be soundly based on the religion, ethnic or national origin, gender, age, class, means or sexual orientation of the judge. Nor, at any rate ordinarily, could an objection be soundly based on his social, educational, service or employment background or history, nor that of any member of his family; nor previous political associations, membership of social, sporting or charitable bodies; nor Masonic associations; nor previous judicial decisions; nor extra-curricular utterances, whether in textbooks, lectures, speeches, articles, interviews, reports, responses to consultation papers; nor previous receipt of instructions to act for or against any party, solicitor or advocate engaged in a case before him; nor membership of the same Inn, circuit, local Law Society or chambers.

By contrast, a real danger of bias might well be thought to arise if there were personal friendship or animosity between the judge and any member of the public involved in the case; or if the judge were closely acquainted with any such member of the public, particularly if that individual's credibility could be significant in the decision of the case; or if in a case where the credibility of any individual were an issue to be decided by the judge, he had, in a previous case, rejected that person's evidence in such outspoken terms as to throw doubt on his ability to approach such a person's evidence with an open mind on any later occasion.

In one way, the Court of Appeal was bound to come to this conclusion. Had it ruled that membership of certain societies, or a particular social background, or the previous political associations of a trial judge *were* grounds for appeal, two consequences would follow. First, there would be a rapid expansion of the use by law firms of special units that monitor and keep files on all aspects of judges' lives. Second, there would be a proliferation of appeals in all departments of the court structure, at the very time when there is such a concerted effort to reduce the backlog of appeals. What this decision leaves us with is a question of profound jurisprudential importance: how far can judges judge in an entirely neutral and socially detached manner?

Question 23

Explain how juries are constituted.

Answer plan

This particular question asks for attention to be focused on the composition of the jury, rather than the jury system generally, and seeks to elicit information about how the composition is determined and how it can be interfered with. The following procedure would address those issues:

- detail the process whereby a jury is actually selected, distinguishing between 'panels of jurors' and juries;
- consider how random this process is in practice;
- consider the need for racially mixed juries and whether randomness is always fair;
- consider rights of the defence and prosecution to challenge potential jurors;
- explain the process of jury vetting and consider its general legitimacy;
- offer a conclusion as to whether randomness is fundamentally necessary or, indeed, valuable *per se*.

Answer

The procedure of deciding cases on the basis of the deliberations of a jury is an ancient one, and one that has attracted much praise within the British legal system. The implicit assumption underlying the whole jury system is that the presence of 12 ordinary lay persons, randomly introduced into the trial procedure to be the arbiters of the facts of the case, strengthens the legitimacy of the legal system. It supposedly achieves this end by introducing a democratic, humanising element into the abstract, impersonal trial process, thereby reducing the exclusive power of the legal professionals who would otherwise command the legal stage and control the legal procedure without reference to the opinion of the lay majority. A corresponding assumption is that jury service is a public duty that citizens should readily undertake, although it is made compulsory and failure to perform one's civic responsibility is subject to the sanction of a £1,000 fine. According to the Lord Chancellor's Department, around 200,000 people serve as jurors in any one year.

The procedure for determining the actual composition of the jury to hear any particular case is as follows. An officer of the court summonses a randomly selected number of qualified individuals and, from that group, draws up panels of potential jurors for various cases. The actual jurors are then randomly selected, by means of a ballot in open court.

The **Juries Act 1974**, as amended by the **Criminal Justice Act 1988**, the **Criminal Justice and Public Order Act 1994** and the **Criminal Justice Act 2003** sets out the law relating to juries. It provides that any person between the ages of 18 and 70, who is on the electoral register and who has lived in the UK for at least five years, is qualified to serve as a juror. The dependency on electoral rolls to determine and locate jurors, however, raises a very real shortfall from the ideal assumptions made in relation to the jury system. The problem arises from the fact that electoral registers tend to be inaccurate. Generally, they have misreported the number of young people who are in an area, due to the fact that such people tend to have a greater degree of mobility than older people and, as a result, tend not to appear on the electoral roll of the place they currently live in. Electoral registers have also under-reported the true number of members of ethnic minorities, who have simply declined to notify the authorities of their existence.

Prior to the **Criminal Justice Act (CJA) 2003**, the general qualification for serving as a juror was subject to a number of exceptions.

For example, a number of people were deemed to be ineligible to serve on juries on the basis of their employment or vocation. Amongst this category were judges, justices of the peace, members of the legal profession, police and probation officers, and members of the clergy or religious orders. Those suffering from a mental disorder were also deemed to be ineligible. **Paragraph 2 of Sched 33 to the CJA 2003** removed the first three groups of persons ineligible, the judiciary, others concerned with the administration of justice and the clergy, leaving only mentally disordered persons with that status.

The provisions of the **CJA 2003** as regards eligibility to serve were challenged, as being contrary to **Art 6** of the **ECHR**, in *R v (1) Abdroikov (2) Green (3) Williamson* (2005), three otherwise unrelated cases. Each of these appellants appealed against their convictions on the grounds that the jury in their respective trials had contained members who were employed in the criminal justice system. The juries in the trials of the first and second appellants had contained serving police officers. The jury in the trial of the third appellant had contained a person employed as a prosecuting solicitor by the Crown Prosecution Service. Their proposal was that, as prior to the **CJA 2003** there would have been no doubt that the presence of such people on juries would have been unlawful, so their presence in the current cases ran contrary to the need for trials to be free from even the taint of apparent bias. The Court of Appeal rejected such arguments as spurious, holding that the expectations placed on ordinary citizens in relation to jury service had to be extended to members of the criminal justice system.

The House of Lords decided that these cases did not involve the ordinary prejudices and predilections to which people were prone, but rather the possibility of bias, possibly unconscious, which flowed from the presence on the jury of people professionally committed to one side of the adversarial trial process. The expectation that each doubtful case would be resolved by the trial judge was not met if neither the judge nor counsel knew that the juror was a police officer or CPS solicitor, as appeared to be the practice. N's case was not one which turned on a contest between the evidence of the police and of N, and it would have been difficult to suggest that unconscious prejudice, if present, would have been likely to operate to N's disadvantage. The Court of Appeal had reached the right conclusion in N's case. However, in G's case, there was a crucial dispute on the evidence between G and the police officer who was the alleged victim. The victim and the police officer on the jury shared the same local service background. In those circumstances the instinct of a police officer juror to prefer the evidence of a brother officer to that of a drug-addicted defendant would be judged by the fair-minded and informed observer to be a real and possible source of unfairness, beyond the reach of standard judicial warnings and directions. G was not tried by a tribunal which was and appeared to be impartial, and his appeal was allowed. In W's case, it was clear that justice was not seen to be done where one of the jurors was a full-time, salaried, long-serving employee of the prosecutor. W's convictions were quashed. There were situations where police officers and CPS solicitors would meet the tests of impartiality. However, that did not mean they would always do so.

In an endeavour to maintain the unquestioned probity of the jury system, certain categories of persons are disqualified from serving as jurors. Amongst these is anyone who has been sentenced to a term of imprisonment, or youth custody, of five years or more. In addition, anyone who, in the past 10 years, has served a sentence, or has had a suspended sentence imposed on them, or has had a community punishment order made against them, is also disqualified. The **CJA** makes a number of amendments to reflect recent, and forthcoming, developments in sentencing legislation. Thus juveniles sentenced under **s 91** of the **Powers of Criminal Courts (Sentencing) Act 2000** to detention for life, or for a term of five years or more, will be disqualified for life from jury service. People sentenced to imprisonment or detention for public protection, or to an extended sentence under **ss 227** or **228** of the Act are also to be disqualified for life from jury service. Anyone who has received a community order (as defined in **s 177** of the Act) will be disqualified from jury service for 10 years. Those on bail in criminal proceedings are disqualified from serving as a juror in the Crown Court.

Certain people were excused as of right from serving as jurors on account of their jobs, age or religious views. Amongst these were members of the medical professions, members of Parliament and members of the armed forces together with anyone over 65 years of age. **Paragraph 3** of **Sched 33** to the **CJA** repeals **s 9(1)** of the **Juries Act 1974** and consequently no one will in future be entitled to excusal as of right from jury service.

It has always been the case that if a person who has been summoned to do jury service could show that there was a 'good reason' why their summons should be deferred or excused, **s 9** of the **Juries Act 1974** provided discretion to defer or excuse service. With the abolition of most of the categories of ineligibility and of the availability of excusal as of right, it is expected that there will be a corresponding increase in applications for excusal or deferral under **s 9** being submitted to the Jury Central Summoning Bureau (see below).

Grounds for such excusal or deferral are supposed to be made only on the basis of good reason but there is at least a measure of doubt as to the rigour with which such rules are applied.

A Practice Note issued in 1988 (now *Practice Direction (Criminal: Consolidated)*

[2002] 1 WLR 2870 para 42) stated that applications for excusal should be treated sympathetically and listed the following as good grounds for excusal:

(a) personal involvement in the case;
(b) close connection with a party or a witness in the case;
(c) personal hardship;
(d) conscientious objection to jury service.

The traditional procedure for determining the composition of the jury to hear any particular case is in the process of being modernised by the introduction of a central summoning bureau, based at Blackfriars Crown Court Centre in London. The new bureau uses a computer system to select jurors at random from the electoral registers and issues the summonses, as well as dealing with jurors' questions and requests. It is intended to link the jury summoning system to the national police records system, to allow checks to be made against potentially disqualified individuals.

The aim of the new procedure is to ensure that all jurors are treated equally and fairly and that the rules are enforced consistently, especially in regard to requests to be excused from service and thus to reduce at least some of the potential difficulties mentioned above.

Under s 12(6) of the **Juries Act 1974**, both prosecution and defence have a right to challenge the array, where the summoning officer has acted improperly in bringing the whole panel together. Such challenges are rare, although an unsuccessful action was raised in the *Danvers case* (1982).

As regards individuals, the defence until fairly recently had the right to issue peremptory challenges, that is, challenges without reason, to potential jury members, up to a maximum of three. In spite of arguments for its retention on a civil liberties basis, the right was abolished in the **Criminal Justice Act 1988**. The defence, however, still has the power to challenge any number of potential jurors for cause, that is, with reason; however, following the attempt of the defence to exclude numerous classes of people from the jury in the *Angry Brigade* trial in 1972, the Lord Chief Justice issued a Practice Direction in which it was laid down that potential jurors were not to be excluded on account of race, religion, politics or occupation.

In *Danvers*, the defence had sought to challenge the array on the basis that a black defendant could not have complete confidence in the impartiality of an all-white jury. The question of the racial mix of a jury has exercised the courts on a number of occasions. In *Ford* (1989), the trial judge's refusal to accept the defendant's application for a racially mixed jury was supported by the Court of Appeal, on the grounds that 'fairness is achieved by the principle of random selection', as regards the make-up of a jury, and that to insist on a racially balanced jury would be contrary to that principle and would be to imply that particular jurors were incapable of impartiality.

To deny people of colour the right to have their cases heard by representatives of their own race on the basis of a refusal to recognise the existence of racially discriminatory attitudes cannot but give the appearance of a society where such racist attitudes are institutionalised. Without suggesting that juries, as presently constituted, are biased, it remains arguable that if, in order to achieve the undoubted appearance of fairness, jury selection has to be manipulated to ensure a racial mix, then it should at least be considered. This was apparently the view of the Runciman Commission, which suggested that in exceptional circumstances, it should be possible for either the prosecution or the defence to apply to the judge before the commencement of a trial to ensure that the jury should contain up to three people from ethnic minority communities, with at least one from the same ethnic minority as the defendant or victim. The report of Sir Robin Auld into the criminal justice system (2001) also suggested that provision should be made to enable ethnic minority representation on juries where race is likely to be relevant to an important issue in the case.

Of perhaps even more concern than challenges by the defence is the extent to which the prosecution can challenge potential jurors for, in addition to the right to challenge for cause, the prosecution also has the option of excluding particular individuals simply by asking them to 'stand by' until a jury has been empanelled. The manifest unreasonableness of this procedure, in view of the limited power of the defence, led to the Attorney-General issuing a *Practice Note* ([1988] 3 All ER 1086) to the effect that the Crown should only exercise its power to stand down potential jurors in the following two circumstances:

(a) to prevent the empanelment of a 'manifestly unsuitable' juror;
(b) where the Attorney-General has approved the vetting of the potential jury members, and that process has revealed that a particular juror might be a security risk, and the Attorney-General has approved the use of the 'stand by' procedure.

This latter point leads, naturally, to another contentious subject, that of jury 'vetting', the process in which the Crown checks the background of potential jurors. The practice of vetting potential jurors developed after *Angry Brigade* (1972), but did not become public until the **Official Secrets Act** case, known as the *ABC Trial*, in 1978. Subsequently, the Attorney-General published the guidelines for vetting panels. The most recent guidelines were published in 1988 and, interestingly, they support the general propositions that jury members should normally be selected randomly from the panel and should be disqualified only on the grounds set out in the **Juries Act 1974**. The guidelines do, however, make reference to exceptional cases of public importance where potential jury members might properly be vetted. Such cases are broadly identified as those involving national security, where part of the evidence may be heard *in camera*, and terrorist cases. Vetting is a twofold process. An initial check in police criminal records and police Special Branch records should be sufficient to reveal whether a further investigation by the security services is required. This further investigation cannot take place without the prior approval of the Attorney-General. The purpose of the vetting is to ensure that jury members will not be likely to divulge any secrets made open to them in the course of a trial, or to ensure that jurors with extreme political views do not get the opportunity to permit those views to influence the outcome of a case.

In conclusion, therefore, it can be seen that juries are by and large random, subject to some particular and important shortcomings. However, as has been suggested above, randomness is not necessarily a virtue in itself, especially if it leads to ethnically unrepresentative juries.

Question 24

Assess the impact of the **Criminal Justice Act (CJA) 2003** on who can be required to attend for jury service.

Answer plan

This question requires respondents to consider the changes in requirements for jury service introduced by the **CJA 2003**, but that in turn requires a consideration of the very important case of *R v Abdroikov* (2005), in which the House of Lords used its powers under the **Human Rights Act (HRA) 1998** to effectively overturn the expressly stated will of parliament (this case may be used as an alternative source in relation to Question 50 below). A possible structure for answering the question would be as follows:

- an introduction explaining the previous system and its inherent shortcomings;
- a detailed account of the provisions introduced by the **CJA 2003**;
- in relation to eligibility, reference *must* be made to *R v Abdroikov* (2005);
- the best answers will make some comment on the use of the courts' powers under the **HRA 1988** to avoid express statutory provisions.

Answer

Prior to the **CJA 2003**, the general qualification for serving as a juror was subject to a number of exceptions and as a result it had been suggested that jury service almost amounted to a self-selecting system, under which those who did not wish to serve, were under no real compulsion to do so, just as long as they could provide a reason for not serving. Following the recommendations of the Auld review of the criminal justice system in 2001, the government enacted the **CJA 2003** with the declared intention of not only increasing the numbers of people who would in future be required to serve as jurors, but also limiting the available excuses for not serving. However, as will be seen below, these intentions have been effectively undermined by the judges of House of Lords.

Ineligibility

A variety of people were deemed to be ineligible to serve on juries on the basis of their employment or vocation. Amongst this category were: judges; Justices of the Peace; members of the legal profession; police and probation officers; and members of the clergy or religious orders. Those suffering from a mental disorder were also deemed to be ineligible. **Paragraph 2 of Sched 33** to the **CJA 2003** removed the first three groups of ineligible persons, the judiciary, others concerned with the administration of justice, and the clergy, leaving only mentally disordered persons with that status.

The above reform came into effect in April 2005. However, the eligibility provisions of the **CJA 2003** were challenged, as being contrary to **Art 6** of the **European Convention on Human Rights**, in *R v (1) Abdroikov (2) Green (3) Williamson* (2005), three otherwise unrelated cases. Each of the appellants appealed against their convictions on the grounds that the jury in their respective trials had contained members who were employed in the criminal justice system. The juries in the trials of the first and second appellants had contained serving police officers. The jury in the trial of the third appellant had contained a person employed as a prosecuting solicitor by the Crown Prosecution Service. Their proposal was that, as prior to the **CJA 2003** there would have been no doubt that the presence of such people on juries would have been unlawful, so their presence in the current cases ran contrary to the need for trials to be free from even the taint of apparent bias.

The Court of Appeal rejected such arguments as spurious, holding that the expectations placed on ordinary citizens in relation to jury service had to be extended to members of the criminal justice system. However, by a majority of three to two the House of Lords held that the appeals of Green and Williamson should succeed, but that Abdroikov's appeal must fail. Lords Rodger and Carswell, in the minority, held that all appeals should fail. In reaching its decision the majority looked at the reports of previous committees which had been tasked with examining the operation of juries. Thus they referred to the findings of the 1965 committee chaired by Lord Morris of Borth-y-Gest which recommended that the police and those professionally concerned in the administration of the law should continue to be ineligible. Then in 2001, Auld LJ reviewed the issue and recommended that everyone should be eligible for jury service save for the mentally ill. He recognised that the risk of bias could not be totally eradicated and envisaged that any question about the risk of bias on the part of any juror could be resolved by the trial judge on the facts of the case. His recommendation was given effect by the **CJA 2003 s 321**. However, as the House of

Lords made clear, Auld LJ's expectation that each doubtful case would be resolved by the trial judge could not be met if neither the judge nor counsel knew that the juror was a police officer or CPS solicitor. The House of Lords recognised that there were situations where police officers and CPS solicitors would meet the tests of impartiality; however, that did not mean they would always do so or do so automatically.

However, according to Lords Rodger and Carswell in the minority, Parliament had endorsed the view that universal eligibility for jury service was to be regarded as appropriate. In reaching that conclusion Parliament had to be taken to have been aware of the test for apparent bias. It must, therefore, be taken to have considered that the risk of bias in the case of serving police officers or CPS solicitors was manageable within the system of jury trial. The consequence of the House of Lords' majority decision was pointed out by Lord Rodger in the clearest of terms:

> I can see no reason why the fair-minded and informed observer should single out juries with police officers and CPS lawyers as being constitutionally incapable of following the judge's directions and reaching an impartial verdict. It must be assumed, for instance, that the observer considers that there is no real possibility that a jury containing a gay man trying a man accused of a homophobic attack will, for that reason alone, be incapable of reaching an unbiased verdict, even though the juror might readily identify with a fellow gay man. Despite this – if Mr Green's appeal is to be allowed – the observer must be supposed to consider that there is, inevitably, a real possibility that a jury will have been biased in a case involving a significant conflict of evidence between a police witness and the defendant, just because the witness and a police officer juror serve in the same borough or the juror serves in a force which commits its work to the trial court in question. Similarly, if Mr Williamson's appeal is allowed, the observer must be taken to consider that the same applies to any jury containing a CPS lawyer whenever the prosecution is brought by the CPS. In my view, an observer who singled out juries with these two types of members would be applying a different standard from the one that is usually applied. For no good reason, the observer would be virtually ignoring the other 11 jurors . . . your Lordships' decision to allow two of the appeals will drive a coach and horses through Parliament's legislation and will go far to reverse its reform of the law, *even though the statutory provisions themselves are not said to be incompatible with Convention rights*. Moreover, any requirement for police officers and CPS lawyers balloted to serve on a jury to identify themselves routinely to the judge would discriminate against them by introducing a process of vetting for them and them alone. Parliament cannot have considered that such a requirement was necessary since it did not impose it. The rational policy of the legislature is to decide who are eligible to serve as jurors and then to treat them all alike.

Disqualification

In an endeavour to maintain the unquestioned probity of the jury system, certain categories of persons are disqualified from serving as jurors. Amongst these are anyone who has been sentenced to a term of imprisonment, or youth custody, of five years or more. In addition, anyone who, in the past 10 years, has served a sentence, or has had a suspended sentence imposed on them, or has had a community punishment order made against them, is also disqualified. The **CJA 2003** makes a number of amendments to reflect recent and forthcoming developments in sentencing legislation. Thus, juveniles sentenced under **s 91** of the **Powers of Criminal Courts (Sentencing) Act 2000** to detention for life, or for a term of five years or more, will be disqualified for life from jury service. People sentenced to imprisonment or detention for public protection, or to an extended sentence under **s 227** or **s 228** of the Act are also to be disqualified for life from jury service. Anyone who has received a community order (as defined in **s 177** of the Act) will be disqualified from jury service for 10 years. Those on bail in criminal proceedings are disqualified from serving as a juror in the Crown Court.

Excusal

Certain people were excused as of right from serving as jurors on account of their jobs, age or religious views. Amongst these were members of the medical professions, Members of Parliament and members of the armed forces, together with anyone over 65 years of age. **Paragraph 3** of **Sched 33** to the **CJA 2003** repeals **s 9(1)** of the **Juries Act (JA) 1974** and consequently no one will in future be entitled to excusal as of right from jury service.

It has always been the case that if a person who has been summoned to do jury service could show that there was a 'good reason' why their summons should be deferred or excused, **s 9** of the **JA 1974** provided discretion to defer or excuse service. With the abolition of most of the categories of ineligibility and of the availability of excusal as of right, it is expected that there will be a corresponding increase in applications for excusal or deferral under **s 9** being submitted to the Jury Central Summoning Bureau (see below).

Grounds for such excusal or deferral are supposed to be made only on the basis of good reason, but there is at least a measure of doubt as to the rigour with which such rules are applied.

A Practice Note issued in 1988 (now *Practice Direction (Criminal: Consolidated)* (2002), para 42) stated that applications for excusal should be treated sympathetically and listed the following as good grounds for excusal:

(a) personal involvement in the case;
(b) close connection with a party or a witness in the case;
(c) personal hardship;
(d) conscientious objection to jury service.

However, a new **s 9AA**, introduced by the **CJA 2003**, places a statutory duty on the

Lord Chancellor, in whom current responsibility for jury summoning is vested, to publish and lay before Parliament guidelines relating to the exercise by the Jury Central Summoning Bureau of its functions in relation to discretionary deferral and excusal.

The aim of the guidelines should be to ensure that all jurors are treated equally and fairly and that the rules are enforced consistently, especially in regard to requests to be excused from service, and thus to reduce at least some of the potential difficulties mentioned above.

Chapter 5

The Criminal Process

INTRODUCTION

The official purpose of the criminal justice system (CJS) is 'to deliver justice for all, by convicting and punishing the guilty and helping them to stop offending, while protecting the innocent'. It is responsible for detecting crime and bringing it to justice; and carrying out the orders of court, such as collecting fines, and supervising community and custodial punishment.

The key goals for criminal justice are to help reduce crime by bringing more offences to justice, and to raise public confidence that the system is fair and will deliver for the law-abiding citizen. That includes increasing the satisfaction of victims and witnesses with the treatment they receive. Together with other partners, the CJS works to prevent crime from happening in the first place, to meet the wider needs of victims, and to help turn offenders away from crime.

The CJS is designed to operate as a coherent whole. It is comprised of: the National Criminal Justice Board, 42 Local Criminal Justice Boards across England and Wales, and the Office for Criminal Justice Reform.

The Ministry of Justice was created in 2007 to provide a stronger focus on the criminal justice system, and to reduce re-offending. Many changes have been made since by the **Criminal Justice and Immigration Act 2008**. Among other things, the Act:

- introduces a minimum tariff of two years for prisoners serving indeterminate public protection sentences;
- ends automatic discounts for offenders given an indeterminate sentence after the initial sentencing decision has been judged unduly lenient;
- gives powers for courts to make dangerous offenders given a discretionary life sentence serve a higher proportion of their tariff before being eligible for parole;
- creates a presumption that trials in magistrates' courts will proceed in the event the accused fails to appear;
- provides for non-dangerous offenders who breach the terms of their licence to be recalled to prison for a fixed 28-day period;
- creates a Youth Rehabilitation Order – a generic community sentence for children

115

and young offenders – this will target the causes of offending behaviour and will simplify the current sentencing framework;
- creates the Youth Conditional Caution for children and young offenders;
- brings compensation for those wrongly convicted broadly into line with compensation for victims of crime.

Checklist

In particular, you should be familiar with the following recommendations and changes in the law.

Appeals
- The work of the Criminal Cases Review Commission.
- The powers for the Court of Appeal.
- The Court of Appeal's decision in *Secretary of State for the Home Department ex p Hickey and Others* (1995).

Trial by jury
- The provisions of the **Criminal Justice Act 2003, ss 43–50 and 321**.

Right to silence
- **Sections 34–37** of the **Criminal Justice and Public Order Act (CJPOA) 1994**, which explain what inferences may now be drawn in what circumstances from the silence of the accused.

Confessions
- **Sections 32–33** of the **CJPOA 1994**, which abolish the rules requiring the court to give the jury a warning about convicting the accused on the uncorroborated evidence of a person who is an accomplice or, in sexual cases, the victim.

Plea bargaining

Limited introduction was recommended by Runciman – reduced sentences for guilty pleas.

In general, you will need to know the major provisions of the **Police and Criminal Evidence Act (PACE) 1984** and other provisions relating to criminal procedure:

- the general powers of arrest – **s 24** of **PACE**;

The Criminal Process

- the general arrest conditions – **s 25** of **PACE**;
- the common law powers of arrest;
- procedure on arrest;
- information on arrest;
- stop and search – **ss 1 and 2** (and revised Code A) of **PACE**;
- search of arrested person – **s 32** of **PACE**;
- search on detention – **s 54** of **PACE**;
- search of premises – **ss 17, 18 and 32** of **PACE**;
- search warrants – **ss 8, 15 and 16** of **PACE**;
- interrogation, confession and admissibility of evidence;
- bail – the **CJPOA 1994** changes;
- plea bargaining.

Question 25

How far is it correct to say that the right to silence has been abolished in the English legal system? Discuss the arguments for and against the changes that have been made to this area of law by the **CJPOA 1994**.

Answer plan

A good response to this type of question will incorporate the following:

- an explanation of the 'right to silence';
- a brief explanation that the right has not been 'abolished';
- consideration of pre-Act law, in relation to silence when questioned by police and silence in court;
- examination of the background to the 1994 reform;
- discussion of the consequences of **ss 34–37** of the Act;
- some description of the alleged advantages of the changes;
- some description of the alleged disadvantages of the changes;
- conclusions.

Answer

Several meanings have been credited to the phrase 'the right to silence'. Six such meanings were identified by Lord Mustill in *Director of Serious Fraud Office ex p Smith* (1993). These ranged from the right to refuse to co-operate with a police inquiry to the principle against self-incrimination. The changes made by the **CJPOA 1994** are concerned with the legal effect of a suspect or accused failing to respond to questions by police officers, or failing to give evidence in his defence in court.

Notwithstanding the new Act, any person may refuse to answer questions put to him out of court. There are only a few exceptions to this (as with **s 2** of the **Criminal Justice Act 1987**, which concerns the investigation of serious fraud and requires certain questions to be answered, under pain of punishment for refusal) and they existed before the new Act. The **CJPOA 1994** does not alter the position of the accused person as a witness – he remains a competent but not compellable witness in his own defence (**s 35**) – although now the prosecution, as well as the judge, may comment upon such a failure to give evidence (**s 168**). Thus, the Act does not really 'abolish the right to silence'; a person can quite legally remain silent when questioned, although adverse comment may be made about such silence in some circumstances.

Except in so far as the new law makes changes, the old law still applies and this needs to be considered briefly first, in order properly to explain how far the **CJPOA** changes the legal framework.

Answering police questions and the right to silence

The police are free to ask anyone any questions. The only restriction is that all questioning is supposed to cease once a suspect has been charged.

There is no obligation on a citizen to answer police questions. A person cannot be charged, for example, with obstructing the police in the execution of their duty simply by failing to answer questions nor, before the **CJPOA 1994**, could the judge or prosecutor suggest to the jury that such silence was evidence of guilt. This was confirmed in *Rice v Connolly* (1966), where Lord Parker CJ said:

> It seems to me quite clear that, though every citizen has a moral duty or, if you like, a social duty to assist the police, there is no legal duty to that effect and, indeed, the whole basis of the common law is the right of the individual to refuse to answer questions put to him by persons in authority, and to refuse to accompany those in authority to any particular place; short, of course, of arrest.

There was an established common law rule that neither the prosecution nor the judge could make adverse comment on the defendant's silence in the face of questions from police officers at the time of arrest. The dividing line, however, between proper and improper judicial comment was a matter of great debate. There are many reasons why a suspect might remain silent when questioned (for example, fear, confusion, reluctance to incriminate another person) and the 'right of silence' has been a long-established general principle in English law. Thus, in *Davis* (1959), a judge was ruled on appeal to have misdirected the jury when he told them that:

> ... a man is not obliged to say anything, but you are entitled to use your common sense ... can you imagine an innocent man who had behaved like that not saying anything to the police? ... He said nothing.

Silence in court

Before the Act, the law relating to a defendant who did not give evidence in court was neatly summed up by the Lord Chief Justice, Lord Taylor, in *Martinez-Tobon* (1994). Where a defendant did not testify at his trial, the trial judge should have given the jury a direction that the defendant was under no obligation to testify and the jury should not assume that he is guilty because he had not given evidence. The judge could, however, comment on the defendant's failure to give evidence where the defence case involved alleged facts which were at variance with prosecution evidence, provided that the judge did not equate silence with guilt. In this case, involving charges of importing cocaine, the judge, commenting on the defence argument, had said that if the appellant 'thought it was emeralds and not drugs, one might have thought he would be very anxious to say so' (defence *counsel* had made this suggestion but this cannot be evidence). The judge's observations were held by the Court of Appeal to be quite proper, as he had also given a standard direction to the jury explaining that silence does not necessarily imply guilt.

Reform

The right to silence was considered by the Runciman Royal Commission on Criminal Justice. In a study commissioned by the Lord Chancellor's Department, only 2 per cent of 527 suspects exercised their right to silence. The Runciman Royal Commission eventually decided to recommend retaining the right to silence. Its report (1993) states:

> The majority of us believe that adverse inferences should not be drawn from silence at the police station and recommend retaining the present caution and trial direction [para 82].

The Commission did, however (para 84), recommend the retention of the current law regarding silence in investigations of serious and complex fraud, under which adverse consequences can follow from silence. The report notes that a large proportion of those who use the right to silence later plead guilty. The majority of the Commission felt that the possibility of an increase in convicting the guilty by abolishing the right would be outweighed by the considerable extra pressure on innocent suspects in police stations. The Commission did, however, meet the police and CPS's concern about 'ambush defences' where a defence is entered late in a trial, thus leaving the prosecution no time to check and rebut the defence. The Commission recommends that if the defence introduces a late change or departs from the strategy it has disclosed in advance to the prosecution, then it should face adverse comment (para 136). Professor Zander, however, issued a note of dissent that the principle must remain that the burden of proof always lies with the prosecution. He stated that:

> The fundamental issue at stake is that the burden of proof throughout lies with the prosecution. Defence disclosure is designed to be helpful to the prosecution and, more generally, to the system. But it is not the job of the defendant to be helpful either to the prosecution or the system.

The Government ignored the recommendation of the Royal Commission. The general purpose of the Act was to assist in the fight against crime. The Government took the view that the balance in the criminal justice system had become tilted too much in favour of the criminal and against the public in general and victims in particular. The alleged advantage of the change in law is that it helps convict criminals who, under the old law, used to be acquitted because they took advantage of the right to keep quiet when questioned, without the court or prosecution being able to comment adversely upon that silence. Introducing the legislation, the Home Secretary said that the change in the law was desirable because 'it is professional criminals, hardened criminals and terrorists who disproportionately take advantage of and abuse the present system'.

The new law is contained in **ss 34–37** of the Act. **Section 34** states that where anyone is questioned under caution by a police officer, or charged with an offence, then a failure to mention a fact at that time which he later relies on in his defence will allow a court to draw such inferences as appear proper about that failure. Inferences may only be drawn if, in the circumstances, a suspect could reasonably have been expected to mention the fact when he was questioned. The inferences which can be drawn can be used in determining whether the accused is guilty as charged. The section, however, permits adverse inferences to be drawn from silence in situations that do not amount to 'interviews', as defined by Code C of **PACE** and thus which are not subject to the safeguards of access to legal advice and of contemporaneous recording, which exist where a suspect is interviewed at the police station. The amended caution to be administered by police officers reads as follows (with appropriate variants for **ss 36** and **37**):

> You do not have to say anything. But it may harm your defence if you do not mention when questioned something which you later rely on in court.

As Card and Ward have warned, a temptation may arise for police officers to give this caution at the earliest possible stage in any situation in which they are talking to someone in connection with a crime, given that the caution may be understood (incorrectly) by some suspects as creating an obligation to speak:

> The Act does not affect earlier law on alibi defences. Under s 11 of the **Criminal Justice Act 1967**, the defence at trial on indictment cannot adduce evidence in support of an alibi defence (that is, where the accused claims to have been away from the crime at the time of its occurrence) unless notice of the details of that defence have been served on the prosecution within seven days of the transfer for trial. Nevertheless, this rule does not prevent an adverse inference being drawn by a court from a failure to have disclosed that alibi at an earlier stage (when, for instance, the accused was arrested).
>
> *The Criminal Justice and Public Order Act 1994*, 1994

Section 35 allows a court or jury to infer what appears proper from the refusal of an accused person, aged 14 or over, to testify in his own defence, or from a refusal without good cause to answer any question at trial. Section 36 permits inferences to be drawn from the failure or refusal of a person under arrest to account for any object, substances or mark in his possession, on his person, in or on his clothing or footwear, or in any place at which he was at the time of arrest. **Section 37** permits inferences to be drawn from the failure of an arrested person to account for his presence at a particular place where he was found.

Thus, as Lord Taylor, the late Lord Chief Justice, has observed, the legal changes do not, strictly speaking, abolish the right to silence:

> If a defendant maintains his silence from first till last, and does not rely on any particular fact by way of defence, but simply puts the prosecution to proof, then [ss 34–37] would not bite at all.

This is, of course, correct, but it ignores the change in the general structure of proofs. **Article 6** of the **European Convention on Human Rights** aims to protect the rights of a suspect to a fair trial. It states that:

> Everyone charged with a criminal offence shall be presumed innocent until proved guilty in accordance with law.

The European Commission on Human Rights has already ruled as admissible a complaint that provisions in the law of Northern Ireland equivalent to those in **ss 34–37** infringe **Art 6**, and the point can now be taken as applicable in the UK, since the **Human Rights Act 1998** came into force in October 2000.

Since the abolition of the court of Star Chamber in 1641, no English court has had the power to use torture or force to exact confessions from suspects. The so-called 'right to silence' really meant that a suspect could remain silent when questioned by police or in court, without prosecution counsel or the judge being allowed to make adverse comment to the jury about such a silence. Traditionally, silence could not be used in court as evidence of guilt.

In support of the old rule, it could be said that:

(a) people are innocent until proven guilty of a crime by the state;
(b) people should never be under force to condemn themselves; and
(c) there are several reasons other than genuine guilt why someone may wish to remain silent in the face of serious accusations – he might be terrified, confused, retarded, wish to protect someone else or fear that the truth would get them in some other type of trouble. The 11th Report of the Criminal Law Revision Committee (1972) gives several examples. The accused might be so shocked at an accusation that he forgets a vital fact which would acquit him of blame; his excuse might be embarrassing, such as being in the company of a prostitute; or he may fear reprisals from another party.

The 'right' is widely protected in other aspects of society: the police, for example, when facing internal disciplinary charges, are not bound to answer questions or allegations put to them.

Limitation of the right to silence has been widely and strongly opposed by lawyers, judges and legal campaign groups. Liberty, for example, has said that drawing adverse inferences from silence would undermine the presumption of innocence. Silence is an important safeguard against oppressive questioning by the police, particularly for the weak and vulnerable.

Michael Mansfield, the leading QC opposing the planned undermining of the right, pointed out that the Government was ignoring the recommendations of no fewer than three Royal Commissions (1929, 1981 and 1993), all of which had resolved in favour of keeping the right intact. He stated that:

> The presumption of innocence should be across the board – I do not think anyone should have to prove their innocence or we will be going towards an inquisitorial system.

John Alderson, former Chief Constable of Devon and Cornwall (1973–82) and a respected writer on constitutional aspects of policing, has written of the impending danger when police are able to 'exert legal and psychological pressure on individuals held in the loneliness of their cells'. He states that:

> History tells us that when an individual has to stand up against the entire apparatus of the modern state, he or she is very vulnerable. That is why, in criminal cases, the burden of proof has always rested on the state rather than on the accused. The Founding Fathers of America amended their constitution to that effect in 1791.

Undermining the right to silence may constitute a significant constitutional change in the relationship between the individual and the state. It may be doubted whether the majority of suspects should be put under greater intimidation by the system because of the conduct of a few 'hardened criminals' – the justification for the legislation given by the Home Secretary when he introduced the legislation.

In conclusion, however, two points should be noted to put the debate in its proper historical context. First, it should not be forgotten that there were, prior to the Act, several instances in English law where there was already a legal obligation for a suspect to answer questions. These included the obligation to speak under **s 2 of the Criminal Justice Act 1987** (above); the obligations under **ss 431–441 of the Companies Act 1985** (concerning investigations in respect of company officers and agents whose companies are being investigated by the Department of Trade and Industry); the obligations under **ss 22 and 131 of the Insolvency Act 1986** (concerning inquiries upon the winding up of companies); **s 18 of the Prevention of Terrorism (Temporary Provisions) Act 1989** (concerning information relating to terrorism); and the law under **s 11** (as amended) of the **Official Secrets Act 1911**.

Second, in the few cases where the right to silence was used under the pre-Act law, we need to ask how far juries were genuinely sympathetic to the judge's directions that they could not assume guilt from silence. Juries convicted in half of such cases, so there is evidence that jurors were suspicious and sceptical about people who exercised the right, just as they may be today when someone exercises the right (that is, remains silent from arrest until the jury retires, without relying on any fact he could have mentioned earlier).

NOTE

The decision in *Heaney and McGuiness v Ireland* (2001) will also be useful in answering some questions on this theme. Under the **Offences Against the State Act 1939**, it was a criminal offence punishable with imprisonment for a detained person to refuse to give a full account to the police of his actions and movements during a specified period. The court found a violation of **Art 6(1) and (2)**. While the right to silence and the right against self-incrimination are not absolute, the degree of compulsion created by the threat of a prison sentence in effect destroyed the very essence of these rights, in a manner incompatible with the **ECHR**.

Question 26

After a shop has been set on fire late one night, Detective Constables Whistle and Cuff, in a nearby road, hear about the incident on their car radio. They then see two youths, Gas and Spark, running down the road away from the area of the shop. The officers stop the youths, who smell of petrol, and ask them some questions. Gas and Spark are then arrested for arson and taken to the police station.

Before questioning, the officers untruthfully told Gas that his fingerprints had been discovered on a discarded bottle of petrol found in the burnt out shop. The solicitor, unaware of the deceit, advised Gas to disclose any involvement he had had in the incident and Gas admitted having taken part.

Spark declined to accept any legal advice after the proper notices about its availability had been given to him. Spark was a drug addict and after a session of relentless questions being fired at him for over two hours, he asked whether the police would agree to bail if he admitted to being involved in the incident. The officer in the room agreed and Spark made a statement, in which he said he was at the shop at the time the fire was just becoming serious, and had gone in to see if any property could be salvaged, but he had not started the fire.

Advise Gas and Spark on the admissibility of their statements.

Answer plan

Advice to Gas

In your advice to Gas, you should:

- explain the significance of **s 82(1)** of the **Police and Criminal Evidence Act (PACE) 1984**;
- explain the relevance of **ss 76** and **78** of **PACE**;
- explain and apply *Sang* (1980);
- explain and apply *Mason* (1988).

Advice to Spark

When advising Spark, include discussion of:

- the rule in *Zavekas* (1970);
- **s 76** of **PACE**, Code C and *Sharp* (1988);
- *Goldenberg* (1988) and the drug issue;
- three possible arguments on appeal, **ss 76, 78** and **82** of **PACE**;
- precedent on 'oppressive', for example, *Miller* (1986).

THE CRIMINAL PROCESS

Answer

Advice to Gas

A confession is defined in **s 82(1)** of **PACE** as a statement 'wholly or partly adverse to the party who made it'. Gas, within these terms, appears to have made a confession. The admissibility of a confession is governed by several sections of **PACE**. Section 76(2) states that in relation to confessions which have allegedly resulted from 'oppression', or in consequence of anything said or done which was likely, in the circumstances existing at the time, to render unreliable any confession made, the court shall not admit the evidence unless the prosecution proves that the confession was not obtained in such a manner.

Section 78 allows a court to refuse to admit evidence if it appears, having regard to all the circumstances including the circumstances in which the evidence was obtained, that admission of the evidence would have such an adverse effect on the fairness of the proceedings that the court ought not to admit it. It was held by the Court of Appeal in *Mason* (1988) that regardless of whether the admissibility of a confession falls to be considered under **s 76(2)**, a judge has the discretion to deal with it under **s 78**.

Section 82 states that 'nothing in this part of the Act [Pt VIII, dealing with evidence] shall prejudice any power of a court to exclude evidence'. The general view is that **s 82** preserved the whole of the common law existing prior to **PACE**, so that a confession could also be excluded under decisions like that of the House of Lords in *Sang* (1980). That case permitted exclusion of evidence where its prejudicial effect outweighs its probative value. Lord Diplock thought that a discretion only existed at common law with regard to admissions and confessions and 'generally with regard to evidence obtained from the accused after commission of the offence'. One observation of Lord Diplock's which is especially helpful to Gas (although *obiter dicta*) is that the purpose of such judicial discretion is to ensure that an accused was not induced to incriminate himself by deception.

It would be possible for Gas to argue for the exclusion of his admission on all three of the above sections (**ss 76, 78 and 82**).

In *Mason* (1988), on facts similar to those in question, the defendant was tricked into making an admission of instigating an arson attack on the car of an enemy, after a police officer had told both him and his solicitor that the defendant's fingerprints had been found on a bottle of inflammable liquid used in the attack. Following the solicitor's advice to give an explanation, the defendant then admitted his role in the arson. The Court of Appeal quashed the defendant's conviction as having such an adverse effect on the fairness of the proceedings (**s 78**) that the court should have excluded it. It is not certain, however, that this case would assist Gas. In *Mason*, the trial judge had admitted the evidence of the defendant's admission, but, in saying the trial judge wrongly exercised his discretion, the Court of Appeal said he had omitted one 'vital factor' from his considerations: that of the deceit practised on the defendant's solicitor. Evidently, a deceit practised only upon the defendant – as in our case – would not in itself warrant discretionary exclusion of the admission.

Advice to Spark

Zavekas (1970) was a case decided using the old Judges' Rules, which held that admissions, to be admissible, had to be voluntary in the sense of being obtained without 'fear of prejudice or hope of advantage, exercised or held out by a person in authority'. The Court of Appeal quashed a conviction, because the trial judge had admitted a confession made after the defendant asked the police whether he could have bail if he made a statement and, receiving an affirmative reply, proceeded to confess. Such law has, however, been effectively overruled by **s 76(2)(b)** of **PACE** and Code C, which give a much narrower compass to the notion of unreliability in respect of confessions. Spark's admission is 'mixed', in that it contains parts which are incriminating (he was at the scene of the crime and he did go into the shop) and parts which are self-serving and self-exculpatory (he did not start the fire). The combination of the provisions of **PACE** and the decisions of the House of Lords in *Sharp* (1988) and *Aziz* (1996) appear to have put the law on this subject beyond doubt. Their Lordships in both *Sharp* and *Aziz* specifically approved the judgment of Lord Lane in *Duncan* (1981), which held that the simplest method and, therefore, the one most likely to produce a just result is for the jury to consider the whole statement, both the incriminating parts and the excuses and explanations, in deciding where the truth lies. **Section 82(1)** of **PACE** defines 'confession' as including 'any statement wholly or partly adverse to the person who made it'. Accordingly, statements of 'mixed' content count as confessions and are admissible in evidence, subject to **s 76** of **PACE** being satisfied.

The Code says that if a suspect asks an officer a 'direct question' as to what action will be taken in the event of his answering questions, making a statement or refusing to do either, 'the officer may inform him what action he proposes to take in that event provided that the action itself is proper and warranted' (Code C, para 11.3).

Provided that the police officer, in stating that the police would agree to bail in consequence of an admission, was answering a direct question from Spark, then the police conduct is lawful and the evidence not rendered inadmissible or vulnerable to exclusion.

The fact that Spark was a drug addict and might have been sufficiently desperate for more drugs to have admitted to anything in order to get bail would not, on current case law, appear to affect the matter provided, of course, that his confession was not prompted by any other factor of police conduct in breach of the Act or the Codes. In *Goldenberg* (1988), the defendant, a heroin addict, requested an interview five days after his arrest and, during this interview, he allegedly gave information about someone whom he claimed had supplied him with heroin. At trial, counsel for the defendant argued that the evidence of the interview might be unreliable under s 76:

(a) because the admissions were made in an attempt to get bail; and
(b) because of his addiction, it might be expected that the defendant would do or say anything – however false – to get bail and thus be able to feed his addiction.

This latter argument was rejected both at trial and on appeal. There was no argument that the interviewing officer had said or done anything improper, and the words 'in consequence of anything said or done' in s 76(2)(b) meant said or done by someone other than the suspect.

If it can be shown that the police interview with Spark was 'oppressive', then the argument for the exclusion of the confession could be run in any or all of three ways: (a) that it should be excluded by virtue of s 76(2)(a), as the police conduct was oppressive *simpliciter*, or that in conjunction with the fact of Spark's addiction and in view of the *ratio* of *Goldenberg* (where the appeal was dismissed because of no evidence of police misconduct), it was a confession gained by oppression; or (b) that it should be excluded by virtue of s 78 (see advice to Gas, above); or (c) that it should be excluded by virtue of s 82, as its prejudicial effect greatly outweighs its probative value and it is within Lord Diplock's formula from *Sang* (1980) of protecting a suspect's right not to incriminate himself.

It will be difficult to show that the police interview was 'oppressive', as the courts have been very reluctant to make such findings. In *Fulling* (1987), the Court of Appeal gave 'oppression' its dictionary meaning, which involves 'the exercise of power or authority in a burdensome, harsh or wrongful manner'. *Fulling* was applied in *Emmerson* (1991). Questioning that was 'rude and discourteous', with a raised voice and some bad language and which gave the impression of 'impatience and irritation', was not considered oppressive. *Paris* (1994) produced a different result. The police were held to have behaved oppressively after shouting at a suspect what they wanted him to say over 300 times, after he had denied involvement in the offence charged. However, in *L* (1994), tactics similar to those employed in *Paris* appear to have been regarded as acceptable. The length of the interviews and the nature of the questioning are, of course, the important considerations.

Rules in Code C govern how interviews should be conducted. It is provided (Code C, para 12.7) that breaks from interviewing shall be made at recognised meal times and that 'short breaks for refreshment shall also be provided at intervals of approximately two hours'. An officer has the discretion to delay a break, but only where there are reasonable grounds for believing that the break would:

(a) involve a risk of harm to persons or serious loss or damage to property; or
(b) unnecessarily delay the suspect's release from custody; or
(c) otherwise prejudice the outcome of the investigation.

It thus seems unlikely that Spark's interview, which lasted 'for over two hours' (but, presumably, nearer to two than three hours), was oppressive, unless he can show that it was deliberately aimed at producing a state of confusion, or that it transgressed the fairly wide Code rules.

One final consideration is that Spark is described as a 'youth'. Code C, para 1.5 says that if anyone appears to be under the age of 17, then he shall be treated as a juvenile. Code C, para 11.14 states that a juvenile, whether suspected or not, must not be interviewed or asked to provide or sign a written statement in the absence of an appropriate adult (unless **para 11.1** or **Annex C** applies, allowing an interview to take place if a delay in interviewing the suspect would lead to interfering with evidence or witnesses).

Question 27

After a series of burglaries in Grimtown, Pat and Billy were arrested by police and taken to the local police station. Pat and Billy were taken to separate rooms for interrogation.

Pat asked to see a solicitor. A police officer wrote something down, went out of the room and came back saying that there would need to be a little delay, as: 'We would not want word to get out to the wrong people that you're in here.' The officer then said: 'You know the ropes, Pat, we would just like to ask you a few simple questions.' Pat then made some confessions which were admitted in court and he was convicted for offences of burglary.

In the other room, Billy also asked about a lawyer. 'We can arrange for one or you can have your own', he was told. Billy thought for a moment and then replied that it would probably be too expensive, so he would not opt for legal advice. Billy asked the police to inform the president of the Civil Freedom League of his arrest. A senior officer told Billy that would not be possible. Billy has now also confessed to certain burglaries and has been tried and convicted.

Advise Pat and Billy on the possibility of appealing against their convictions.

Answer plan

Advice to Pat

In your advice to Pat, you should:

- give the meaning of s 58 of the **Police and Criminal Evidence Act (PACE) 1984;**

- explain the significance of **s 116**, 'serious arrestable offence';
- state whether burglary falls within this category – see **s 24(1)(b)**;
- explain and apply *McIvor* (1987);
- explain and apply *Smith (Eric)* (1987), *Samuel* (1988) and *Parris* (1989);
- explain and apply Code C, Annex B, Note B4.

Advice to Billy

In your advice to Billy, you should examine:

- his entitlement to free advice: revised Code C, para 3.1;
- the meaning of 'friend or relative' (**s 56(6)**);
- the application of *Beycan* (1990);
- the relevance of **s 76(2)(b)**.

Answer

Advice to Pat

PACE came into effect in 1986 and, since that time, the access a suspect in a police station has to a lawyer has been governed by the Act. **Section 58(1) of PACE** states that a person arrested and held in custody in a police station shall be entitled, if he so requests, to consult a solicitor at any time. The request must be recorded in the custody record and the request must be granted 'as soon as is practicable', except to the extent that delay is permitted by the section. Delay in compliance with Pat's request is only permitted by the section if he is being held in connection with a 'serious arrestable offence' and an officer of at least the rank of superintendent authorises it. 'Serious arrestable offences' are defined in **s 116** and **Sched 5**. The term includes named offences such as murder and rape and also any arrestable offence which has, *inter alia*, led to 'substantial financial gain to any person' (**s 116(6)(e)**) or 'serious financial loss to any person' (**s 116(6)(f)**).

Burglary is an 'arrestable offence' by virtue of **s 24(1)(b) of PACE** as someone over 21 (without previous convictions) could, upon conviction for it, be sentenced to a term of imprisonment of five years. It is arguable whether Pat has been arrested in connection with a 'serious arrestable offence'. It would depend on the value of the stolen goods and on the respective financial positions of:

(a) those who were burgled; and

(b) Pat.

It was held in *McIvor* (1987) that the theft of 28 beagles worth £880 from a hunt was not a serious arrestable offence. The theft of the dogs, which were owned collectively by the hunt, did not cause 'serious financial loss'. In *Smith (Eric)* (1987), a robbery from Woolworths involving two video recorders (valued at £800) plus cash of £116 was regarded by the trial judge as probably not a serious arrestable offence: the loss to such a large national store would be small and the gain to the robbers would not necessarily be substantial.

Under Code C, Annex B, Note C1, an officer of at least the rank of superintendent may only delay Pat's access to a solicitor on the grounds stated in **s 58** of **PACE**. He must have 'reasonable grounds' for believing that such access will:

(a) lead to interference with, or harm to, evidence connected with a serious arrestable offence, or interference with, or physical injury to, other persons; or

(b) lead to the alerting of other persons involved in the offence but not yet arrested; or

(c) hinder the recovery of any property obtained as a result of the offence.

The words used by the officer to Pat, 'We would not want word to get out to the wrong people that you're in here', are consistent with any of the statutory reasons in (a) to (c) above. The Act says, however, that if the delay is authorised, then the suspect must be told the reason for the delay and the reasons must be recorded on the custody sheet. The officer's words here are quite vague, so neither of the requirements (the explanation to Pat and the recording of the reason) appear to have been complied with.

Moreover, it was held in *Samuel* (1988) that it was insufficient for an officer simply to believe that giving a suspect access to a solicitor might lead to the alerting of accomplices: the defendant was being questioned about offences of burglary and robbery. His request to see a solicitor was refused, on the grounds that the offences were serious and that there was a risk of accomplices being inadvertently alerted. The defendant subsequently made confessions which were admitted at trial. The Court of Appeal quashed his conviction, stating that access to a solicitor was a 'fundamental right' of a citizen and that a police officer who sought to refuse access had to justify the refusal by reference to the specific circumstances of the case. The court noted that 'solicitors are intelligent professional people', whereas most suspects were 'not very clever', so the likelihood of the latter being able to hoodwink the former into inadvertently passing on a coded message to fellow criminals was very low. This would probably only be a sustainable point in very few cases.

In *Parris* (1989), it was held that where the lawyer called was the duty solicitor, there would usually be no grounds for the police fearing that he would alert other parties to the crime. Here, the court quashed a conviction for armed robbery because of breaches of **s 58**. In *Davidson* (1988), it was held by the Court of Appeal that the police had to be 'nearly certain' that a solicitor granted access to the suspect would warn another criminal or get rid of the proceeds of the crime. The power to delay access to a solicitor could not be exercised until the suspect had nominated an actual solicitor. This was not the case here; the court excluded the confessions given by the suspect without legal advice and, as a result, the prosecution's case collapsed.

The revised Code of Practice (Code C, Annex B, Note B4) clarifies the position further. This says that the officer may only authorise a delay if he has reasonable grounds to believe that the specific solicitor in question will, inadvertently or otherwise, pass on a message from the detained person which will lead to the alerting of accomplices, or interference with evidence. It is uncertain from the question whether Pat is asking to see a specific solicitor. Unless this is the case and the officer has reasonable grounds for the relevant suspicions, then he will be in breach of the Code and **s 58**. Such a breach, though, does not entail automatic exclusion by the court of any resulting statement made by the suspect. The court will evaluate all the circumstances.

In *Dunford* (1990), the defendant had a record and was aware of his right not to answer any questions put by the police. Before reaching the police station, he had refused to answer questions and had, thereafter, answered several questions with the phrase 'no comment'. In such circumstances, the Court of Appeal ruled that the judge had been entitled to allow the confession made in the police station. Moreover, the Court of Appeal ruled in *Walsh* (1990) that an 'adverse effect on the fairness of proceedings' within the meaning of **s 78** would no doubt follow from a 'significant and substantial breach' of **s 58**, but that did not necessarily mean that the evidence thus obtained had to be excluded. The court had to decide, not simply whether there had been an adverse effect on the fairness of proceedings, but whether it had been such an adverse effect that justice required the evidence to be excluded.

In sum, Pat's appeal could succeed if he could persuade the Court of Appeal that **s 78** should have been used to exclude evidence of his confessions because of significant breaches of **s 58** and Code C, which had such an adverse effect on the fairness of proceedings that justice requires they be excluded. Pat's access to a lawyer is delayed, but was **s 58** of **PACE** complied with? The officer 'wrote something down', but was this the required entry on the custody sheet? He went out of the room, but was it to get the required permission of the superintendent? Was the vague reason given to Pat for the delay sufficient to exclude Pat's 'fundamental right'? There are also significant doubts about whether the offence was a 'serious arrestable offence' and whether, if so, the police had reasonable grounds to believe that any of the criteria in **s 58(8)** were applicable. Overall, this gives a strong case to Pat, only slightly counterposed by virtue of Pat's possible criminal record (that is, '. . . you know the ropes, Pat . . .') by the decisions in *Dunford* and *Walsh*.

Advice to Billy

The duty solicitor schemes at police stations, set up under **PACE**, are run by the Legal Aid Board. The provision of legal advice to suspects at police stations is not means tested; it is paid for by the state. Research has shown that many suspects who previously did not take up the opportunity for legal advice abstained because they were unaware that it was free. The revised Code of Practice (April 1995) dealt with this problem by requiring the police to inform the suspect that the advice is free (Code C, para 3.1(ii)). The Code also requires (para 6.3) that a poster advertising the right to have free legal advice must be displayed prominently in the charging area of every police station.

We are not told whether there is a poster for Billy to see, but in not informing Billy that advice is free, the officer is in breach of the Code.

Under **s 56** of **PACE**, an arrested person held in custody, like Billy, has the right to have someone informed of his arrest. The person to be informed must be a 'friend or relative or other person who is known to him or who is likely to take an interest in his welfare'. Whether the president of the Civil Freedom League is within this category is a moot point. He would be if he was a friend or associate of Billy's and even, possibly, in his capacity as someone publicly concerned with civil liberties but, if the only link was the latter one, it is uncertain whether this would be sufficient. A circular issued to police to assist them with the operation of **s 56**'s forerunner (**s 62** of the **Criminal Law Act 1977**) excluded public figures, like pop stars and football players, from the sorts of person who could be notified. Those groups, however, are of course not related to civil liberties.

The only other reasons given in the Act to justify a delay in notifying a specified person are when, in a case of a serious arrestable offence (see under advice to Pat), an officer of at least the rank of superintendent authorises it for any of the reasons in **s 56(5)**, which are the same as those dealt with in Pat's case under **s 58(8)**. **Section 56(6)** states that the suspect must be told of the reason for the delay and it must be recorded on the custody sheet, neither of which appear to have been done in this case.

It seems more likely that there has been a breach of Code C (in respect of the notification of free legal advice) than of **s 56**, but, even if there were only such a breach of the Code, it is quite possible that the Court of Appeal would quash Billy's conviction, as he was deprived of his fundamental right to legal advice as a result of the breach. In *Beycan* (1990), the Court of Appeal quashed a conviction based on a confession when the suspect had been arrested, taken to the station and asked: 'Are you happy to be interviewed in the normal way we conduct these interviews without a solicitor, friend or representative?' Billy's case is arguably stronger, as he has actually expressed a desire for advice and only proceeded reluctantly without it.

It may be possible to construe these events, in respect of Billy, in a way which shows him 'changing his mind' about taking legal advice. Thus, there could also be a possible breach of Code C, para 6.6(d):

> When the person who wanted legal advice changes his mind, the interview may be started without further delay provided the person has given his agreement in writing or on tape to being interviewed without receiving legal

advice and that an officer of the rank of inspector or above has given agreement . . .

In *Wadman* (1996), the defendant, having initially declined legal advice, changed his mind and then, while arrangements were being made, reverted to saying that he did not wish to have a solicitor. The police failed to comply with para 6.6(d) of Code C. The judge held that the Code was not 'mandatory' and admitted the evidence. On appeal, the conviction was quashed. The court ruled that the judge's approach to the Code was flawed; he confused the discretion he had on the *voir dire* – whether to admit the evidence – with the absence of discretion for police officers when complying with the Code: it was a disciplinary offence not to do so. It was not a case where the court should exercise its own discretion.

The appeals of both Pat and Billy could also be argued under **s 76(2)(b)**, which permits the court not to allow the confession if it was gained in consequence of:

> . . . anything said or done which was likely, in the circumstances existing at the time, to render unreliable any confession which might be made by him in consequence thereof.

The basis of the argument would be the same as for **s 78**.

Question 28

After a serious assault on an old woman by a group of youths, PCs East and Wood stopped Peter in the street late at night. He had blood on his hands. When asked some simple routine questions, Peter became abusive and very hostile to the officers. He told the officers that his name was 'Mickey Mouse' and refused to answer any questions.

The following day, Mary and Paul are arrested for taking part in the assault. During questioning by police, Mary sat with her boyfriend, who is a law student. Before being cautioned, she answered some questions, but not others and, at her trial, the judge suggested to the jury that she 'might have remained silent to avoid incriminating herself'.

Paul remained silent after being cautioned, refusing to answer police questions and, at trial, the judge invited the jury to consider whether an innocent man would have behaved in such a manner.

Peter has been convicted of obstructing the police officers in the execution of their duty. Mary and Paul have now been convicted of the assault. Advise Peter, Mary and Paul about their possible grounds of appeal.

> **Answer plan**
>
> **Advice to Peter**
>
> When advising Peter:
>
> - apply *Rice v Connolly* (1966) – consider what constitutes 'obstruction';
> - apply *Ricketts v Cox* (1982) – 'the manner of a person together with his silence';
> - consider whether the decisions are distinguishable.
>
> **Advice to Mary**
>
> When advising Mary:
>
> - apply *Davis* (1959) – improper directions to a jury;
> - consider the rule in *Parkes* (1976), where people are speaking on equal terms;
> - discuss the decision in *Chandler* (1976);
> - evaluate which case is closer to the facts of the problem.
>
> **Advice to Paul**
>
> Your advice to Paul should include:
>
> - the basis for an appeal – the **Criminal Appeal Act 1968**;
> - application of *Chandler* (1976).

Answer

Advice to Peter

Peter might have an appeal against his conviction for obstructing the police officers in the execution of their duty if he was not legally obliged to answer the questions put to him by the officers. Normally, the citizen is entitled to remain silent in the face of police questions, without this either being the subject of a charge of obstructing the police in the execution of their duties, or being commented on adversely by the prosecution or judge at trial.

This rule is established by the important Divisional Court decision in *Rice v Connolly* (1966). The appellant was seen by officers at night in an area where burglaries had been committed. He refused to tell the police where he had come from or where he was going. He identified himself only by his surname and a street name where he said he lived. He refused to accompany the police to a police box to further verify his identity. His conviction for an offence under s 51(3) of the **Police Act 1964** (resisting or wilfully obstructing a police officer in the execution of his duty) was quashed, as the Divisional Court said he had the right not to answer the questions. Lord Parker CJ stated that a proper conviction would require proof that the action was 'wilful', which means not only done intentionally, but also done without lawful excuse. Citizens, he said, had a moral duty and perhaps a social one to help the police with their inquiries, but there was no such legal duty.

The decision in *Rice v Connolly* was unanimous, but James J noted that he would not go so far as to say that silence combined with conduct could not amount to an obstruction. It would be a matter for the courts to decide on the facts of any particular case. In *Ricketts v Cox* (1982), on facts similar to those in question here, the defendant's appeal against a conviction under s 51(3) was dismissed. Two police officers questioned the defendant and another man in the early hours of the morning, following a serious assault. The defendant was uncooperative and shouted in obscene language at the officers, and then tried to walk away without answering any questions. The court found that this was an instance where 'the manner of a person together with his silence' could amount to obstruction. This decision probably accounts for Peter's conviction, in view of his obstreperous conduct coupled with the evidently false name he gave.

The decision in *Ricketts v Cox* has been widely criticised (Glanville Williams; Smith and Hogan; and Bailey, Harris and Jones) as flawed and at odds with *Rice v Connolly*. If a refusal to answer questions is lawful, which it clearly is, then how can this important constitutional right be cancelled merely because the questioned party is abusive? Peter's appeal could be based upon this point, inviting the Court of Appeal to deal with the confusion promoted by the two Divisional Court decisions by overruling *Ricketts v Cox*. Peter could possibly be acquitted if the facts of his case were governed simply by the decision in *Rice v Connolly*. Even though, unlike the appellant in the 1966 case, Peter had gone beyond simple reticence and told the officers his name was 'Mickey Mouse', this could perhaps be argued to be so self-evidently false as tantamount to saying, 'I shall not tell you my name'. The court agreed, in *Rice v Connolly*, that to tell a 'cock and bull' story to the police would obviously be an obstruction. This would clearly cover Peter had he said his name was Tom Smith and misled the police as to his true identity, but his sarcastic reference to a cartoon character could be regarded as not seriously misleading, and lawful, as he is not legally obliged to reveal his name. It does not look like Peter was under caution when he refused to answer police questions. If he was, then his failure to answer could be made the subject of comment (see below, under 'Advice to Mary') by the trial judge under s 34 of the **Criminal Justice and Public Order Act (CJPOA) 1994**.

Advice to Mary

Mary's conviction could be quashed if it can be shown that the trial judge's words to the jury amounted to a misdirection. Before the **CJPOA 1994**, the 'right to silence' was regarded as a well entrenched principle of law. The common law position is that everyone still has the right to remain silent in the same circumstances as they did before the **1994 Act**; what has changed is the entitlement of the judge or prosecuting counsel to make adverse comment on such a silence. There are many reasons why a suspect might remain silent when questioned (for example, fear, confusion, reluctance to incriminate another person) and, generally, failure or refusal to answer questions does not amount to evidence against the person concerned, unless it can be said that the defendant was on 'equal terms' with the questioner. In *Parkes* (1976), the Privy Council ruled that a judge could invite the jury to consider the possibility of drawing adverse inferences from silence from a tenant who had been accused by a landlady of murdering her daughter. The landlady and tenant, for this encounter, were regarded as having parity of status, unlike a person faced with questions from the police. Failure to answer questions put by a police officer, or someone in a similar position, is unlikely to lead to adverse inferences being drawn at any trial. In *Chandler* (1976), the suspect, in the company of his solicitor, refused to answer some questions asked by a police officer before the caution. The judge told the jury that they should decide whether the defendant's silence was attributable to his wish to exercise his common law right, or because he might incriminate himself. The Court of Appeal thought the presence of Chandler's solicitor meant that the parties were on 'even terms' but, on the facts, quashed Chandler's conviction, since the judge had gone too far in suggesting that silence before a caution could be evidence of guilt.

The alleged advantage of the change of law is that **ss 34–38** of the **CJPOA 1994** help convict criminals who, under the old law, used to be acquitted because they took advantage of the right to keep quiet when questioned, without the court or prosecution being able to comment adversely upon that silence. However, the dangers entailed in undermining the right of silence are most acute in respect of police questioning scenarios. In *R v Condron* (1997), the Court of Appeal said that the guidelines set out in *R v Cowan* (1996), regarding the drawing of adverse inferences where the accused fails to testify, are equally applicable where the accused fails to answer questions when being interviewed by the police. More detailed guidance was given in *R v Argent* (1997), where the Court of Appeal set out the conditions which have to be satisfied before adverse inferences can be drawn from a person's failure to answer police questions (**s 34** of the **CJPOA 1994**). The conditions include:

(a) the failure to answer has to occur before a defendant was charged;
(b) the alleged failure must occur during questioning under caution;
(c) the questioning must be directed at trying to discover whether and by whom the offence has been committed;

(d) the failure must be a failure to mention any fact relied on in the person's defence; and

(e) the fact that the defendant failed to mention has to be one which this particular defendant could reasonably be expected to have mentioned when being questioned, taking account of all the circumstances existing at that time (for example, the time of day, the defendant's age, experience, mental capacity, state of health, sobriety, personality and access to legal advice).

Therefore, s 34(1) only applies in respect of questioning under caution. If no caution is administered, no inference can be drawn from the failure to mention a fact in response to such questioning. A person must be cautioned where there are grounds to suspect him of an offence, before any questions are put to him regarding involvement or suspected involvement in that offence (Code C, para 10.1 of the **Police and Criminal Evidence Act (PACE) 1984**) and a person must normally be cautioned on being arrested (Code D, para 10.3). A caution need not be administered if the questions are put for other purposes. **Section 34** permits adverse inferences to be drawn from silence in situations that do not amount to 'interviews', as defined by Code C of PACE, and thus which are not subject to the safeguards of access to legal advice and of contemporaneous recording, which exist where a suspect is interviewed at a police station. An 'interview' is defined by Code C, para 11.1(a) as being:

> ... the questioning of a person regarding his involvement or suspected involvement in a criminal offence or offences which by virtue of para 10.1 of Code C is required to be carried out under caution.

Sections 36 and **37** of the **CJPOA 1994** permit inferences to be drawn from the failure of an arrested person to account for an object, substance or mark, etc, or to account for his presence at a particular place where he is found. The main differences between **s 34** and **ss 36** and **37** are that **s 34** applies where the suspect has been cautioned, but **ss 36** and **37** only apply where the suspect has been arrested; **ss 36** and **37** apply whether or not a fact is relied upon in a person's defence, whereas **s 34** applies only in respect of failure to mention a fact relied upon in a person's defence.

Mary could appeal against her conviction if prosecution evidence is obtained as a result of unfair or unlawful police conduct under **ss 76** and **78** of **PACE**. The questioning of Mary at the station prior to a caution being given may be in contravention of **s 34** of the **CJPOA 1994** and the Codes of Practice in **PACE** (Code C, para 10 and Code D). Cautions need not be given if the questions put did not constitute an 'interview' and were 'questions put for other purposes', but these considerations would not be applicable here, as Mary was already arrested at the material time of being questioned. If Mary failed to answer questions subsequently, under caution or on being charged, **s 34** applies only to facts which she later relies on in her defence. The section has no function if she makes no attempt to put previously undisclosed facts forward at trial.

The common law position continues to apply where the new statutory provisions do not apply. Mary could appeal against her conviction on the grounds that she was not on 'equal terms' with the officer who interviewed her as, unlike the defendant in *Chandler*, she was not accompanied by a lawyer, but merely a law student.

Advice to Paul

Prior to 1996, the Court of Appeal would allow an appeal if they thought that: (a) the conviction was unsafe and unsatisfactory; (b) the judgment of the court trial should be set aside on a wrong decision on any question of law; and (c) there had been a material irregularity in the course of the trial. The **Criminal Appeal Act 1995** abolishes the three grounds of appeal, replacing them with a single test, namely, that the court thinks the conviction is unsafe. The Act does not contain any definition of the word 'unsafe'. Much of the former law will therefore be relevant in deciding what is liable to render a conviction unsafe. In particular, the court may still apply the 'lurking doubt' test enunciated in *R v Cooper* (1969):

> . . . whether we are content to let the matter stand as it is, or whether there is not some lurking doubt in our minds which makes us wonder whether an injustice has been done.

As noted above, **ss 34–38** of the **CJPOA 1994** constitute a major curtailment of the 'right of silence'. Thus, although Paul retains his 'right' to remain silent both at the trial and the interrogation, 'proper' inferences may be drawn from his failure to mention certain facts when questioned under caution or on being charged (**s 34**).

Paul's appeal could succeed if he can show that **s 78** of **PACE** should have been used to exclude adverse inferences of his silence because of significant breaches of **s 34** of the **CJPOA 1994**. If he simply contends that there is no case to answer, that he has no fact which he could have contributed and he does not rely on a particular defence, **s 34** can have no effect. There can be no conviction on silence alone. **Section 38** applies to all four provisions of the **1994 Act** which operate to permit the drawing of inferences, and stipulates that a defendant cannot be convicted or have a case to answer solely on the basis of an inference drawn from silence. There must, therefore, be some other evidence in addition to any inference to be drawn.

Question 29

After an armed robbery at the Upland Bank in Oldcastle, the police arrested Karl for his involvement in the crime. An hour later, having interviewed Karl at the police station, the police went to his parents' home to remove for forensic examination a car parked in the driveway. Tony, Karl's father, resisted the police attempts to remove the vehicle and punched PC Grit. Tony was eventually overpowered and PC Grit then searched the garage and found a collection of plastic bank cards with different names and a pile of correspondence about crimes, including some letters bearing advice from Karl's solicitor.

Karl has been charged with involvement in the bank robbery and crimes relating to the stolen bank cards. Tony has been charged with assaulting an officer in the execution of his duty. Advise Karl and Tony.

Answer plan

Advice to Karl

You should include:

- an explanation and application of **s 78** of the **Police and Criminal Evidence Act (PACE) 1984**;
- an explanation and application of **s 18** of **PACE**;
- an explanation and application of **s 32** of **PACE**;
- an application of *Badham* (1987);
- consideration of Code B (revised) on searches and **s 67(11)** on exclusions;
- discussion of the ambit of **s 19** of **PACE**.

Advice to Tony

Include:

- an explanation of the effect of **s 117** of **PACE** in the context of the legality of the searches under **s 18** or **s 20**;
- discussion of **s 51** of the **Police Act 1964**.

Answer

Advice to Karl

The police appear to have had sufficient evidence on which to arrest Karl before any examination of the car in his driveway. Nevertheless, the car seems to be very significant evidence as the police went back to get it. It is important to discover, therefore, whether the police were legally entitled to act as they did. If not, then the evidence obtained might be excluded under **s 78** of **PACE**, if it is likely to have, in all of the circumstances, an adverse effect on the trial.

The answer to this particular question – whether the police search was lawful –

will also determine whether Tony was legally justified in acting as he did, so this matter shall be returned to again later.

Karl has been arrested for robbery, which is an arrestable offence by virtue of the fact that Karl, if he was over 21 (even without previous convictions), could be sentenced to a term of imprisonment for five years or more upon conviction (**s 24** of **PACE**). **Section 18** of **PACE** empowers an officer to enter premises 'occupied or controlled by a person arrested for an arrestable offence' to search for evidence related to that or connected offences. He must, however, have 'reasonable grounds' for believing that there is evidence on the premises that relates to the offence in question or to some offence 'which is connected with or similar to that offence'. Searching for the vehicle suspected of being used in the armed robbery would be within the section's ambit, provided that Karl was an occupant of the address in the sense that he lived or stayed there. We know that letters to Karl from his solicitor were found in his father's garage, which suggests that Karl lived at that address. The search of the garage which results in the discovery of the cards and letters would also be within the section's scope, if crimes relating to stolen bank cards can be regarded as 'similar to' the crime of bank robbery. The element of violence or its threat involved in robbery would probably, however, put it in a different class from matters of deception and fraud.

The section also states that any officer making such a search must have prior authorisation in writing from a fellow officer of at least the rank of inspector, or subsequent approval, if such is necessary for the 'effective investigation of the offence'. The authorising officer must make a record of the search and, if the search was authorised in advance, it must show the nature of the evidence that was sought, in order to avoid 'fishing expeditions'. Failure to conform with these rules courts the risk that evidence, thus obtained, will not be admissible in court. Many searches of this type are conducted some time after arrest, so the lapse of an hour before the police come to search Tony's premises and take the evidence does not appear to affect the lawfulness of the conduct.

It may be that Karl did not live with or stay with his parents, in which case the search would not be lawful under **s 18**. There is, however, the possibility that the search could have been lawful under **s 32**, which authorises the search, *inter alia*, of any premises on which the arrest took place. The search can be for anything relating to the offence for which a person has been arrested. If the search was made under this power, then it would be lawful in respect of the car (allegedly, used in the robbery), but not in respect of the bank cards or letters. We do not know where Karl was arrested, but, if he was arrested at his parents' home, then **s 32** would legitimise the police search. The delay, however, might be more significant here. According to the decision in *Badham* (1987), a search of the home where the defendant lived with his father, which took place three hours after the defendant's arrest was not lawful. The Act gave no time-limit, but the section was headed 'Search upon arrest' and the power was an immediate one. The Crown Court held that it would be wrong to permit an open-ended right to go back to the premises where the arrest had taken place. Here, PC Grit goes to Tony's house only an hour after Karl's arrest, but the *ratio decidendi* of *Badham* would apply just as much to this shorter, but still considerable, delay. **Section 32** might perhaps permit an officer escorting an arrested suspect back to the station to turn around after two minutes' walking and return to search the premises where the arrest was made, but not after an hour.

It is a requirement of the revised Code B (April 1995) that when conducting a search, the police shall give to the occupier a written notice of powers and rights showing which powers have been exercised. This applies to searches made under several powers, including those under **ss 18** and **32**. The notice must specify under which power the search is being made. The notice must also explain the rights of the occupier and the owner of any property seized. The Codes of Practice are not technically 'law'. If Karl can show that evidence (that is, relating to the car) has been obtained in breach of the Code, then the trial judge or Appeal Court can be invited to exclude that evidence (**s 67(11)**).

There is no common law power to enter and search premises after an arrest, so any search not lawful under **ss 18** or **32** would be unlawful.

Under **s 19**, an officer who is lawfully searching any premises is authorised to seize any article (if it is not covered by legal professional privilege) if he reasonably believes that it is evidence relating to the offence which he is investigating, or 'any other offence', and that it is necessary to seize it in order to prevent it from being 'concealed, lost, damaged, altered or destroyed'. It would be possible for the police to make a convincing case for the car (if there was evidence connecting it to the robbery) and the bank cards to be seized. It seems likely, however, that the solicitor's letters would be protected within the status of professional legal privilege, as **s 10(1)(a)** defines items 'subject to legal privilege' as including 'communications between a professional legal adviser and his client made in connection with giving legal advice to the client'.

In sum, Karl might be able to show that any evidence obtained relating to the car should be excluded by **s 78**. The search might not be lawful under **s 18** if:

(a) Karl was not an occupant of his father's house; or

(b) the search was not properly authorised in writing by an inspector; or

(c) there were no reasonable grounds to believe that there was evidence at Tony's address which related to the robbery.

Additionally, the search might not be lawful under **s 32** if it was not the site of Karl's arrest. Furthermore, Karl might be able to show that the conduct of the search was not in accordance with Code B if, for example, the written notice of rights and powers was not given to Tony.

Advice to Tony

If the search of Tony's premises is lawful under either **s 18** or **s 32**, then **s 117** of **PACE** confers power on the police to use force in order to carry out their search, provided that the force used is reasonable and necessary. In such circumstances, PC Grit would have been acting in the execution of his duty and Tony would be guilty of an assault under **s 51** of the **Police Act 1964**. If, however, PC Grit's search was unlawful, so that he was not acting in the execution of his duty, then Tony would be entitled to use force to resist the intrusion onto his premises. There are many decisions to vindicate Tony's actions if the search was unlawful. The convictions of *Badham* (1987) and *Churchill* (1989), for obstructing a police officer in the execution of his duty and assault occasioning actual bodily harm respectively, were quashed on appeal, because the searches in both cases were not justifiable within the provisions of **PACE**. If the search was unlawful for the reasons discussed in the advice to Karl, then the prosecution of Tony for the assault might fail.

Question 30

Ben was walking home in the early hours of the morning. He was approached by two constables, PC Blue and PC Green, and asked to stop. He then, reluctantly, answered some questions about who he was and where he had been. By now fed up, he started to walk away as PC Blue was checking his details over the radio. PC Green tried to stop Ben and was punched in the face.

Later, but before dawn, PC Blue saw Dodger, who appeared scruffy and panicked and whom he suspected was carrying a set of 'skeleton keys' to fit various types of household door. He stopped Dodger and asked, 'Okay if we have a look at what you have got on you?' and then, receiving no reply, searched him very thoroughly. Dodger then protested and PC Blue replied: 'Look, this is quite legal, I am PC Blue of Fenwick Street station and I think you are up to no good.' PC Blue found 'skeleton' keys on Dodger, who has, as a result, now been convicted of 'going equipped to steal'.

Ben has been charged with assaulting a constable in the execution of his duty and Dodger wishes to appeal against his conviction. Advise Ben and Dodger.

Answer plan

Advice to Ben

Consider:
- whether PC Green was acting in the course of his duty;

- the *de minimis* rule;
- any application of *Bentley v Brudzinski* (1982).

Advice to Dodger

You should:

- explain the statutory setting: **ss 1, 67 and 78** of the **Police and Criminal Evidence Act (PACE) 1984** and revised Code A;
- apply this to the facts;
- discuss **s 2** of **PACE** and the legality of the search;
- apply *Fennelley* (1989).

Answer

Advice to Ben

In order to discover whether Ben has assaulted the constable in the execution of his duty, we need to determine whether PC Blue was acting 'in the course of his duty'. If not, then Ben cannot be convicted of the crime charged, although it is worthy of note that had he been charged with common assault, he could have been found guilty, according to *obiter dicta* of Donaldson LJ in *Bentley v Brudzinski* (1982).

In *Kenlin v Gardiner* (1967), a police officer took hold of the arm of a boy whom he wanted to question about the latter's suspicious conduct. The boy did not believe the man was a policeman; despite having been shown a warrant card, he punched the officer in order to escape. Another boy who he was with behaved similarly and their convictions for assaulting an officer in the execution of his duty were quashed by the Divisional Court. The court held that the boys were entitled to act as they did in self-defence, as the officer's conduct in trying to physically apprehend them had not been legal. There is no legal power of detention short of arrest. As Lawton LJ observed in *Lemsatef* (1977), the police do not have any powers to detain somebody 'for the purposes of getting them to help with their enquiries'. This reasoning would assist Ben, assuming that PC Green was not in fact trying to stop Ben in order to arrest him.

It is important, however, to examine the precise circumstances of the detaining officer's conduct, because there are cases to suggest that if what the officer does amounts to only a *de minimis* interference with the citizen's liberty, then forceful 'self-defence' by the citizen will not be justified. In *Donnelly v Jackman* (1970), an officer approached a suspect to ask some questions. The suspect ignored the request and walked away from the officer. The officer followed and made further requests for the suspect to stop and talk. He tapped the suspect on the shoulder and the suspect reciprocated by tapping the officer on the shoulder and saying, 'Now we are even, copper'. The officer tapped the suspect on the shoulder again, which was replied to with a forceful punch. Mr Donnelly's conviction was upheld and the decision in *Kenlin v Gardiner* was distinguished as, in the earlier case, the officers had actually taken hold of the boys and detained them. The court stated that:

> ... it is not every trivial interference with a citizen's liberty that amounts to a course of conduct sufficient to take the officer out of the course of his duties.

In *Bentley v Brudzinski*, the facts were very close to those in question. A constable stopped two men who had been running barefoot down a street in the early hours. He questioned them about a stolen vehicle, as they fitted the description of suspects in an earlier incident. They waited for about 10 minutes while the officer checked their details over a radio and then they began to leave. Another constable, who had just arrived on the scene, then said, 'Just a minute', and put his hand on the defendant's shoulder. The defendant then punched that officer in the face. Unlike the decision in *Donnelly v Jackman*, the Divisional Court held here that the officer's conduct was more than a trivial interference with the citizen's liberty and amounted to an unlawful attempt to stop and detain him. The respondent was thus not guilty of assaulting an officer in the execution of his duty. We know that PC Green 'tried to stop Ben'. If this attempt involved physical restraint, then the authorities suggest that Ben's resistance would not have amounted to the crime of assaulting an officer in the execution of his duty, because the officer would not have been acting within his powers. Conversely, if the attempt amounted to nothing more than a tap on the shoulder, Ben would probably be guilty as charged.

Advice to Dodger

Under **s 1** of **PACE**, PC Blue is entitled to stop and search someone whom he reasonably suspects of carrying certain items, including an article 'made or adapted for use in the course of or in connection with ...' (**s 1(7)(b)(i)**) '... burglary' (**s 1(8)(a)**). 'Skeleton keys' would fall within such a category. It might be, however, that PC Blue is in breach of the rules in the Codes of Practice, in particular, Code A for the exercise by police officers of statutory powers of stop and search. The Codes are not technically law although they were mistakenly labelled as having 'statutory authority' by Russell LJ in *McCay* (1991). A judge may, however, exclude evidence which has been obtained in breach of the rules and an appeal court may quash a conviction where the judge failed to do so (**s 67(11)**). Additionally, **s 78** of **PACE** allows the exclusion of evidence which has been obtained in breach of the Act. The court, after considering all the circumstances, including the circumstances in which the evidence was obtained, will not admit evidence which would have 'an adverse effect on the fairness of the proceedings that the court ought not to admit it'.

What, if anything, has PC Blue done wrong? Did he have reasonable grounds for suspecting that Dodger was carrying 'skeleton' keys? Reasonable suspicion requires an objective basis. In favour of PC Blue's case is the fact that it was in the early hours and Dodger was 'panicked'. Code A states that reasonable suspicion may exist where 'a person is seen acting covertly or warily'. It would perhaps be difficult to bring 'panic' within the categories cited by the Code. The Code specifically states that 'hairstyle', 'manner of dress' and knowledge of 'previous convictions' cannot alone or in combination give grounds for suspicion.

The current Code A (May 1997) was amended to provide some clarification of police powers in relation to groups and gangs. The additional sections (Code A, para 1.6(a) and Code A, para 1.7(aa)) state that where there is reliable information that members of a group or gang who habitually carry knives, weapons or controlled drugs and wear a distinctive item of clothing or other means of identification to indicate membership of it, then police officers may use that identifying item as the basis of their suspicion.

We are not informed as to what basis PC Blue thinks he has for his suspicions, but as he suspects Dodger to be carrying 'skeleton keys', in particular, we might infer that PC Blue knows Dodger from a previous encounter, perhaps one which resulted in Dodger's arrest and subsequent conviction. Even this, coupled with Dodger's scruffiness, would not suffice as a reasonable ground. 'Time and place' and 'behaviour' are factors which can constitute the necessary reasonable grounds and it is just possible that the panic of Dodger in the early hours in the street would lend support to the officer's case, but he would still have to address the question of why he suspected Dodger of carrying 'skeleton keys'.

Under **s 2** of **PACE**, the police officer who proposes to carry out a search must state his name and police station (which PC Blue does, but only after the search has begun), the purpose of the search and the grounds for the search. PC Blue fails to comply with these latter rules. A failure to give grounds, as required by **s 2(3)(c)**, will render the search unlawful (*Fennelley* (1989)) and, in view of the very generalised explanation given by PC Blue, 'I think you are up to no good', it seems that the officer is in breach of the Act. The *Fennelley* decision shows that the courts are prepared to be quite strict in their interpretation of the rules. The defendant (F), a heroin addict, was seen by plain clothes police officers in the street. They believed they witnessed him selling drugs on the street. F was stopped, questioned and asked what he had in his pockets. He was searched and no drugs were found but, during a later strip search at the police station, some heroin was found in his underpants. F was charged with possession with intent to supply the drug, but the Crown Court decided that the evidence found by the police officers during the search should be excluded, using **s 78** of **PACE**, as the police officers had failed to abide by the Act and the Codes in a number of respects. Significantly for our concerns here, they had failed to comply with the mandatory requirements of **s 2(3)**, in that they had not informed F about their grounds for suspicion, nor about the purpose of their search. It was argued that these breaches affected the fairness of the trial, because F had not been given the chance to answer the suspicions of the police at the earliest opportunity. If he had, he might have been able to give an explanation which would have resulted in his being charged with mere possession, rather than possession with intent to supply.

The Act also requires that a search in the street must be limited to outer clothing and gloves (s 2(9)). We know that Dodger has been searched 'very thoroughly' and if that has entailed the removal of more than a coat, jacket or gloves in the street, then the rule has been broken.

The Act, however, does not apply to voluntary searches. If Dodger 'consents' to be stopped and searched, then PC Blue is not exercising any power. Dodger's protests come only towards the end of the search, so his acquiescence at the outset could be construed as consent. The revised Code A now states that juveniles or mentally handicapped people should not be subject to voluntary searches. If Dodger was in either category, then even a voluntary search would be in breach of the rules.

Thus, Dodger might be able to succeed on appeal if he can show that key evidence leading to his conviction should have been excluded as having been obtained in breach of the Act or the Codes and in a way that had an adverse effect on the proceedings. The weak grounds for his original suspicions, the failures properly to inform Dodger about the grounds for, and the purpose of, the search and the nature of the search itself are all in question and could separately, or together, form the basis of an appeal. This is provided that the search was not by consent.

Question 31

Dozy went shopping at his local supermarket. He picked an apple from the shelf and ate it while doing his other shopping in the store. Dozy then paid for the items in his trolley and walked towards the exit. Before he left, Dozy was apprehended by Peter, a store detective, who said, 'You cannot leave this store'. Dozy asked why not and was informed that he was not being arrested, but that the store manager wished to see him. Dozy was then taken by force to the manager's office where he was made to wait for an hour until the manager returned from his lunch. When the manager arrived, he told Dozy that the store's policy was to always prosecute shoplifters and that the police would now be called to take Dozy away.

Dozy has now been acquitted on a charge of stealing the apple and he wishes to sue the supermarket. Advise Dozy.

> ### Answer plan
> You should consider:
> - grounds for Dozy's civil action;
> - the legal definition of an 'arrest';
> - the lawfulness of the arrest;
> - *Walters v WH Smith & Son Ltd* (1914);
> - *Self* (1992);
> - *John Lewis & Co Ltd v Tims* (1952).

Answer

Dozy might have an action for damages against Peter or the store (if vicarious liability applies) for false imprisonment. The answer to this question would largely depend upon whether the action of Peter was lawful.

There is no legal power to detain a suspect without arrest. 'Arrest', however, is a matter of fact, not a legal concept. In *Spicer v Holt* (1977), Lord Dilhorne said that:

> Whether or not a person has been arrested depends not on the legality of the arrest, but on whether he has been deprived of his liberty to go where he pleases.

Thus, Dozy may have been arrested if he was prevented from leaving (the use of force on him to take him back to the manager's office helps support such an argument), but whether the arrest was lawful will depend on other matters, namely, the conditions specified in **s 24** of the **Police and Criminal Evidence Act (PACE) 1984**. Aside from the technicalities of whether there has been an arrest, there seems clear *prima facie* evidence of false imprisonment. Having been forcibly taken to the manager's room, it seems likely that force or its threat was used to keep Dozy there, but, even if not, an action for false imprisonment would still exist. The claimant need not even know he has been restrained. In *Meering v Grahame White Aviation Co Ltd* (1919), Lord Atkin stated that a person could be 'imprisoned' within the terms of the tort, even if they were asleep or drunk at the time and thus remain unaware of their captivity.

Peter, though, may have arrested Dozy. If this was so, the question remains whether the arrest was lawful.

Dozy was evidently not informed of why he was being arrested. **Section 28(3)** of **PACE** states that an arrest is not lawful unless the person arrested is informed of the ground for the arrest at the time of, or as soon as practicable after, the arrest. It was, however, recognised in *Christie v Leachinsky* (1947), and remains good law today, that the rule does not apply where the arrest is by a private citizen and the ground of arrest is obvious. If Peter's actions, despite his words, do amount to an arrest, then it could be regarded as having taken place in circumstances which made it obvious why it was being carried out. Even if the arrest is regarded as unlawful for failure to inform of the relevant ground, the illegality will not operate retrospectively to vitiate the whole arrest. It will, according to the Divisional Court in *DPP v Hawkins* (1988), render the arrest unlawful, as from the moment when it would have been practicable for the arrestor to have given a reason. Thus, any damages which Dozy could claim would be limited to those reflecting his experience during the time in the office, from when he should have been informed about why he had been arrested, until the time he was told of the reason for his arrest by the police.

An arrestable offence is one for which the sentence is fixed by law or for which a person over 21 may be sentenced on the first occasion to at least five years' imprisonment (s 24 of **PACE**). Theft, fitting in the second category, is an arrestable offence and **ss** 24 and 25 of **PACE** give a general power of arrest without warrant for 'arrestable offences'. The Act, however, preserves an old common law distinction in respect of the powers of constables and private individuals when making such arrests. Where an arrest is being made *after* an offence is thought to have been committed, then **PACE** confers narrower rights upon the private individual than on the police officer.

In *Walters v WH Smith & Son Ltd* (1914), the defendants had reasonably suspected that Walters had stolen books from a station bookstall. At his trial, Walters was acquitted as the jury believed his statement that he had intended to pay for the books. No crime had therefore been committed in respect of any of the books. Walters sued the defendants, *inter alia*, for false imprisonment, a tort which involves the wrongful deprivation of personal liberty in any form, as he had been arrested for a crime which had not in fact been committed. The Court of Appeal held that to justify the arrest, a private individual had to show, not only reasonable suspicion, but also that the offence for which the arrested person was given over into custody had in fact been committed, even if by someone else. A police officer making an arrest in the same circumstances could legally justify the arrest by showing 'reasonable suspicion' alone, without having to show that an offence was in fact committed.

This principle is now incorporated into **PACE** and Peter appears to have fallen foul of the provision, because the *de facto* arrest takes place after the alleged crime of shoplifting but, as events fall, the criminal courts have acquitted Dozy of any crime. If there was no crime, then Peter could not rely on s 24(5), which only allows an individual to arrest a suspect whom he has reasonable grounds to believe has committed the offence 'where an arrestable crime has been committed'.

It is worthy of note that the less prudent arrestor who acts against a suspect when the latter is suspected of being in the act of committing an arrestable offence (**s** 24(4)) can justify his conduct simply by showing that there were 'reasonable grounds' on which to base the suspicion. He need not show that an offence was in fact being committed.

This analysis is supported by the decision in *Self* (1992), on facts very similar to the question's. The defendant was seen by a store detective in Woolworth's to pick up a bar of chocolate and leave the store without paying. The detective followed him out into the street and, with the assistance of a member of the public, she arrested the suspect under the powers of **s 24(5)** of **PACE**. The suspect resisted the arrest and assaulted both his arrestors. He was subsequently charged with theft of the chocolate and with offences of assault with intent to resist lawful apprehension or detainer, contrary to **s 38** of the **Offences Against the Person Act 1861**. At his trial, he was acquitted of theft (apparently, for lack of *mens rea*), but convicted of the assaults. These convictions were quashed by the Court of Appeal on the grounds that as the arrest had not been lawful, he was entitled to resist it. The power of arrest conferred upon a citizen (**s 24(5)**) in circumstances where an offence is thought to *have been committed* only applies when an offence *has* been committed and, as the jury decided that Mr Self had not committed any offence, there was no power to arrest him.

We know that Dozy has been acquitted of any crime, so it looks as if any arrest made by Peter (*de facto* and, therefore, in law) would be invalidated by virtue of **s 24(5)** of **PACE**, which provides that the offence must have 'been committed'. However, despite Dozy's acquittal, it might be possible to contend that a crime had still 'been committed'. Such a contention was not possible in *Walters v WH Smith*, because there Mr Walters had denied the *mens rea* of the offence of theft, a vital ingredient of the crime, and the jury had accepted this version, thus denying that a crime had taken place. In different circumstances, perhaps, than those in the question, it might be that the defendant in any criminal proceedings (Dozy) was acquitted by way of a successful 'excusatory defence', for example, insanity, which would not deny that a crime had occurred, simply that the defendant could not be legally responsible. In such circumstances, the arrest would be lawful, as a crime would have 'been committed'.

A question would then arise as to the period of detention for over an hour. In *John Lewis & Co v Tims* (1952), Mrs Tims and her daughter were arrested by store detectives for shoplifting four calendars from the appellant's Oxford Street store. It was a regulation of the store that only a managing director or a general manager was authorised to institute any prosecution. After being arrested, Mrs Tims and her daughter were taken to the office of the chief store detective. They were detained there until a chief detective and a manager arrived to give instructions whether to prosecute. They were, eventually, handed over to police custody within an hour of arrest. In a claim by Mrs Tims for false imprisonment, she alleged that the detectives were obliged to give her into the custody of the police immediately upon arrest. The House of Lords held that the delay was reasonable in the circumstances, as there were advantages in refusing to give private detectives a 'free hand' and leaving to a superior official the determination of such an important question as whether to prosecute.

Dozy's case may be distinguishable (although the distinction is not a compelling one) as here, the reason for the delay is concerned with the comfort the manager will enjoy by not interrupting his lunch, rather than any matter of company business. The evidence in the *John Lewis* case was that the manager came without any delay and listened to the evidence; any delay (which was evidentially in doubt) occurred while the accounts of the store detectives were being given in the presence of the suspects.

It is true that Dozy has not suffered any real damage to his person but, as Lord Porter observed in the *John Lewis* case, when 'the liberty of the subject is at stake, questions of the damage sustained become of little importance'.

Question 32

On the one hand, English law rightly presumes that everyone is innocent until proven guilty, so it would be wrong to keep anyone in custody (normally a punishment) unless they have been convicted. On the other hand, some of those charged with serious crimes are likely to try to abscond or interfere with witnesses or evidence unless they are kept secure until trial. Framing rules to govern this conflict is a question of balance.

In the light of recent changes to the principles of bail in the English legal system, discuss whether current law has the balance right.

Answer plan

Answers should incorporate:

- discussion of the background to key legal changes in 1993–94;
- explanation of the current legal framework;
- **s 27** of the **Criminal Justice and Public Order Act (CJPOA) 1994** – extension of police powers in relation to bail;
- the **Bail Act 1976** and the presumption of bail;
- **s 25** of the **CJPOA 1994** and the denial of bail where there has been earlier conviction for murder, etc;
- appeals and repeated applications;
- the **Bail (Amendment) Act 1993**;
- conclusions.

Answer

There is in most circumstances a strong legal presumption that for an unconvicted suspect, liberty must prevail over incarceration. In *Hurnam v State of Mauritius* (2005), the Privy Council held that the seriousness of an offence cannot be treated as a conclusive reason for refusing bail to an unconvicted suspect. The right to personal liberty is an important constitutional right, and a suspect should remain at large unless it is necessary to refuse bail in order to serve one of the ends for which detention before trial was permissible.

In the early 1990s, the UK government took the view that bail was too easily granted and that too many crimes were being committed by those on bail who deserved to be in custody while awaiting trial. The **Bail (Amendment) Act 1993** and the **CJPOA 1994 (ss 25–30)** emanate from that philosophy, their aim being to restrict the granting of bail. A case which caught public sympathy for this view involved a young man who had many convictions for car crime and joyriding. Whilst on bail, he was joyriding in a vehicle when he smashed into a schoolgirl. She clung to the bonnet but he shook her off and thus killed her. The Home Secretary commented publicly that the new legislative measures would prevent such terrible events.

Each year, about 50,000 offences are committed by people on bail. A study by the Metropolitan Police in 1988 indicated that 16 per cent of those charged by that force were already on bail for another offence. Another study in 1993 from the same force showed that of 537 suspects arrested in one week during a clampdown on burglary, 40 per cent were on bail. Some had been bailed 10 or 15 times during the preceding year.

Before examining how recent legislation changes the law, it is appropriate to set out the general principles of bail. In the criminal process, the first stage at which bail is raised as an issue is at the police station. If a person is arrested on a warrant, this will indicate whether he is to be held in custody or released on bail. If the suspect is arrested without a warrant, then the police will have to decide whether to release the suspect after he has been charged. After a person has been charged, **s 38(1)(a)** of the **Police and Criminal Evidence Act (PACE) 1984** states that a person must be released unless: (a) his name and address are not known; or (b) the custody officer reasonably thinks that his detention is necessary for his own protection, or to prevent him from injuring someone or damaging property; or (c) because he might abscond or interfere with the course of justice. Most arrested people are bailed by the police. In 1990, 83 per cent of those arrested in connection with indictable offences and 88 per cent of those arrested for summary offences (other than motoring offences) were released. This area has been amended by **s 28** of the **1994 Act**. A custody officer can now, in the case of an imprisonable offence, refuse to release an arrested person after charge if the officer has reasonable grounds for believing that the detention of that person is necessary to prevent him from committing *any* offence. Previously, many cases were caught by (b) above, and the police officer was able to keep a dangerous person in custody, but some sorts of conduct that the arrested person was likely to go out and commit (for example, drink driving) were not the sort of thing that the police were entitled to use to refuse bail.

Section 27 of the 1994 Act amends ss 38 and 47 of **PACE** so as to allow the police to grant conditional bail to persons charged. The conditions can be whatever is required to ensure that the person surrenders to custody, does not commit an offence while on bail, or does not interfere with witnesses or otherwise obstruct the course of justice. The new powers of the custody officer, however, do not include a power to impose a requirement to reside in a bail hostel. By amending **Pt IV** of **PACE**, **s 29** of the **1994 Act** gives the police power to arrest without warrant a person who, having been granted conditional police bail, has failed to attend at a police station at the appointed time.

The **Bail Act 1976** created a statutory presumption of bail. It states (**s 4**) that subject to **Sched 1** and amendments made by **s 25** of the **1994 Act** about murder, manslaughter, etc (see below), bail shall be granted to a person accused of an offence in a magistrates' court or a Crown Court and to convicted people who are being remanded for reports to be made. The court must therefore grant bail (unless one of the exceptions apply), even if the defendant does not make an application. **Schedule 1** provides that a court need not grant bail to a person charged with an offence punishable with imprisonment if it is satisfied that there are substantial grounds for believing that if released on bail, the defendant would:

(a) fail to surrender to custody;

(b) commit an offence while on bail; or

(c) interfere with witnesses, or otherwise obstruct the course of justice.

The court can also refuse bail if it believes that the defendant ought to stay in custody for his own protection, or if it has not been practicable 'for want of time to obtain sufficient information to enable the court to make its decision on bail'.

When the court is considering the grounds stated above, all relevant factors must be taken into account, including the nature and seriousness of the offence, the character, antecedents, associations and community ties of the defendant and his record for satisfying his obligations under previous grants of bail.

If the defendant is charged with an offence not punishable with imprisonment, **Sched 1** provides that bail can only be withheld if he has previously failed to surrender on bail and if the court believes that in view of that failure, he would fail again to surrender if released on bail.

Section 25 of the **CJPOA 1994** provides that in some circumstances, a person who has been charged with or convicted of murder, attempted murder, manslaughter, rape or attempted rape must not be granted bail. The circumstances are simply that the conviction must have been within the UK and that in the case of a manslaughter conviction, it must have been dealt with by way of a custodial sentence. The term 'conviction' is given a wide meaning and also includes anyone found 'not guilty by way of insanity'.

There has been debate about whether the changes wrought by s 25 are justifiable. A Home Office minister, defending the section, stated that it would be worth the risk if it prevented just one murder or rape, even though there might be a few 'hard cases', that is, people eventually acquitted of crime who were remanded in custody pending trial. As Card and Ward have remarked in a commentary on the Act (*Criminal Justice and Public Order Act 1994*, 1994), the Government, when pushed, was unable to cite a single case where a person released on bail in the circumstances covered by s 25 reoffended in a similar way. There is no time-limit on the previous conviction and there is no requirement of any connection between the previous offence and the one in question. Card and Ward suggest that there is a world of difference between a person who was convicted of manslaughter 30 years ago on the grounds of complicity in a suicide pact and who is now charged with attempted rape (of which he must be presumed innocent), and the person who was convicted of rape eight years ago and now faces another rape charge. The first person is not an obvious risk to society and it is, they argue, regrettable that bail will be denied to him. There is also argument to be had with the contents of the s 25 list. Why should some clearly dangerous and prevalent crimes like robbery be omitted from it? In any case, it may have been better had the offences in the list raised a strong presumption against bail as opposed to an absolute ban, as the former could be rebutted in cases where there was, on the facts, no risk.

The **Criminal Justice Act 2003** made a number of changes to the law in respect of bail. It enables action to be taken to reduce breaches of bail by introducing a new presumption against bail in certain circumstances. The Act enables the immediate grant of bail at the scene of arrest ('street bail') if there is no immediate need to deal with the arrested person at a police station. It gives police the discretion to decide when and where an arrested person should attend a police station for interview. It also enables reviews of the continuing need for detention without charge to be conducted over the telephone rather than in person at the police station as was previously the case.

Part II (ss 13–21) of the **2003 Act** gives effect to the Law Commission's recommendation that minor amendments needed to be made to the **Bail Act 1976** to ensure that its compliance with the **European Convention on Human Rights** is beyond dispute. The earlier law which purported to make it an exception to the right to bail that an offence appears to have been committed while the defendant was on bail for another offence was repealed, and replaced with a presumption that bail will not be granted in these circumstances to a defendant aged 18 or over unless the court is satisfied that there is no significant risk of his reoffending on bail. There is also a presumption that a defendant aged 18 or over who, without reasonable cause, has failed to surrender to custody will not be granted bail, unless the court is satisfied that there is no significant risk that he would so fail if released.

This Act also gives effect to recommendations of Lord Justice Auld in his *Review of the Criminal Courts of England and Wales* for simplifying the bail appeals system, including the removal of the High Court's bail jurisdiction where it was concurrent with that of the Crown Court. The right of the prosecution to appeal to the Crown Court against a decision by magistrates to grant bail is extended to cover all imprisonable offences (and not just, as earlier, those carrying a maximum penalty of five years or more).

The **2003 Act** creates a presumption that bail will not be granted for a person aged 18 or over who is charged with an imprisonable offence, and tests positive for a specified Class A drug, if he refuses to undergo an assessment as to his dependency or propensity to misuse such drugs, or following an assessment, refuses any relevant follow-up action recommended unless the court is satisfied that there is no significant risk of his reoffending on bail.

Bail can be granted as conditional or unconditional. Where it is unconditional, the accused must simply surrender to the court at the appointed date. Failure to appear without reasonable cause is an offence under s 6 of the **Bail Act 1976** and can result, if tried in a Crown Court, in a sentence of up to 12 months' imprisonment or a fine. Conditions can be attached to the granting of bail where the court thinks that it is necessary to ensure that the accused surrenders at the right time, does not interfere with witnesses or commit further offences. There is no statutory limit to the conditions the court may impose and the most common include requirements that the accused reports daily or weekly to a police station, resides at a particular address, surrenders his passport or does not go to particular places or associate with particular people.

Section 7 of the **1976 Bail Act** gives the police power to arrest anyone on conditional bail whom they reasonably suspect is likely to break the conditions, or who has already done so. Anyone arrested in these circumstances must be brought before a magistrate within 24 hours. The magistrate may then reconsider the question of bail.

Personal recognisances, by which the suspect agreed to pay a sum if he failed to surrender to the court, were abolished by the **1976 Act**, except in cases where it is believed that he might try to flee abroad. The Act did retain the court's right to ask for sureties as a condition of bail. By putting sureties in a position where they can have large sums of money 'estreated' if the suspect does not surrender to the court, a significant pressure (not using the resources of the criminal justice system) is put on the accused. The proportion of those who do not answer to bail is very small – consistently about 4 per cent of those given bail. **Section 9** of the Act strengthens the surety principle by making it a criminal offence to agree to indemnify a surety. This sort of thing could happen, for example, if the accused agreed to reimburse the surety in the event that the accused skipped bail and the surety was requested to pay.

The rules which govern how someone who has been refused bail might re-apply and appeal have also been framed with a view to balancing the interests of the accused with those of the public and justice. The original refusal should not be absolute and final but, on the other hand, it is seen as necessary that the refusals are not reversed too easily.

If the court decides not to grant the defendant bail, then s 154 provides that it is the court's duty to consider whether the defendant ought to be granted bail at each subsequent hearing. At the first hearing after the one at which bail was first refused, he may support an application for bail with any arguments, but at subsequent hearings, the court need not hear arguments as to fact or law which it has heard before. The **Criminal Justice Act 1982** enables a court to remand an accused in his absence for up to three successive one week remand hearings, provided that he consents and is legally represented. Such repeated visits are costly to the state and can be unsettling for the accused, especially if he has to spend most of the day in a police cell only to be told the case has been adjourned again without bail. If someone does not consent, they are prevented from applying for bail on each successive visit if the only supporting arguments are those that have been heard by the court before (*R v Nottingham Justices ex p Davies* (1980)).

To avoid unproductive hearings, that is, to promote courts being able to adjourn a case for a period within which reasonable progress can be made on a case, **s 155** of the **Criminal Justice Act 1988** allows for adjournments for up to 28 days, provided that the court sets the date for when the next stage of the proceedings should take place. What began as an experiment under this section has now, by statutory order (**SI 1991/2667**), been extended to all courts.

The interests of the accused are also served by the variety of appeals he may make if bail has been refused. If bail has been refused by magistrates, then, in limited circumstances, an application may be made to another bench of magistrates. Applications for reconsideration can also be made to a judge in chambers (through a legal representative) or to the Official Solicitor (in writing). Appeal can also be made to the Crown Court in respect of bail for both pre-committal remands and where a defendant has been committed for trial or sentence at the Crown Court.

Section 3 of the **Bail Act 1976** allows for an application to vary the conditions of court bail to be made by the person bailed, or the prosecutor or a police officer. Application may also be made for the imposition of conditions on unconditional court bail. As amended by the **CJPOA 1994**, s 3 of the **Bail Act 1976** now allows for the same thing in relation to police bail, although the new provisions do not allow the prosecutor to seek reconsideration of the decision to grant bail itself. Under the **Bail (Amendment) Act 1993**, however, the prosecution does now have a right to appeal against the grant of bail by a court. This right applies to offences which carry a maximum sentence of imprisonment of five years, or more, and to offences of taking a vehicle without consent (joyriding). When this right of appeal is exercised, the defendant will remain in custody until the appeal is heard by a Crown Court judge, who will decide whether to grant bail or remand the defendant in custody within 48 hours of the magistrate's decision. Parliament was concerned that this power could be abused and has stated that it should be reserved 'for cases of greatest concern, when there is a serious risk of harm to the public' or where there are 'other significant public interest grounds' for an appeal.

Although this area of law was subject to a comprehensive revision after a Home Office special working party reported in 1974, and has been legislatively debated and modified five times since the **1976 Act**, it is still a matter of great importance, both to those civil libertarians who consider the law too tilted against the accused, and to the police and some commentators who believe criticism of the law from both sides to the debate might indicate a desirable state of balance reached by the current regulatory framework.

Question 33

What difficulties are involved in designing rules to govern plea bargaining and how successful is the English system in this respect?

Answer plan

Any answer on this theme should take account of the research findings presented to the Royal Commission on Criminal Justice and the recommendations made by the Commission:

- definition of terms;
- explanation of the guidelines in *Turner* (1970);
- difficulties in applying the *Practice Direction (Turner Rules)* (1976);
- discussion of the points in *Pitman* (1991);
- whether the Court of Appeal can attract proper guilty pleas whilst not engaging in injudicious disclosure of the possible sentence;
- recommendations of the Runciman Commission and the Auld Report;
- conclusion.

Answer

'Plea bargaining' has been defined as 'the practice whereby the accused enters a plea of guilty in return for which he will be given some consideration that results in a sentence concession' (Baldwin and McConville, *Negotiated Justice*, 1977). In practice, this can refer to a situation either where there has been a plea arrangement for the accused to plead guilty to a lesser charge than the one with which he is charged (charge bargaining), or where there is simply a sentencing discount available on a plea of guilty by the accused (sentence bargaining).

For a guilty defendant and for the prosecution, such a negotiated settlement represents a mutually valuable compromise, because the prosecution has gained a guilty plea and the defendant a sentence concession. Additionally, there will have been a significant saving to the state in the cost of a trial. Such bargains, however, are fraught with legal difficulties, chiefly because they can be construed as circumstances where undue pressure has been put on the accused to plead guilty. Many convictions have been quashed for just such a reason.

There is a limited way in which 'plea bargaining' is already part of the English legal system. The **Serious Organised Crime and Police Act 2005** introduced a formalised system of plea bargaining. The current general system of judges giving indications of how they might sentence if the court were given a guilty plea, and judges giving sentence discounts for early pleas, is not affected by the Act. Such a system, though, is open and controlled by a judge. The **2005 Act** gives power to prosecutors to grant full and conditional immunities to putative or actual defendants. It is possible for the agreements to be supported by formal contracts. Thus, if a witness granted immunity from prosecution subsequently fails to testify as agreed against his or her co-conspirators, the contract is repudiated, and that defendant is again liable to prosecution.

A commitment to implement such principles was announced in 2007 (*The Times*, 15 March, 2007) as part of reforms to the handling of large-scale fraud cases. Lord Goldsmith, QC, the Attorney-General, cited such agreements among measures aimed at tackling fraud, now estimated to be costing Britain £20 billion a year. Other plans include tougher jail terms, the maximum term expected to be increased to 14 years' imprisonment.

Research conducted by Professor Zander for the Royal Commission on Criminal Justice (Runciman Report, Cm 2263, 1993) found that in a study of 900 Crown Court cases, 90 per cent of barristers and two-thirds of judges were in favour of formalising plea bargaining based on sentence discounts. The study suggests that 11 per cent of those who pleaded guilty in fact maintained their innocence, but wanted to secure a reduction in sentence.

A plea of guilty by the accused must be made freely. He must only be advised to plead guilty if he has committed the crime in question. In *Turner* (1970), Lord Parker CJ set out guidelines on plea bargaining. He stated that:

(a) it may sometimes be the duty of counsel to give strong advice to the accused that a plea of guilty with remorse is a mitigating factor which might enable the court to give a lesser sentence;
(b) the accused must ultimately make up his own mind as to how to plead;
(c) there should be open access to the trial judge and counsel for both sides should attend each meeting, preferably in open court; and
(d) the judge should never indicate the sentence which he is minded to impose, nor should he ever indicate that on a plea of guilty, he would impose one sentence, but that on a conviction following a plea of not guilty, he would impose a more severe sentence. The judge could say what sentence he would impose on a plea of guilty (where, for example, he has read the depositions and antecedents), but without mentioning what he would do if the accused were convicted after pleading not guilty. Even this would be wrong, however, since the accused might take the judge to be intimating that a more severe sentence would follow upon conviction after a guilty plea. The only exception to this rule is where a judge says that the sentence will take a particular form, following conviction, whether there has been a plea of guilty or not guilty.

These guidelines were subsequently embodied in the Court of Appeal's *Practice Direction (Turner Rules)* (1976). A number of difficulties have been experienced in applying these principles. Perhaps the greatest problem has resulted from the fact that although the principles state in (d) that a judge should never say that a sentence passed after a conviction would be more severe than one passed after a guilty plea, it is a generally known rule that guilty pleas lead to lesser sentences. In *Cain* (1976), it was stressed that in general, defendants should realise that guilty pleas attract lesser sentences. Lord Widgery said: 'Any accused person who does not know about it should know about it.' The difficulty is that the trial judge must not mention it, otherwise he could be construed as exerting pressure on the accused to plead guilty.

In *Turner*, the defendant pleaded not guilty on a charge of theft. He had previous convictions and, during an adjournment, he was advised by counsel in strong terms to change his plea; after having spoken with the judge, which the defendant knew, counsel advised that in his opinion, a plea of guilty would result in a non-custodial sentence, whereas if he persisted with a not guilty plea and thereby attacked police witnesses, there was a real possibility of receiving a custodial sentence. The defendant changed his plea to not guilty and then appealed on the ground that he did not have a free choice in changing his plea. His appeal was allowed on the basis that he might have formed the impression that the views being expressed to him by his counsel were those of the judge, particularly as it was known by the accused that counsel had just returned from seeing the judge when he gave his advice to the accused.

The advantages for the prosecution in gaining a guilty plea are obvious but, as the *Code for Crown Prosecutors* notes, administrative convenience in the form of a rapid guilty plea should not take precedence over the interests of justice. Justice demands that the court should be able to pass a proper sentence, consistent with the gravity of the accused's actions and, if a plea is accepted, then the defendant can only be sentenced on the basis of the crime that he has admitted. It is noteworthy that the judge is not bound to accept a plea arrangement made between the sides. The Farquharson Committee on the Role of Prosecuting Counsel thought that there is a general right for the prosecution to offer no evidence in respect of any particular charge, but that where the judge's opinion is sought on whether it is desirable to reassure the public at large that the right course is being taken, counsel must abide by the judge's decision. Where the judge thinks that counsel's view to proceed is wrong, the trial can be halted until the Director of Public Prosecutions (DPP) has been consulted and given the judge's comments. In the notorious case of *Sutcliffe* (1981) (the 'Yorkshire Ripper' case), the prosecution and defence had agreed that Sutcliffe would plead guilty to manslaughter on the grounds of diminished responsibility, but the trial judge rejected that agreement and, after consultations with the DPP, Sutcliffe was eventually found guilty of murder.

The extent of the difficulties in framing rules on plea bargaining which achieve clarity and fairness can be judged by the remark of Lord Lane CJ in the case of *Pitman* (1991):

> There seems to be a steady flow of appeals to this court arising from visits by counsel to the judge in his private room. No amount of criticism and no amount of warnings and no amount of exhortation seems to be able to prevent this from happening.

In this case, on counsel's advice, the appellant pleaded not guilty to causing death by reckless driving. On cup final day in 1989, he had driven, having been drinking all afternoon, in a car without a rear view mirror. He had crashed into another car, killing one of its passengers, whilst having double the permitted level of alcohol in his blood.

During the trial, the judge called both counsel to his room and stated that he did not think there was a defence to the charge. Counsel for the appellant explained that although the appellant had admitted that his carelessness caused the accident, the advice to plead not guilty was based on the fact that the prosecution might not be able to prove the necessary recklessness. The trial judge replied that the appellant's plea was a matter for the appellant himself and not counsel and that if the appellant accepted responsibility for the accident, he ought to plead guilty and if he did so, he would receive 'substantial credit' when it came to sentencing.

Counsel for the appellant then discussed this with the appellant, who changed his plea to guilty and was sentenced to nine months' imprisonment and was disqualified for four years. His appeal was allowed, as the judge had put undue pressure on the appellant and his counsel to change his plea to guilty and his remarks had suggested that his chances of acquittal were slight if he pleaded not guilty and that if he was found guilty, having pleaded not guilty, he would certainly be sentenced to imprisonment. Lord Lane CJ emphasised that a judge should not initiate discussions in private and that where, at the behest of counsel, they are absolutely necessary, they should be recorded by shorthand or on a recording device.

Another problem here concerns framing the guidelines so that they are sufficiently permissive to allow counsel access to the judge in his private room in cases in deserving instances, but avoiding the problems of confidentiality. As Mustill LJ said in *Harper-Taylor and Bakker* (1988):

> The need to solve an immediate practical problem may combine with the more relaxed atmosphere of the private room to blur the formal outlines of the trial.

There is a risk that counsel and solicitors may hear something said to the judge which they would rather not hear, putting them into a state of conflict between their duties to their clients and their obligations to maintain the confidentiality of the private room. Reviewing the current state of the law, Curran (see [1991] Crim LR 79) has written that the effect of cases like *Bird* (1977) and *Agar* (1990) (the latter not a plea bargaining case, but one which hinged on a judge's ruling in his private room as complied with by counsel to the appellant's detriment) is that defence counsel has a duty to disclose to his client any observations made by the judge in his room which significantly affect the client's case, whether or not the judge expresses them to be made confidentially.

The Royal Commission on Criminal Justice, chaired by Viscount Runciman, reported in July 1993. It recommended (pp 156–159) a clearly articulated system of sentence discounts, with earlier pleas attracting higher discounts. Lord Runciman pointed out that this was not 'plea bargaining' in the American sense, in which the prosecution can suggest the appropriate sentence. The proposal was supported by law enforcement officers, like the DPP, who regard it as a way to tackle 'cracked trials': those which abort at the last minute through a change of plea to guilty. In 1994, 83 per cent of defendants who elected for trial at the Crown Court changed their plea to guilty. The proposal was, however, opposed by groups like Liberty and Justice, who believe that these changes might pressurise innocent people, intimidated by the system, into a guilty plea. It can be seen as subtly undermining the presumption of innocence and the requirement that the prosecution proves its case.

Further recommendations have been put forward by the Auld Report (2001), which proposed (para 12) the introduction of a scheme of discounts on sentencing on a graduated scale, so that the earlier the plea of guilty is entered, the higher the discount for it. Such a scheme should be coupled with a system of advance indication of sentence for a defendant who is considering pleading guilty.

Sanders and Young (*Criminal Justice*, 1994) have argued that it is artificial and unrealistic for the law to encourage guilty pleas through the sentence discount, whilst simultaneously denying the defence the opportunity to discover exactly what, if anything, is on offer from the judge in a particular case. They contend that, in practice, both defence counsel and judges have abused their right to meet in private and have, despite the Court of Appeal's guidance, engaged in sentence bargaining on a wide scale.

The Court of Appeal has consistently indicated that the information should not be given to defendants, because that might put undue pressure on them to plead guilty, but sentence discounts are legally recognised (see Thomas, in *Current Sentencing Practice*, para A8 2(b)), a guilty plea attracts a lighter sentence, and the extent of the reduction is usually between one-quarter and one-third of what would have otherwise been the sentence. Moreover, Lord Widgery has stated (above) that defendants should know about them. The pressure could scarcely be increased by informing a defendant with details, rather than leaving it to his general knowledge. If anything, Zander has argued, it would diminish the pressure by making it clear that the defendant's fears about the penalty for pleading not guilty are exaggerated.

There is, however, reason for anxiety with such a call for more openness. Sanders and Young regard it as 'an idealistic notion' that one can improve the effectiveness of the system in convicting the guilty without also increasing its effectiveness in convicting the innocent (*Criminal Justice*, 1994). In one Home Office study (1992), Hedderman and Moxon found that 65 per cent of those pleading guilty in Crown Court cases said that their decision had been influenced by the prospect of receiving a discount in sentence. Even the Royal Commission recognised that not all those pleading guilty are, in fact, guilty; some may have just capitulated to the pressure of taking the reduced sentence, rather than run the risk of the full sentence. As Sanders and Young contend, this issue goes to the heart of constitutional principles. Only if the state acts properly in collecting and presenting evidence can punishment be justified, according to commonly accepted principles. Even the guilty are entitled to due process of law. A system of plea bargaining may undermine such principles, since it allows the state to secure convictions based on unproven allegations.

Question 34

How far should the law allow witnesses to be prepared by the advocates who will examine them in criminal courts?

Answer plan

Your answer should:

- explain the importance of witnesses to the court process;
- introduce the important case of *Momodou* (2005), and the Bar Code provisions;
- mention civil case rules, just to help set the scene for the criminal case issues which are the main focus of this essay;
- differentiate lawful 'witness familiarisation' from improper 'witness coaching';
- explain the dangers of witness coaching to the legal process;
- explain the Court of Appeal's test to distinguish the acceptable forms of witness preparation from the unacceptable forms;
- explain the Attorney-General's 2005 proposals for change;
- explain the objections to his proposals.

Answer

This question concerns matters central to the way the English legal system deals with evidence. Witnesses are integral parts of criminal and civil cases in the English legal system. They are arguably the most important feature of the process by which courts aim to get to the truth in a dispute. Can and should court witnesses be prepared by their advocate before giving their testimony?

These issues were recently addressed by the Court of Appeal in *R v Momodou* (2005). The legal background to this case is in a rule of the Bar Code of Conduct: Part VII – Conduct of Work. It explains (rule 705) that:

A barrister must not:
(a) rehearse practise or coach a witness in relation to his evidence;
(b) encourage a witness to give evidence which is untruthful or which is not the whole truth.

In civil cases a barrister can 'give general advice to a witness about giving evidence for example speak up, speak slowly, answer the question, keep answers as short as possible, ask if a question is not understood, say if you cannot remember and do not guess or speculate . . .' (Miscellaneous Guidance, Part F, para 9). In criminal cases a barrister can have contact with a witness before the case 'with a view to introducing himself to the witness, explaining the court's procedure . . . and answering any questions on procedure which the witness may have'. Barristers are also permitted to put a witness through some questions before the case in order to test his recollection and the quality of his evidence.

In *Momodou*, the Court of Appeal criminal division clearly defines the difference, in *a criminal case* context, between the proper process of 'witness familiarisation' and the improper use of 'witness training or coaching'. The case concerned defendants who had been convicted of violent disorder during a serious disturbance at the Yarls Wood Detention Centre, in Bedfordshire, in 2002. The Court rejected claims that unlawful pre-trial coaching of security guard prosecution witnesses had led to the wrongful conviction of two asylum-seekers involved in the riot at the detention centre.

The Court of Appeal held that, although two key security guard witnesses had attended a programme operated by a legal training firm, the safety of the convictions had not been undermined.

Lord Justice Judge observed that the dangers in witness coaching included that a dishonest witnesses might learn, during a rehearsal, how to 'improve' his testimony. The danger augmented if the coaching was not one-to-one but conducted collectively because prospective witnesses might 'bring their respective accounts into what they believe to be better alignment with others'. Pre-trial arrangements to familiarise a witness with the layout of the court, court processes, and the way evidence should be given, will be fine provided the trainers, preferably lawyers, have no knowledge of the actual issues in the forthcoming trial. Lord Justice Judge explained the core of the reasoning of the Court of Appeal on this issue. He said there is a dramatic distinction between witness training or coaching, and witness familiarisation. Training or coaching for witnesses in criminal proceedings (whether for prosecution or defence) is not permitted. This is the logical consequence of the well-known principle that discussions between witnesses should not take place, and that the statements and proofs of one witness should not be disclosed to any other witness. He noted: 'The witness should give his or her own evidence, so far as practicable uninfluenced by what anyone else has said, whether in formal discussions or informal conversations' (para 61).

The rule reduces, indeed hopefully avoids any possibility, that one witness may tailor his evidence in the light of what anyone else said, and equally, avoids any unfounded perception that he may have done so. These risks are inherent in witness training.

Lord Justice Judge also said: 'An honest witness may alter the emphasis of his evidence to accommodate what he thinks may be a different, more accurate, or simply better remembered perception of events. A dishonest witness will very rapidly calculate how his testimony may be "improved" '(para 61).

The Court ruled that this familiarisation process should normally be supervised or conducted by a solicitor or barrister, or someone who is responsible to a solicitor or barrister with experience of the criminal justice process, and preferably by an organisation accredited for the purpose by the Bar Council and Law Society. None of those involved should have any personal knowledge of the matters in issue. Records should be maintained of all those present and the identity of those responsible for the familiarisation process, whenever it takes place. The programme should be retained, together with all the written material (or appropriate copies) used during the familiarisation sessions. None of the material should bear any similarity whatever to the issues in the criminal proceedings to be attended by the witnesses, and nothing in it should play on or trigger the witness's recollection of events.

In December 2004, not long before the Court of Appeal's February 2005 decision, the Attorney-General, Lord Goldsmith QC, issued a statement in which he advocated the case for prosecutors being able to speak with witnesses privately, and off the record before the trial. This is an utterance not in perfect harmony with the views expressed by the Court of Appeal in *Momodou*.

The Attorney-General said that many people would be surprised to learn that prosecutors in England and Wales are not entitled to interview witnesses before trial, even when they are key prosecution witnesses whose credibility may be critical to whether a prosecution should go ahead or not. He said the practice should change, arguing that: 'It is striking that it is only in England and Wales that prosecutors do not have direct access to witnesses even in order to assess their credibility and reliability.'

The conclusions reached by the Attorney-General included that prosecutors should be permitted to speak to witnesses – including children and vulnerable witnesses – about matters of evidence. He said prosecution witness interviews should be conducted for the purpose and the extent that, in the view of the prosecutor, such an interview is necessary in order to assess the reliability of or clarify a witness's evidence.

Where possible, he argued, an interview should generally take place once the prosecutor considers that he/she has sufficient information and evidence for an interview to be of value, but before the prosecutor reaches a decision to proceed.

However, prosecutors should, he said, be permitted to hold witness interviews *at any stage of the proceedings* including, therefore, just before trial. He argued that this was particularly so if further evidence or material, casting doubt on the reliability of a witness's evidence, came to light at a later stage in the proceedings or if further witnesses came to light after a decision to prosecute has been reached.

The Attorney-General contended that interviews should be conducted informally with the prosecutor, the witness, where possible a police officer, and independent support if the witness so wishes. He suggested that interviews should be conducted in the absence of the defence, and that police officers should be permitted to be present at interviews.

One sharply expressed objection to this came during a House of Lords' debate. The eminent lawyer Lord Thomas of Gresham said (Lords *Hansard* text for 17 January 2005 (250117–22) Column 626):

> In subtle ways, the complainant in a criminal case is beginning to be treated as the client of the prosecutor. The essential impartiality of prosecuting counsel is, in my view, being undermined. He is being asked to take sides and to become involved in the emotions and personalities of complainants and their families. Achieving justice, objectively, between the state and the individual should be at the heart of the criminal justice system – not, as the Government so often states, victims and witnesses.

He argued that justice cannot be done if a witness is so intimidated that he does not come forward or if his account is incomplete. But that, he said, is a matter for the police to investigate and not counsel. Similarly, the voluntary witness service does a great deal to ease the fears of complainants and witnesses where the court proceedings are in themselves intimidating. The prosecutor should not be involved at all in some kind of calming and comforting role.

He contended that, generally, the American experience shows how undesirable witness coaching is. Prosecutors have the ability, consciously or unconsciously, to strengthen the case by questions and suggestions that cause the witness to fill gaps in memory, eliminate ambiguities or contradictions, sharpen language, create emphasis, and alter demeanor. He asked 'Do we in this country really want to get involved in suspicions of horse shedding?'

The expression 'horse shedding' is a nineteenth-century American expression and refers to the practice whereby lawyers would coach witnesses in the horse sheds near the court houses in rural parts of the United States.

How far we do now go down that road is a political decision to be taken in the legislature on behalf of society at large, and it is clear that this apparently technical legal issue is in fact quite a contentious political issue of balancing the interests of the state and the individual.

CHAPTER 6

CIVIL PROCESS AND LEGAL SERVICES

INTRODUCTION

The purpose of the Civil Justice Council is that of 'ensuring that this country retains a fair and effective justice system'. How far that system is fair and effective is the key theme of this chapter.

The county courts are the main platform on which the civil law rights and duties of British citizens are played out. If something goes badly wrong here, as the evidence suggests is happening now, then the rights of British citizens are prejudiced on a significant scale.

There are 218 county courts in England and Wales, dealing with claims for matters such as personal injury, debt, house repossessions and breaches of contract. All but the most complicated and momentous civil cases are dealt with by the county courts.

In February 2007, Judge Paul Collins, London's most senior county court judge, told BBC Radio 4's *Law in Action* programme that low pay and high turnover amongst administrative staff mean that serious errors are commonplace and routinely lead to incorrect judgments in court. Judge Collins said:

> We are operating on the margins of effectiveness and with further cuts looming we run the risk of bringing about a real collapse in the service we're able to give to people using the courts.

According to Judge Collins, the lack of resources is causing mistakes. A common problem is one in which someone who is being sued files a defence but the papers are not passed on to the judge by overburdened court staff. The judge will automatically award damages to the person who brought the claim, assuming that the person being sued does not want to defend it. According to Judge Collins:

> This happens on a regular basis and although these errors can be put right it takes work to put them right, producing more to do for already hard pressed court staff and judges.

Staff in the court service are amongst the poorest paid of all government departments. In Judge Collins' own court in Central London, the number of people employed had been cut from 125 in 1992 to just 80 at the time he spoke out. The quantity of work, however, had not diminished. Roughly speaking, therefore, the remaining staff were having to cover between them about a third more work than when there were 125 staff. It is no wonder that county court staff are becoming stressed and losing files.

County courts are no longer subsidised through general taxation. Instead, they are expected to generate all their income from fees charged to court users. This was intended to protect the courts from having to compete with other public services for government funds. The courts' budgets are fixed by government, and although the courts more than covered their costs last year, the surplus raised from fees was spent on other services.

Problems in the administration of the courts have, in Judge Collins' experience, been further exacerbated by cuts in the availability of legal aid. He stated that:

> There is plenty of anecdotal evidence that this has led to an increase in the number of people representing themselves without the help of a qualified lawyer. These cases inevitably take up more time and as a result court proceedings last longer to the detriment of others using the courts.

One clear way in which the system has improved in recent times has been in respect of the accessibility of its information. Since 2005, the website of the Civil Division of the Court of Appeal contains links to all the most recent judgments of the court and to the relevant Civil Procedure Rules. The website is www.civilappeals.gov.uk. Another very useful website for regularly updated information about the civil process is that of the Courts Service, www.hmcourts-service.gov.uk.

Since 1999, the civil process and the provision of legal services have undergone a major change. The **Civil Procedure Rules (CPR)**, the most fundamental changes in civil process for over a century, have radically altered the operation of civil justice. Part of the rationale of the new rules was to expedite the way cases were dealt with and to allow more cases to be settled early, through negotiation between the parties or alternative dispute resolution (ADR). In this respect, there is some evidence of success.

The overriding objective of the **CPR** is to enable the court to deal justly with cases. The first rule reads:

> 1.1(1) These rules are a new procedural code with the overriding objective of enabling the court to deal with cases justly.

This objective will include ensuring that the parties are on an equal footing and saving expense. When exercising any discretion given by the **CPR**, the court must, according to r 1.2, have regard to the overriding objective and a checklist of factors, including the amount of money involved, the complexity of the issue, the parties' financial positions, how the case can be dealt with expeditiously and by allotting an appropriate share of the court's resources, while taking into account the needs of others. In future, as Judge John Frenkel observes ('On the road to reform' (1998)):

'The decisions of the Court of Appeal are more likely to illustrate the application of the new rules to the facts of a particular case, as opposed to being interpretative authorities that define the meaning of the rules.'

Another area of change concerns conditional fee arrangements (CFAs). In the first version of CFAs, only people who expected to win money from their case could benefit from conditional fees. This was the only way that most people could afford to pay the success fee, but it meant that a successful litigant would not receive all the money he had been awarded. So, in 2000, the Government took the power, in the **Access to Justice Act 1999**, to make it possible for the winning party to recover the success fee and any insurance premium from the losing party. This will ensure that it is the person or organisation that has committed the legal wrong who pays, and it will allow defendants and claimants (other than in family law cases), whose case is not about money, to use CFAs.

Legal services have also undergone very significant change in recent times. Expanded rights of advocacy for solicitors and others (including patent agents) have changed the traditional picture of the courts as the domain of barristers. In 2005, there were over 2,500 qualified solicitor-advocates. The introduction of the Legal Services Commission (LSC) and the Community Legal Service (CLS) marks a sea-change in the delivery of publicly funded law and the impending change, to a public defender system, carries the potential for far-reaching implications for both the legal system and for the public, as consumers of its services.

Checklist

You should be familiar with:
- the main provisions of the 1996 Woolf Report on Civil Justice;
- the purpose and main provisions of the new **CPR**;
- the arguments both for and against the proposition that the reforms can work and have worked well in practice;
- the main provisions of the **Access to Justice Act 1999**;
- the role and purpose of the LSC and the CLS;
- CFAs;
- the nature and purpose of the proposed Salaried Defence Service and critical commentary on this system;
- recent changes concerning rights of audience and legal liability of the legal professions.

Question 35

Explain the process of judicial review, and state how the process is different from an appeal.

Answer plan

- Set the structure of the answer by outlining the basic difference between a judicial review and an appeal.
- Turn to an example of a judicial review case and expound it: *The Queen on the Application of Greenpeace Ltd v Secretary of State for Trade and Industry* (2007).
- Explain the basic mechanics (prerogative remedies) of the judicial review.
- Cite and explain *Associated Provincial Picture Houses Ltd v Wednesbury Corporation* (1948).
- Explain the case's significance in respect of the 'reasonableness' principle.

Answer

The process of judicial review is a part of the civil process categorised as administrative law. It is the process whereby the High Court can check that public bodies make their decisions using only legal and fair procedures. This process is different from an appeal, because the bodies that the High Court finds are in violation of the requirements of legal and fair decision making cannot be ordered to come to *different* decisions, but merely to reconsider the issue in question acting within the legal rules and fairly. Unlike a successful appeal, a successful judicial review does not result in the original decision being reversed, but merely invalidated.

A recent example can be found in the decision *The Queen on the Application of Greenpeace Ltd v Secretary of State for Trade and Industry* (2007). The High Court decided that a consultation process carried out by the Government on the future production of electricity was inadequate. Mr Justice Sullivan ruled that in attempting to canvass public opinion about the use of nuclear power plants, having said in a White Paper (a governmental proposal and discussion document) that it would allow 'the fullest public consultation', the Government's subsequent consultation exercise was procedurally unfair. There was a breach of the 'legitimate expectation' that there would be a full public consultation. The exercise was too rushed and confined by a tight deadline. The government had later stated that as a result of its consultation, 'The Government believes that nuclear has a role to play in the future UK generating mix alongside other low carbon generating options'. The judicial review was brought by Greenpeace Ltd, which wanted to make a considered response to the consultation. The Court did not rule that the Government's decision to build another nuclear power plant was 'wrong as a matter of policy', it ruled simply that a political decision that condoned the development of further nuclear plant had not been made in an appropriate way. Mr Justice Sullivan held that (para. 120):

> [T]here was a breach of the claimant's legitimate expectation to fullest public consultation; that the consultation process was procedurally unfair; and that therefore the decision in the Energy Review that nuclear new build 'has a role to play . . .' was unlawful.

The essence of successful judicial review like this is not that a court says that a public body made a *wrong* decision but that it made a decision in a *wrong way*. Here, the Government had, in July 2006, come out in favour of new nuclear power stations without fulfilling its earlier documented promise to carry out 'the fullest consultation'. Whether the UK opts for new nuclear power stations is a *political* decision which the people (via our Government), not the law courts, will make. But in making the decision, proper process must be followed, so even mighty politicians must obey the rules of decision making. If they promise to consult fully then they must do just that.

Consulting the public is an important governmental activity. The people are an intrinsic part of government in the modern European setting. The European Court of Justice in 1980 referred to: '. . . the fundamental democratic principle that the peoples [of democratic countries in Europe] should take part in the exercise of power . . .' (Case 138/79, *SA Roquette Frères v Council*, 1980 ECR 3333, 3360, para 33).

Judicial review is the procedure by which *prerogative* remedies (coming from the inherent power of the court) have been obtainable in the High Court against lower courts, tribunals, and administrative authorities from which there is no formal appeal process. So, where there is no procedure for an appeal to reconsider the merits of a decision (like the decision to approve new nuclear power stations), it is very important that the decision-making panel's approach to its task is impeccably fair. The primary purpose of judicial review is to control any actions of public authorities that might be made in excess of their proper powers (*ultra vires*) or on the basis of some unreasonable way of coming to a decision.

Judicial review, part of administrative law, has expanded dramatically as a part of law in recent history. In 1981, 552 applications for judicial review were made at the High Court, whereas in 2005, a total of 5,381 applications were made. We have come a long way since 1935 when Lord Chief Justice Hewart dismissed administrative law as worthless 'Continental jargon'.

The foundational precedent for modern cases of judicial review is *Associated Provincial Picture Houses Ltd v Wednesbury Corporation* (1948). This concerned a local authority, in Wednesbury, central England, which had, under the **Sunday**

Entertainments Act 1932, granted a licence to a company for it to open its Gaumont cinema on Sundays. The Act allowed for a licence to be granted with 'such conditions as the authority thinks fit'. The authority imposed the condition that children under 15 were not to be allowed into cinemas on Sundays. The company argued that the provision was 'unreasonable' and therefore *ultra vires*, that is, 'beyond the powers' of the local authority. It argued that the court should be the arbiter of whether a condition was reasonable.

In the Court of Appeal, the reasoning of Lord Greene, the Master of the Rolls, soon crystallised into a hallowed legal proposition. He said that where Parliament had entrusted discretionary powers to another body, like a local authority, the courts could declare that some decisions were 'unreasonable', and therefore beyond what the authority was authorised to do.

In a key passage of his judgment, the Master of the Rolls said:

> The court is entitled to investigate the action of the local authority with a view to seeing whether they have taken into account matters which they ought not to take into account, or, conversely, have refused to take into account or neglected to take into account matters which they ought to take into account. Once that question is answered in favour of the local authority, it may be still possible to say that, although the local authority have kept within the four corners of the matters which they ought to consider, they have nevertheless come to a conclusion so unreasonable that no reasonable authority could ever have come to it. In such a case, again, I think the court can interfere. The power of the court to interfere in each case is not as an appellate authority to override a decision of the local authority, but as a judicial authority which is concerned, and concerned only, to see whether the local authority have contravened the law by acting in excess of the powers which Parliament has confided in them.

The courts, though, could not simply substitute their own opinion for that of the public body. To be unreasonable, the decision would have to be one where an authority had 'taken into account matters which it ought not to take into account, or, conversely, has refused to take into account or neglected to take into account matters which it ought to take into account'. Applying the principles in this case, the court held that that the local authority had not acted unreasonably or *ultra vires* in imposing the condition that those under 15 could not attend the cinema on a Sunday.

Even if the way a decision was made passes that test, the decision could still be challenged in the courts if it was one which 'no reasonable body could have come to'. In other words, if it is a patently mad decision. An example given in an earlier case was if a teacher had been dismissed 'because she had red hair, or for some equally frivolous and foolish reason'.

The principles have since become the touchstone of the courts when deciding judicial review cases, and the legal phrase '*Wednesbury* unreasonable' is shorthand for a decision of a public body or official that violates the criterion of necessary reasonableness established in this case. The judicial control of governmental power is an essential element of democracy.

Question 36

What pressures have been found to encourage litigants to settle claims, even against their best interests, and what approach to this issue is taken by the **CPR**?

> **Answer plan**
>
> You should consider the following:
> - the nature of settlement;
> - fear of costs and uncertainty of outcome;
> - Part 36 payments;
> - the **Civil Procedure Rules (CPR)** and limiting costs;
> - active case management.

Answer

A settlement is a compromise. In the context of litigation, it involves the parties deciding to resolve their dispute out of court, rather than go to a full hearing and have the matter decided by a judge, or even a civil jury. If a litigant is being pushed into giving in when he has a sound legal case and his rights should be vindicated, then a compromise is undesirable. Where, however, a dispute is evenly balanced and would involve a great deal of time, anxiety and resources to resolve in a full trial, then a compromise might well represent a trilateral relief: relief for both sides and the taxpayers who support the legal system.

Most civil disputes are settled out of court. Less than 10 per cent of cases where a claim form is issued actually go to court and, even of those which do go to trial, many are settled before judgment. Evidence presented by the London Passenger Transport Board to the Winn Committee on Personal Injury Litigation (1968), for example, showed that of about 5,000 claims made against it per year, about 4,900 were settled without proceedings. Of the 100 or so cases which were commenced, only about one-quarter were taken to full judgment.

The largest study of this sort was conducted by the Oxford Centre for Socio-Legal

Studies (Harris *et al, Compensation and Support for Illness and Injury*, 1984), which examined a random sample of 1,711 accident victims who had been incapacitated for a minimum of two weeks. Of this group, only 26 per cent had considered claiming damages, only 14 per cent had consulted a solicitor and only 12 per cent were awarded damages. The study looked at the level of damages obtained by the small group (8 per cent) who gained them without the use of solicitors, and concluded that these people appeared to be under-compensated. In the 182 cases (from 1,711 in the sample) in which damages were obtained, the claimant accepted the first offer made in 104 cases (see Genn, *Hard Bargaining: Out of Court Settlements in Personal Injury Claims*, 1987).

Many factors combine to persuade disputants to settle out of court and the fear of prohibitive costs can be a serious deterrent to bringing proceedings. This is particularly so when it is remembered that the basic rule is that 'costs follow the event', that is, the successful party can expect the judge to order the loser to pay some or all of his solicitor's bill. Costs, however, are a discretionary matter, so the whole process is beset with uncertainties. Another gamble the claimant is faced with is the procedure of 'payment into court' (now known as a 'Part 36 payment') where, at any stage after the commencement of proceedings, the defendant may make a payment into court in satisfaction of the claimant's claim. The claimant may accept the payment or continue the action. If the claimant chooses to continue and the damages obtained are not greater than the amount paid in by the defendant, the claimant will be liable for the defendant's taxed costs (that is, costs which are authorised by a court official – a taxing master) from the time of payment in, even though he has won the action. When the judge makes an award of damages, he will not know the amount of any payment into court, so he cannot influence the matter of whether the claimant has to suffer under the rule.

There were 80 cases in the Oxford study which involved abandoned claims and, of these, 16 per cent were abandoned because of fear of legal expenses. Where a claimant is not legally aided, the lawyer may try to persuade him to accept a settlement offer, plus costs, rather than risk a legal action which could fail. This is better for the lawyer, as it assures the payment of costs but, arguably, is not in the best interests of many claimants, because settlement awards are generally lower than damages awarded by courts for the same types of case.

A study of High Court personal injury cases by Zander (1973–74) ((1975) *Law Soc Gazette*, 25 June, p 680) showed that while costs were a relatively low proportion of damages in large claims, they were proportionately very high in small claims. Where the damages were under £1,000, 86 per cent of cases had claimed costs for one side amounting to three-fifths of the damages or more. In 33 per cent of cases, the total costs of both sides amounted to more than the amount in dispute. The CJR found that the average cost to the claimant in High Court personal injury actions in 1984 was £6,830 in London and £2,480 outside London. In the county court, costs were an average of 99 per cent of the claimant's damages recovered, as opposed to about one-quarter in the High Court.

Research conducted for the Woolf Report on the civil justice system threw further light on this area. The Final Report (*Access to Justice*, 1996) includes a survey of Supreme Court Taxing Office taxed bills conducted by Professor Hazel Genn of University College, London. Genn found alarming data on costs (*Hard Bargaining: Out of Court Settlement in Personal Injury Claims*, 1987). Her findings indicate that the average costs among the lowest value claims consistently represented more than 100 per cent of the claim value. They also showed that in cases worth between £12,500 and £25,000, average costs ranged from 40 per cent to 95 per cent of the value of the claim. The system provided higher benefits to lawyers than to their clients.

In the Oxford study, delay was another significant factor influencing people to discontinue claims; 6 per cent of those who abandoned their actions cited it as affecting their decision. Cane (in Atiyah's *Accidents, Compensation and the Law*, 1993) has shown evidence that delay and its attendant anxiety can cause a recognisable state of 'litigation neurosis', a complaint which ceases upon the resolution of the dispute. Delay generally assists the defendant and is sometimes used as a deliberate tactic against weaker opponents, or to alleviate the cashflow problems of the smaller insurance companies.

Another factor putting pressure on litigants to settle is that of the risks and uncertainties entailed in the claim. If the case goes to trial, then the claimant will, to succeed, have to prove his case on the balance of probabilities. The process is beset with legal uncertainties. Is the defendant liable at law for the claimant's loss or injury? Even where the law is clear, there may be evidential difficulties. Genn has presented material to suggest that in many cases, a claimant's solicitor either does not have sufficient resources to undertake proper factual investigations, or does not seek out all available reports. It is also very difficult to contact all relevant witnesses and to assess how persuasive their courtroom evidence would be. Defendants, including or assisted by insurance companies, will often have resources which place them in a good position to fully investigate the circumstances of accidents. Assessing the quantum of damages is another very problematic part of litigation. In an American experiment, 20 pairs of practising lawyers were given identical information about a case and were instructed to negotiate a settlement. Their resultant settlements ranged from the highest of US$95,000 to the lowest of US$15,000, with an average of just over US$47,000.

The Oxford study found that many other factors contributed to the discontinuation of claims, including the fear of affecting a continuing relationship and arguments that the victim's own fault caused the accident. The most cited reason (mentioned by 45 per cent of respondents) was problems over obtaining evidence. There have been some legal changes since the Oxford study in 1984, and it will be interesting to see if future studies detect any significant consequential changes in claimants' behaviour.

The LCD committed itself (in the CJR's General Issues Paper) to the use of new technology, especially for improving the system of county court debt business. The

Production Centre has operated since early 1990, since when, relying on new technology, it has issued over 1.5 million summonses. Dealing more expeditiously with this sort of work could free the courts and thus reduce delays for other types of case.

The courts have made some progress in this area since 1996, although the challenges in the UK are considerable. Lord Justice Brooke, a leading proponent of the use of information and communications technology (ICT) in the courts, has noted that in England at the time, there was no Ministry of Justice with masses of resources at its command, and the LCD, which supports the courts, is a small department and, over the last 10 years, its credibility with the Treasury was damaged because of the way that unbudgeted legal aid expenditure went on soaring. Lord Justice Brooke believes that expenditure on ICT has suffered as a result:

> We have certainly not seen any of the imaginative forward investment in IT which other comparable countries have experienced. In America, for instance, the federal judiciary run the federal courts, and, in 1990, the Senate voted them US$70 million to undertake a programme of computerisation in the court process.
>
> Lord Justice Brooke, *The Changing Jurisdiction, IT and the English and Welsh Courts: The Next 10 Years*, keynote speech to the 13th Bileta Conference, Dublin, 28 March 1998

In 2001, there were only about 140 judges using computers in court, but the number is rising steadily, with consequential improvements in the efficiency of the courts.

Under the **CPR**, there is a greater incentive for parties to settle their differences. The court now takes into account any pre-action offers to settle when making an order for costs. Thus, a side which has refused a reasonable offer to settle will be treated less generously in the issue of how far the court will order their costs to be paid by the other side. For this to happen, the offer, however, must be one which is made to be open to the other side for at least 21 days after receipt (to stop any undue pressure being put on someone with the phrase: 'Take it or leave it, it is only open for one day, then I shall withdraw the offer'). Also, if the offer is made by the defendant, it must be an offer to pay compensation and to pay the claimant's costs.

Several aspects of the new rules encourage litigants to settle rather than take risks in order (as a claimant) to hold out for unreasonably large sums of compensation, or to try to get away (as a defendant) with paying nothing, rather than some compensation. The system of Part 36 payments or offers does not apply to small claims, but, for other cases, it seems bound to have a significant effect. Thus, if at the trial, a claimant does not get more damages than a sum offered by the defendant in what is called a Part 36 payment (that is, an offer to settle or a payment into the court), or obtain a judgment more favourable than a Part 36 offer, the court will order the claimant to pay any costs incurred by the defendant after the latest date for accepting the payment or offer. The court now has a discretion to make a different order for costs than the normal order.

District Judge Frenkel has given the following example: claim, £150,000 – judgment, £51,000 – £50,000 paid into court. The 'without prejudice' correspondence shows that the claimant would consider nothing short of £150,000. The claimant may be in trouble. The defendant will ask the judge to consider overriding principles of **Pt** 1: 'Was it proportional to incur the further costs of trial to secure an additional £1,000?' **Part** 44.3 confirms the general rule that the loser pays, but allows the court to make a different order to take into account offers to settle, payment into court, the parties' conduct, including pre-action conduct and exaggeration of the claim ((1999) 149 NLJ 458).

Similarly, where at trial a defendant is held liable to the claimant for more money than the proposals contained in a claimant's Part 36 offer (that is, where the claimant has made an offer to settle), the court may order the defendant to pay interest on the award, at a rate not exceeding 10 per cent above the base rate, for some or all of the period starting with the date on which the defendant could have accepted the offer.

Active case management imposes a duty on the courts to help parties settle their disputes. A 'stay' is a temporary halt in proceedings and an opportunity for the court to order such a pause arises at the stage when the defence to a claim has been filed. Parties can indicate that they have agreed on a stay to attempt to settle the case and, provided the court agrees, can have an initial period of one month to try to do this. In order to avoid the stay being used as a delaying tactic, the order granting the stay will require the parties to report back to the court within 14 days of the end of the period of the stay to:

(a) inform the court if the matter has been settled either wholly or partly; or

(b) ask for more time for settlement; or

(c) report that the attempt to settle has failed, so that the process of allocation of court track can take place.

The court will always give the final decision about whether to grant the parties more time to use a mediator, or arbitrator, or expert to settle, even if the parties are agreed that they wish to have more time. A stay will never be granted for an indefinite period.

In the Final Report on *Access to Justice*, Lord Woolf recognised the importance of witness statements in cases, but observed that they had become problematic, because lawyers had made them excessively long and detailed in order to protect against leaving out something which later proved to be relevant. He said, 'witness statements have ceased to be the authentic account of the lay witness; instead, they have become an elaborate, costly branch of legal drafting' (para 55). Under the new rules, witness statements must contain the evidence that the witness will give at trial, but they should be briefer than those drafted under the previous rules; they should be drafted in lay language and should not discuss legal propositions. Witnesses are now allowed to amplify on the statement, or deal with matters that have arisen since the Report was served, although this is not an automatic right and a 'good reason' for the admission of new evidence will have to be established.

Overall, it seems likely that as a result of the introduction of the new **CPR**, fewer of the annually settled cases will have been settled for the 'wrong reasons' (that is, because parties are frightened of the possible delays, costs, and uncertainties of proceeding to a full judgment) and more disputants will settle in the truer spirit of compromise, facilitated by an improved legal system.

NOTE

Inordinate delay also raises questions of human rights. Consider this case from the European Court of Human Rights. In *Jose da Conceicao Guerreiro v Portugal* (2002) App No 00045560/99 (G Ress P), 31 January, the applicant complained of a violation of **Art 6(1)** of the **European Convention on Human Rights**, on the basis that civil proceedings to which he was a party had lasted 14 years and two months and had therefore exceeded the 'reasonable time' requirement of the Article. The Court held unanimously that there had been a violation of **Art 6(1)** and the applicant was awarded 5,500 euros (about £3,500) for non-pecuniary and pecuniary damages. Most civil cases in the UK do not last that long, but a great many do endure for longer than five years, with all the attendant cost and the stress that such a period of uncertainty entails.

Question 37

The **Civil Procedure Rules (CPR)** introduced in 1999 have been an unqualified success in changing the legal system.

Discuss.

Answer plan

You will need to consider the following:

- the background to the new rules;
- Burton J's criticisms;
- the assessment of Burns J;

- concealed delays under the new system;
- the Eversheds study;
- judges and lawyers struggling with the new system.

Answer

The new **CPR**, the most fundamental changes in civil process for over 100 years, have radically altered the operation of civil justice. Since the new rules came into force (26 April 1999), they have been regularly reformed. The 21st update came into force in 2001.

Part of the rationale of the new rules was to expedite the way cases were dealt with and to allow more cases to be settled early through negotiation between the parties or alternative dispute resolution (ADR). In this respect, there is some evidence of success. Between May and August 1999, there was a 25 per cent reduction in the number of cases issued in the county courts, compared with the same period the previous year. By the end of January 2000, there was a further fall of 23 per cent. There is also evidence (in a speech by David Lock MP, Parliamentary Secretary to the Lord Chancellor's Department (LCD), 15 October 1999) that changes to pre-action behaviour, as a result of the pre-action protocols, have been partly responsible for the reduction in the number of cases going all the way through to trial.

An interesting assessment of the new rules was presented by Mr Justice Burton of the Queen's Bench Division. Speaking at the city law firm Kennedys, he outlined five benefits of the reforms and five problems ((2000) *Law Soc Gazette*, 10 February).

The five problems with the reforms were: the courts' inflexibility in not allowing parties to agree extensions of time between themselves; the danger of the judiciary pushing time guillotines onto parties; the risk that lawyers and clients could exploit 'standard' disclosure to conceal important documents; single joint experts possibly usurping the role of judges; and summary assessments of costs, leading to judges making assumptions replacing detailed costs analyses. He itemised the benefits as: pre-action protocols; emphasis on encouraging settlement; judicial intervention; Part 24 strike-out provisions; and Part 36 offers to settle.

Mr Justice Burton said that there had been three options for reforming appeals: (1) to extend the present system in order to discourage more than one appeal; (2) to refuse appeals without leave; or (3) to abolish the present system, giving no right to rehearings, only appeals. He said that he regretted that all three had been adopted (in the **Access to Justice Act 1999**). The consequence will be pressure on judges 'to get it right first time' and higher costs for parties.

Richard Burns, a barrister and recorder sitting in the county court, and thus someone who has experienced the new rules from both sides of the Bench, has made some interesting observations about the new system ('A view from the ranks' (2000) 150 NLJ 1829, pp 1829–1830). On the positive side, Judge Burns says that 'the transition has been far smoother than many had anticipated and there have been a number of very worthwhile gains'. He notes, however, that set against the ambitious aims Lord Woolf had set for the reforms, they were a 'relative failure'. Among the gains, the judge lists the unified system of procedure in all civil courts; awareness that the costs of litigation should bear a 'passing resemblance to the value of the claim'; vastly improved pre-action co-operation; more sensible and open pleadings which force the parties to define the issues at an early stage; the wider use of jointly instructed (and, therefore, impartial) experts; and in **Part 36** of the **CPR**, rules cunningly devised to encourage the parties to settle.

One way in which the system is not working properly, according to Richard Burns, is in relation to costs. He argues that the system is, in fact, proving more expensive than the old system for many litigants, as the timetable imposed usually compels the parties 'to spend time and money progressing claims to trial whether or not they expect to settle. Paradoxically, the procedures encouraging, as they do, the front-end loading of expenditure on cases may lead to more trials – certainly, this appears to have been happening in some of the court centres where I appear'.

Another difficulty concerns the system of case management, which Lord Woolf envisaged would be the engine to drive forward the litigation cheaply and expeditiously. Burns regards this as a system which is 'excessively bureaucratic and makes too many demands on the parties'. It is also, he argues, very poorly resourced, as the Court Service received very little extra money to finance the sort of increases in judicial staffing and information technology that Woolf had seen as essential.

Concealed delays are also blighting the system, according to Judge Burns. While recognising that on the whole, cases come to trial more quickly than they did, he notes that:

> The overall delay experienced by litigants is much the same as it ever was. This is because solicitors, feeling daunted by the demands made on them by the **CPR** and lacking the time and resources to manage more than a certain quota of cases through the system, are delaying the issue of proceedings. The delay frequently runs into years.

Eversheds, the corporate law claims firm, has conducted an 'access to justice' survey for five years. It canvassed the opinions and experiences of lawyers and those using the legal system. Results published in 2000, after one year of the Woolf reforms, showed that of its respondents, 54 per cent said that the civil litigation process had improved in the past year, a big increase on 1998's 15 per cent. Some 52 per cent of respondents believed that litigation was quicker, but only 22 per cent thought costs were lower.

John Heaps, head of litigation at Eversheds, has stated (*The Times*, 2 May 2000) that: 'The UK legal system historically has been plagued by unsatisfactory delays and expense. The style of dispute resolution is changing as a result of the Woolf reforms; people no longer seek aggressive uncompromising lawyers, but those who look for commercial solutions.'

The survey sought the views of heads of legal departments of UK companies and public sector bodies; 70 per cent of respondents were in the private sector, with 30 per cent in London. The replies suggest that a change in culture is emerging. Nearly two-thirds of respondents did not think that the reforms would make them less likely to start proceedings, but 43 per cent said that they were settling cases earlier and almost half said that their lawyers were handling disputes differently. Mediation, or ADR, is also becoming more popular: 41 per cent have used it, compared with 30 per cent in 1998.

There is, however, concern that while judges are managing cases more effectively, the courts do not have adequate resources (this was expressed by 50 per cent of respondents). Only 24 per cent believed that litigants were now getting better justice; 44 per cent said that they were not.

On the matter of costs, opinions were sharply divided. Nearly half did not believe costs to have been affected by the introduction of the new rules. Disturbingly, however, 19 per cent said that costs had risen, particularly in the regions. But a conference on Woolf held by CEDR found that although costs had increased at the start of litigation (front-loading), overall, they were down, as settlements came sooner.

Conditional or 'no win, no fee' work is attractive in principle, but little used: 48 per cent of respondents said that they would pay lawyers a higher fee for winning, if they could pay a lower fee, or none, if the case was lost, but only 24 per cent had discussed such a deal.

Litigation may be quicker and less likely to go to court, but 52 per cent of respondents expected to have the same number of business disputes in the following year, with as many being resolved through litigation. One in five were more optimistic and thought fewer disputes would be resolved in court.

John Heaps argues that overall the findings are positive. He has said: 'Over half the respondents feel the speed of resolving disputes has improved. But there are concerns that the aims and aspirations are not matched by court resources.'

A survey carried out by the City Research Group of the firm Wragge & Co obtained similar findings (*The Times*, 2 May 2000). It suggests that among in-house lawyers from FTSE 1,000 companies, a lack of resources has become 'a major stumbling block'. Some 81 per cent of respondents thought that courts did not have the resources to process claims quickly enough and some complained of 'inconsistent interpretation' between courts; however, 89 per cent of respondents backed the changes and said that litigation was quicker, with fewer 'frivolous claims'. Some 41 per cent thought that costs had been cut and there was strong backing for ADR, with 80 per cent saying that it had proved popular. Nine out of 10 lawyers thought that clients were more involved in the management of the dispute, but 38 per cent believed that the reforms had compromised justice at the expense of cost-cutting. As with the CEDR survey, the change singled out for the biggest impact is that which allows either party to make a formal settlement offer at any stage, or potentially face cost penalties.

A senior litigation partner at Wragge & Co, Andrew Manning Cox, observed that the survey mirrored the firm's experiences. Among surprise findings was the low awareness of Woolf among businesses. Their lawyers were apparently not using the new rules to the best tactical advantage of their companies.

Another City law firm, Lovells, found 71 per cent of respondents were now treating litigation as a last resort, with 72 per cent willing, voluntarily, to exchange documents with the other side. Where litigation is unavoidable, it is quicker, with 66 per cent saying that judges now set tighter timetables. Two-thirds found that the court 'rubber stamped' joint requests by the parties to move back dates in the timetable, but this flexibility did not extend to trial dates.

One of the findings that will be very disappointing for many involved with the project of the Woolf reforms is the apparently low use of a jointly appointed expert. According to the survey, only 7 per cent of respondents were involved in cases with such an expert.

The survey also highlights a low level of case management. Only 9 per cent found that the court monitored case progress and chased lawyers to meet deadlines; 42 per cent found the court had sought to narrow the issues as early as it could. The commercial court, Lovells found, was managing cases better than other High Court divisions. Moreover, courts did not penalise parties who failed to comply with the new rules. This certainly ties in with the experience of the barrister and county court judge Richard Burns. He has noted that the burden of work on many civil judges is so heavy that they cannot properly manage each case:

> Their burden in the busier courts is so huge that all they can do is skim the surface of files that cross their desks. It is rare, in my experience, for the same judge to be able to deal with all the interlocutory stages of even the bigger cases and so there is little or no continuity.
>
> (2000) 150 NLJ 1830

Asked for the worst aspect of the reforms, respondents chose the rule on summary assessment of costs in preliminary hearings, criticised as a lottery. In fact, the main deficiency in the new system seems to be one of variable application according to the style or interpretation of them favoured in any given court or region. This, though, may well become more uniform over time and, if that occurs, then the new rules really can claim to have radically and successfully altered the civil process in England and Wales.

NOTES

Research from the Law Society of England and Wales suggests that the cost of engaging in civil litigation has not been reduced by the civil justice reforms introduced in 2000. One of the main purposes of the reforms introduced through the **Civil Procedure Act 1997** was to improve public access to law by reducing its expense. Lord Woolf said that the first defect he had found in the civil justice system was 'that it is too expensive in that the costs often exceed the value of the claim' (Woolf Report, *Access to Justice*, 1996, p 2). Today, lack of proper resources and insufficient enforcement of the rules in civil courts mean that the potential impact of the Woolf reforms is limited. This is the finding of the latest Law Society survey of how the new rules are working (*The Woolf Network Questionnaire*, The Law Society, 2002).

Although there was a generally positive attitude towards the reforms, 70 per cent of respondents said that they had 'some reservations' about the reforms and said that under-resourced courts was one of the main concerns.

One major problem is that Lord Woolf's idea for 'fixed costs' for all disputes up to £15,000 has not been introduced. Instead, the judges assess the costs at the end of each stage of the litigation, and this is itself a time-consuming and costly event.

However, there was support for the new civil justice procedures. Around 84 per cent of solicitors questioned said that they thought the new procedures were quicker, and 70 per cent said that they were more efficient than the old ones. Nonetheless, a high number felt that the procedures were not cheaper for their clients than under the old rules.

In terms of improved efficiency, greater use of telephone case management conferences and more settlements were two of the main issues cited as leading to greater efficiency.

In August 2002, the Government published an updated evaluation of the **CPR** introduced three years earlier. The report, *Further Findings: A Continuing Evaluation of the Civil Justice Reforms*, is a follow-up to the report, *Emerging Findings: An Early Evaluation of the Civil Justice Reforms*, published in 2001. It builds on the earlier evidence and includes additional information. Both reports are available on the LCD website www.lcd.gov.uk.

Question 38

What is meant by legal professional privilege, and what purpose does it serve in the English legal system?

> **Answer plan**
>
> The question calls for an explanation of the doctrine, and then a description of why the privilege is a part of the system. The part of the answer dealing with the purpose of the privilege can be enhanced by an evaluative element.
>
> - Introduce the theme with an example.
> - Explain the principle and its origin.
> - Provide some case law support for the doctrine.
> - Explain the social benefits of client-lawyer confidentiality.
> - Illustrate the limitation of the privilege *R v Cox and Railton* (1884).
> - Conclusion – evaluation of doctrine.

Answer

A special set of rules controls the confidentiality of communications between lawyers and their clients. It is a very important part of the legal system.

The issue of secretly recorded conversations between the lawyer Simon Creighton and his imprisoned client (*The Times*, 5 February 2008) raised for public debate the question: why do we have the principle of 'professional privilege' that protects the lawyer-client relationship?

In essence, the privilege means that communications between a lawyer and client are confidential, and can only be revealed to a law court or the police at the option of the client. The same protection of confidentiality does not extend to doctor-patient, priest-penitent, or accountant-client relationships so it is easier for the legal system to acquire information from those professional communications.

The word 'privilege' comes from the Latin (*privilegium*) for 'private law': a law applying to an individual or small group. Under general law, what citizens say to each other can be used in evidence in law courts. A 'private law' though, applies to lawyers, and gives lawyer-client communications a specially guarded confidentiality.

The justification is simple and compelling. Citizens do not want to live in anarchy, they want to live in a society of laws and rules. As there are hundreds of thousands of laws, citizens do not want to have to become expert themselves on them all, anymore than they want to learn medicine just so they can be their own doctor. People want experts on the laws: lawyers. So, a society should encourage citizens to go to its lawyers for advice whenever they are in difficulties. To ensure the lawyer-client relationship works well, there must be complete trust, and, in order for that to happen, the client must feel assured that client-lawyer communications are completely private and confidential.

It might be argued that 'if a client has done nothing wrong, they've got nothing to worry about if their chats with their lawyer are recorded and later played to a court'. That, though, misses an important point. To be full and frank with lawyers in criminal, family, civil, and commercial cases, many clients have to mention secret, embarrassing or compromising things that are incidental to their main stories but more social good is served by those things remaining confidential, and the law taking its proper course guided by lawyers, than if clients were deterred from telling the bigger truths of their situations to lawyers for fear of the incidental compromising facts being open to be made public.

The rule of privilege is long established. In *Greenough v Gaskell* (1833), Lord Chancellor Brougham said (at 621) that the rule was important to uphold 'the interests of justice'. He said if the rule did not exist, people would be mistrustful of consulting legal experts, and so would end up worsening their own positions with do-it-yourself law. He said 'every one would be thrown upon his own legal resources'.

More recently, in 2003, the Privy Council (the highest appeal court for many commonwealth countries) ruled that lawyer-client privilege is fundamental to the operation of justice and should not be overridden unless the law has specifically said so in a particular circumstance: *B v Auckland District Law Society* (2003). The Privy Council held that the power of a district law society in New Zealand to require the production of documents by legal practitioners when investigating complaints against them under **s 101(3)(d)** of the **Law Practitioners Act 1982**, did not override legal professional privilege, and privilege was not waived by voluntarily making the documents available for limited purposes. The privilege is also protected under European law: Case 155/79 *AM&S Europe Ltd v EC Commission* (1983), and European human rights law: *Campbell v UK* (1992).

The privilege against disclosure does not, however, cover all communications. In a case in 1884, an English appeal confirmed that if a client asks a lawyer for information in order to be guided on how to commit a crime, the lawyer can testify about that to a court despite the client's protests: *R v Cox and Railton* (1884).

Henry Muster, who had been libelled in *The Brightonian*, was awarded damages. But the publisher of the paper, Richard Railton, conspired with a business partner to make a property transaction in order to avoid paying the damages. Railton had asked his solicitor some questions in preparation to do something unlawful. Informed by his solicitor, for example, that he was not allowed to sell property to his own business partner, Railton asked the solicitor 'Does anyone know about the partnership except for you?' After the scam was exposed, the solicitor was called as a prosecution witness and Railton and his partner were convicted.

Allowing client-lawyer privilege does not, as is sometimes said, amount to allowing criminals to thrive. Legally, a lawyer must not assist in the commission of a crime or say to a court anything he knows is untrue – those are very serious offences. Moreover, it is a lawyer's positive duty to disclose information that he knows or suspects relates to particular crimes such as terrorism (under the **Terrorism Act 2000**) or money laundering (under the **Proceeds of Crime Act 2002**).

Sometimes, of course, deciding whether the obligation to report something wrongful to a court puts lawyers in a difficult position. The barrister Rayner Goddard (who became Lord Chief Justice in 1946) asked his first client, during their initial cell interview at the Old Bailey: 'Now, my man, what is your story?' The client replied 'Well, that's rather up to you, guv'nor.'

It might be that the privilege rule means that lawyers get to hear of some immoral or shocking non-criminal aspects of the lives of certain clients, and that those remain secret. That, though, is a small price to pay for a population knowing that the state does not have its eye and an ear in the very offices to which its citizens go when they need help.

Question 39

Explain the circumstances in which an advocate can be held liable for courtroom negligence and assess the public policy arguments in this area.

Answer plan

Look at:

- the decision in *Arthur JS Hall & Co v Simons* (2000);
- the brief historical background;
- the advocate's divided loyalty;
- the 'cab rank' rule;
- the witness analogy;
- collateral attack;
- the need for public confidence in the system.

Answer

In *Arthur JS Hall & Co v Simons* (2000), the House of Lords made a bold change in this area of law. It imposed a duty of care upon courtroom advocates that had not been previously supported in law.

Lawyers are, for the general public, the most central and prominent part of the English legal system. They are, arguably, to the legal system what doctors are to the health system. For many decades, a debate has grown about why a patient injured by the negligence of a surgeon in the operating theatre can sue for damages, whereas a litigant whose case is lost because of the negligence of his advocate cannot sue. It all seemed very unfair. Even the most glaringly obvious courtroom negligence was protected against legal action by a special advocates' immunity. The claim that this protection was made by lawyers (and judges who were lawyers) for lawyers was difficult to refute. In this House of Lords' decision, the historic immunity has been abolished in respect of both barristers and solicitor-advocates (of whom there are now over 2,000 with higher courts' rights of audience) and for both civil and criminal proceedings.

In three cases, all conjoined on appeal, a claimant raised a claim of negligence against a firm of solicitors and, in each case, the firms relied on the immunity attaching to barristers and other advocates from actions in negligence. At first instance, all the claims were struck out. Then, on appeal, the Court of Appeal said that claims could have proceeded. The solicitors appealed to the Lords and two key questions were raised: should the old immunity rule be maintained and, in a criminal case, what was the proper scope of the principle against 'collateral attack'? A 'collateral attack' is when someone convicted in a criminal court tries to invalidate that conviction outside the criminal appeals process by suing his trial defence lawyer in a civil court. The purpose of such a 'collateral attack' is to win in the civil case, proving negligence against the criminal trial lawyer, and thus by implication, to show that the conviction in the criminal case was unfair.

The House of Lords held (Lord Hope, Lord Hutton and Lord Hobhouse dissenting in part) that in the light of modern conditions, it was now clear that it was no longer in the public interest in the administration of justice that advocates should have immunity from suit for negligence for acts concerned with the conduct of either civil or criminal litigation.

Lord Hoffmann (with Lord Steyn, Lord Browne-Wilkinson and Lord Millett delivering concurring opinions) said that over 30 years had passed since the House had last considered the rationale for the immunity of the advocate from suit, in *Rondel v Worsley* (1969). Public policy was not immutable and there had been great changes in the law of negligence, the functioning of the legal profession, the administration of justice and public perceptions. It was, once again, time to re-examine the whole matter. Interestingly, Lord Hoffmann chose to formulate his opinion in a creative mode to reflect public policy, rather than in the tradition of what can be seen as slavish obedience to the details of precedent:

> I hope that I will not be thought ungrateful if I do not encumber this speech with citations. The question of what the public interest now requires depends upon the strength of the arguments rather than the weight of authority.

The point of departure was that, in general, English law provided a remedy in damages for a person who had suffered injury as a result of professional negligence. It followed that any exception which denied such a remedy required a sound justification. The arguments relied on by the court in *Rondel v Worsley* as justifying the immunity had to be considered. One by one, these arguments were evaluated and rejected.

Advocate's divided loyalty

There were two distinct versions of the divided loyalty argument. The first was that the possibility of being sued for negligence would actually inhibit the lawyer, consciously or unconsciously, from giving his duty to the court priority over his duty to his client. The second was that the divided loyalty was a special factor that made the conduct of litigation a very difficult art and could lead to the advocate being exposed to vexatious claims by difficult clients. The argument was pressed, most strongly, in connection with advocacy in criminal proceedings, where the clients were said to be more than usually likely to be vexatious.

There had been recent developments in the civil justice system designed to reduce the incidence of vexatious litigation. The first was r 24.2 of the **CPR**, which provided that a court could give summary judgment in favour of a defendant if it considered that 'the claimant had no real prospect of succeeding on the claim'. The second was the changes to the funding of civil litigation introduced by the **Access to Justice Act 1999**, which would make it much more difficult than it had been in the past to obtain legal help for negligence actions which had little prospect of success.

There was no doubt that the advocate's duty to the court was extremely important in the English justice system. The question was whether removing the immunity would have a significantly adverse effect. If the possibility of being held liable in negligence was calculated to have an adverse effect on the behaviour of advocates in court, one might have expected that to have followed, at least in some degree, from the introduction of wasted costs orders (where a court disallows a lawyer from being able to claim part of a fee for work which is regarded as unnecessary and wasteful). Although the liability of a negligent advocate to a wasted costs order was not the same as a liability to pay general damages, the experience of the wasted costs jurisdiction was the only empirical evidence available in England to test the proposition that such liability would have an adverse effect upon the way advocates performed their duty to the court, and there was no suggestion that it had changed standards of advocacy for the worse.

The 'cab rank'

The 'cab rank' rule provided that a barrister could not refuse to act for a client on the ground that he disapproved of him or his case. The argument was that a barrister, who was obliged to accept any client, would be unfairly exposed to vexatious actions by clients whom any sensible lawyer with freedom of action would have refused to act for. Such a claim, however, was in the nature of things intuitive, incapable of empirical verification and did not have any real substance.

The witness analogy

The argument started from the well established rule that a witness was absolutely immune from liability for anything that he said in court. So were the judge, counsel and the parties. They could not be sued for libel, malicious falsehood or conspiring to give false evidence. The policy of the rule was to encourage persons who took part in court proceedings to express themselves freely. However, a witness owed no duty of care to anyone in respect of the evidence he gave to the court. His only duty was to tell the truth.

There was no analogy with the position of a lawyer who owed a duty of care to his client. The fact that the advocate was the only person involved in the trial process who was liable to be sued for negligence was because he was the only person who had undertaken such a duty of care to his client.

Collateral attack

The most substantial argument was that it might be contrary to the public interest for a court to retry a case which had been decided by another court. However, actions for negligence against lawyers were not the only cases that gave rise to a possibility of the same issue being tried twice. The law had to deal with the problem in numerous other contexts. So, before examining the strength of the collateral challenge argument as a reason for maintaining the immunity of lawyers, it was necessary to consider how the law dealt with collateral challenge in general.

The law discouraged relitigation of the same issues, except by means of an appeal. The Latin maxims often quoted were *nemo debet bis vexari pro una et eadem causa* and interest *rei publicae ut finis sit litium*. The first was concerned with the interests of the defendant: a person should not be troubled twice for the same reason. That policy had generated the rules which prevented relitigation when the parties were the same: *autrefois acquit* (someone acquitted of a crime cannot be tried again for that crime), *res judicata* (a particular dispute decided by a civil court cannot be retried) and issue estoppel (a person cannot deny the fact of a judgment previously decided against him).

The second policy was wider: it was concerned with the interests of the state. There was a general public interest in the same issue not being litigated over again. The second policy could be used to justify the extension of the rules of issue estoppel to cases in which the parties were not the same, but the circumstances were such as to bring the case within the spirit of the rules. Criminal proceedings were in a special category because, although they were technically litigation between the Crown and the defendant, the Crown prosecuted on behalf of society as a whole. So, a conviction had some of the quality of a judgment *in rem*, which should be binding in favour of everyone.

Not all relitigation of the same issue, however, would be manifestly unfair to a party, or bring the administration of justice into disrepute. Sometimes, there were valid reasons for rehearing a dispute. It was, therefore, unnecessary to try to stop any relitigation by forbidding anyone from suing their lawyer. It was, in Lord Hoffmann's words, 'burning down the house to roast the pig; using a broad-spectrum remedy without side effects could handle the problem equally well'.

The scope for re-examination of issues in criminal proceedings was much wider than in civil cases. Fresh evidence was more readily admitted. A conviction could be set aside as unsafe and unsatisfactory when the accused appeared to have been prejudiced by 'flagrantly incompetent advocacy': see *R v Clinton* (1993). After conviction, the case could be referred to the Court of Appeal if the conviction was on indictment, or to the Crown Court if the trial was summary, by the Criminal Cases Review Commission.

It followed that it would ordinarily be an abuse of process for a civil court to be asked to decide that a subsisting conviction was wrong. That applied to a conviction on a plea of guilty, as well as after a trial. The resulting conflict of judgments was likely to bring the administration of justice into disrepute. The proper procedure was to appeal, or if the right of appeal had been exhausted, to apply to the Criminal Cases Review Commission. It would, ordinarily, be an abuse because there were bound to be exceptional cases in which the issue could be tried without a risk that the conflict of judgments would bring the administration of justice into disrepute.

Once the conviction has been set aside, there could be no public policy objection to an action for negligence against the legal advisers. There could be no conflict of judgments. On the other hand, in civil, including matrimonial, cases, it would seldom be possible to say that an action for negligence against a legal adviser or representative would bring the administration of justice into disrepute. Whether the original decision was right or wrong was usually a matter of concern only to the parties and had no wider implications. There was no public interest objection to a subsequent finding that but for the negligence of his lawyers, the losing party would have won.

But, again, there might be exceptions. The action for negligence might be an abuse of process on the ground that it was manifestly unfair to someone else. Take, for example, the case of a defendant who published a serious defamation which he attempted, unsuccessfully, to justify. Should he be able to sue his lawyers and claim that if the case had been conducted differently, the allegation would have been proved to be true? It seemed unfair to the claimant in the defamation action that any court should be allowed to come to such a conclusion in proceedings to which he was not a party. On the other hand, it was equally unfair that he should have to join as a party and rebut the allegation for a second time. A man's reputation was not only a matter between him and the other party. It represented his relationship with the world. So, it might be that in such circumstances, an action for negligence would be an abuse of the process of the court.

Having regard to the power of the court to strike out actions which had no real prospect of success, the doctrine was unlikely, in that context, to be invoked very often. The first step in any application to strike out an action alleging negligence in the conduct of a previous action had to be to ask whether it had a real prospect of success.

Lord Hope, Lord Hutton and Lord Hobhouse delivered judgments in which they agreed that the immunity from suit was no longer required in relation to civil proceedings, but dissented to the extent of saying that the immunity was still required in the public interest in the administration of justice in relation to criminal proceedings.

This decision is of major and historic importance in the English legal system for several reasons. It can be seen as a bold attempt by the senior judiciary to drag the legal profession (often a metonymy for the whole legal system) into the 21st century world of accountability and fair business practice. In his judgment, Lord Steyn makes this dramatic observation:

> ... public confidence in the legal system is not enhanced by the existence of the immunity. The appearance is created that the law singles out its own for protection no matter how flagrant the breach of the barrister. The world has changed since 1967. The practice of law has become more commercialised: barristers may now advertise. They may now enter into contracts for legal services with their professional clients. They are now obliged to carry insurance. On the other hand, today we live in a consumerist society in which people have a much greater awareness of their rights. If they have suffered a wrong as the result of the provision of negligent professional services, they expect to have the right to claim redress. It tends to erode confidence in the legal system if advocates, alone among professional men, are immune from liability for negligence.

The case raises and explores many key issues of the legal system, including the proper relationship between lawyers and the courts, the proper relationship between lawyers and clients, the differences between criminal and civil actions, professional ethics, the nature of dispute resolution and the circumstances under which the courts should make new law. Above all, however, the case has one simple significance: 'It will', in the words of Jonathan Hirst QC, Chairman of the Bar Council, 'mean that a claimant who can prove loss, as the result of an advocate's negligence, will no longer be prevented from making a claim. We cannot really say that is wrong' ((2000) *Bar News*, August, p 3).

NOTES

The case of *Moy v Pettmann Smith (a firm)* (2005) gives some comfort to advocates regarding advice provided to clients at the door of the court, that is when, at the last moment before a case begins, an offer to settle the case is made by the other side and a lawyer has to advise his or her client under some pressure of time whether to accept it. The House of Lords decided that advice given by lawyers in such circumstances does not have to be absolutely perfect in order to be avoid being safe from an action for negligence by a dissatisfied client.

Question 40

Expert witnesses perform an important role in court. Discuss the considerations that influence how their evidence is regulated.

Answer plan

Various approaches could be used in answer to this question. Provided that a structured response is given, and that it provides what the question asks for, it will be satisfactory. The answer here has been structured as follows:

- explain why expert evidence is important;
- explain the dangers of a system that uses experts paid by the side of the case that they are called by;
- explain the temptations that might beset an expert;
- give illustrations of what can happen if an expert is wrong;
- explain how the Woolf reforms sought to reduce the risks in this area of civil process;
- conclude with a suggested improvement to the current system.

Answer

In court, in both criminal cases and civil cases, experts are often needed to get to the truth. All sorts of expertise is needed in order to work out questions like how a traffic accident occurred, whether the way surgery was performed was negligent, whether the financial accounting of a company was fraudulent, whether A is the father of B, whether a council worker was being exposed to unreasonable levels of stress, and so forth. Experts on everything from accountancy to zoology are regularly in court. Obviously, a great deal of the determination of 'justice' therefore swings on experts – in some cases more than it does on the performance of lawyers or judges. How the legal system uses experts is therefore very important.

Recent developments in respect of the way experts work in both criminal and civil cases have highlighted the main issues.

Speaking at the publication of the annual report of the Criminal Cases Review Commission, in 2004, its chairman, Professor Graham Zellick, suggested that high fees were tempting experts to give unequivocal opinions just to secure their next case.

He said expert witnesses can make 'quite a nice living' out of just being expert witnesses, which presupposes they continue to be instructed. He said: 'If they are doubtful or hesitant, they don't get another set of instructions. If money is to be made, it is not always clear that the highest ethical standards apply.'

Professor Zellick called for an inquiry into the legal framework under which expert witnesses operate. He echoed earlier comments made by the Attorney-General by saying that judges needed powers to rule expert evidence inadmissible and a benchmark by which to sort trustworthy witnesses from 'charlatans'.

He said we need very clear rules as to what constitutes the area that can be called expert evidence; who the practitioners are; to whom courts will listen and the extent to which they can give opinions.

The time had come, he suggested, for clarification of the duties of expert witnesses. A good illustration of the point that justice does not come cheaply is the fact that fees paid to expert witnesses in civil and criminal cases cost more than £130 million a year in legal aid funds.

Research by Bond Solon, a firm that trains expert witnesses, has indicated that 8.5 per cent of witnesses charge more than £1,600 a day and another 10 per cent charge above £1,400. Thirty-four per cent charge above £800.

Lord Goldsmith, the Attorney-General, has said that experts should only voice opinions rooted firmly in fact and experience; and should be ready to disclose any flaw or weakness in that opinion.

Professor Zellick argues that unless there is regulation of experts, there could be more miscarriages of justice. Some experts, he notes, appeared to 'make it up as they go along'. He observes that experts only express a view but that 'I am not sure that juries always completely understand that'. One graphic example of the unreliability of expert evidence came with the conviction and subsequent release of the late Sally Clark, a solicitor accused of murdering her two baby sons. She was convicted largely on the evidence of the paediatrician Professor Sir Roy Meadow, who said that the chance of two such children dying of cot death was 'one in 73 million'. This figure was later criticised by statisticians and the judge at Mrs Clark's appeal. She was subsequently released. Yet Sir Roy's opinions on the reasons for sudden child deaths had been instrumental in the conviction of a number of other mothers. Angela Cannings, also jailed for supposedly murdering her children, was released late last year as a result of continuing doubts over his testimony. In July 2005, Professor Meadow was struck off the medical register by the General

Medical Council for 'serious professional misconduct' in respect of his evidence in court cases.

In the civil courts, there is an growing concern among the medical and legal professions that the views of expert witnesses can be partial and ill-informed. Yet medical expert witnesses can earn up to £400 an hour, and easily clock up £50,000 a year, in addition to payment from their main employer – usually the NHS. The professional opinions they give are key in determining whether patients get compensation for medical errors.

The worlds of law and medicine are closely connected. Medical negligence claims are rising and there is a substantial need for expert medical opinion. The medical expertise called for ranges from preparing reports for insurance companies, or assessing civil damages claims for simple injuries, like whiplash injury, to high-profile medical negligence cases requiring courtroom testimony. About 2,000 doctors regularly act as expert witnesses to the courts.

The partisan 'hired gun' expert was supposed to have been largely removed from the legal system by the Woolf Reforms. Following a major review of the civil justice process, led by Lord Woolf, an overhaul and redesign of the civil cases system was instituted by the **Civil Procedure Act 1998**. One of the changes was, in cases requiring non-legal expertise, to require a single expert beholden to the court alone unless the sides could not agree on an expert and the court agreed to more than one. Nonetheless, bad practice still occurs. One abuse takes place where an expert writes an independent report for a civil action, but is invited by the solicitors who are engaging him or her to delete parts because they believe that those sections might prove problematic in court under cross-examination.

Another allegation is that the current system of legal aid funding is the root of the problem. Using the evidence of experts, a solicitor advises the Legal Services Commission (which allocates legal aid funding) whether a case deserves legal aid – even though the solicitor and the expert witness stand to gain financially from a positive decision. That means that it must be very tempting for some solicitors in some cases to find an expert willing to provide very strong evidence that a claimant's claim has a good evidential foundation, so that the case gets funded by the state and therefore promises payments for both the lawyer and the expert. One possible area of improvement would be for an independent expert to be appointed by the court to evaluate both sides of the case.

NOTES

In 2007, Gene Morrison, a conman from Hyde, in Cheshire, was convicted of 22 crimes, including deception offences and perjury, after having posed for years as a forensic psychologist. He had used the title 'Dr' but when asked by police from where he gained that qualification, he replied (on film) 'Er, I have forgotten that.'

Worryingly, he was able to have given testimony in over 700 cases without being exposed by lawyers or judges as a fake.

Many legal disputes need the evidence of experts. Expert opinion is much more than what an American judge once condemned as 'only an ordinary guess in evening clothes'. Every week thousands of specialists like consultant doctors, accountants, authorities on art, and shipping experts, deliver testimony. Such expertise makes the discovery of truth much easier. But it does present occasional problems.

When justice is miscarried because someone has given sham evidence from the witness box, the repercussions can be catastrophic: people get imprisoned, companies collapse, and children can be taken from parents.

An abiding challenge is that a judge or a jury has to evaluate intricate testimony to do with science, technology, or finance, and to conclude which side of a case is supported by stronger evidence. Sometimes a trial does not get as much expertise as is later seen to be helpful. In February 2007, in a retrial, Ian and Angela Gay were acquitted of having killed the three-year-old Christian Blewitt, by poisoning him with salt. In this second trial, a new medical expert witness presented an alternative theory about Christian's fatally high sodium level. He showed how the boy's blood-salt concentration could have been attributable to osmoreceptor dysfunction – a medical condition that results in the body not being able to regulate its sodium levels properly.

In civil cases, one problem has sometimes been a profusion of specialist testimony, leaving the court, as one judge said adapting a line of Milton, 'dark with excessive brightness'. To avoid a trial becoming overborne by an abundance of obscure expertise, a court now has the power under the **Civil Procedure Rules** to direct that evidence is given by a *single* expert to serve 'both sides' of the case. **Rule 35.7(3)** says that where the parties cannot agree who should be the expert, the court may select the expert from a list provided by the parties, or chosen in another manner 'as the court may direct'.

It is also important that when technical evidence is adduced (cited as proof of something) in court, that it can be understood by people outside of whatever discipline it comes from. Medical evidence, for example, however abstruse must be able to be explained in non-medical terms. And arguments about whether something is good practice must be such as could persuade a court not just a panel of doctors. In a House of Lords' decision in 1997 (*Bolitho v City and Hackney Heath Authority*), Lord Browne-Wilkinson said that medical evidence must be 'capable of withstanding logical analysis' (that is from a non-doctor) and that if it was not, 'a judge is entitled to hold that the body of opinion is not reasonable or responsible'.

Another point about expert evidence is that those giving it have a duty to justice above their duty to the person paying for their services. In criminal cases, expert witnesses have an obligation to assist the court, and they must remain objective and express only genuinely held opinions which are not biased in favour of either party.

Experts should ensure that developments in scientific thinking and techniques are not kept from the court, even where they remain at the stage of a mere hypothesis. This duty is facilitated by the **Criminal Procedure Rules** which enable opposing experts to consult together before the trial and, if possible, to settle their points of agreement or disagreement with a summary of their reasons.

Similarly, in civil trials, experts must be more than hired proponents of their side's case. The **Practice Direction on Civil Procedure Rule 35** states that 'It is the duty of an expert to help the court' and that this duty 'is paramount and overrides any obligation to the person from whom the expert has received instructions or by whom he is paid'. The rules are strict and demand that an expert should provide objective, unbiased opinion, and should not assume 'the role of an advocate'.

The court is a perfect place to allow expertise to be applied to real problems in an unrushed, balanced way, to be expounded during an examination with a guiding advocate, and tested during cross-examination.

CHAPTER 7

ALTERNATIVE DISPUTE RESOLUTION

INTRODUCTION

This part of the English legal system has undergone significant development in recent times. English legal system courses tend to focus too much attention on the operation of the traditional court system. Whilst the courts are of fundamental importance, one should not overlook the increasing importance of alternative methods of deciding disputes. It should never be forgotten that tribunals actually deal with more cases than the county courts and High Court combined. The use of specialist tribunals to decide problems has a long history in England, but it has to be realised that the huge growth in the number of tribunals is a product of the growth of the interventionist welfare state and represents, at one level, an attack on the traditional legal system. These alternative mechanisms may also be seen as highlighting the weaknesses in the adversarial court system, in that they emphasise conciliation over conflict and, to that extent at least, they may well represent an advance on the traditional system of dispute resolution. It should also be borne in mind, however, that such informal procedures themselves are not without weaknesses.

Litigation is an extremely costly procedure. This is so not just for the parties concerned in any action who have to pay the costs of their legal representatives, but also for the state which has to provide the legal framework within which the action is taken, that is, courts, judges and other staff. This has been a great impetus for potential litigants to resort to alternative dispute resolution (ADR) and, in particular, to mediation – the use of a neutral third party to assist the disputants to reach a compromise. Most civil cases are settled at the door of the court, but by the time they arrive there, most parties have spent much time and money. Mediation aims to encourage disputants to reach such an agreement earlier. One private mediation company, Mediation UK, already mediates in over 5,000 neighbour disputes a year.

Checklist

You should:
- have at least a minimal understanding of the social historical process that has seen the substantial development of tribunals;

- have particular knowledge of the operation of a substantial number of tribunals;
- be able to compare the advantages and disadvantages of alternative dispute resolutions, as against traditional court mechanisms;
- be able to distinguish and write about arbitration, mediation and conciliation;
- be prepared to answer a specific question relating to the **Arbitration Act 1996**;
- be prepared to answer a question on the county court small claims procedure (this may stand you in good stead for questions on court structure or civil procedure as well).

Question 41

Explain the operation of tribunals as alternatives to the court system and assess the need for the proposed reforms included in the **Tribunals, Courts and Enforcement Act (TCEA) 2007**.

Answer plan

This question invites a relatively straightforward comparison of tribunals and courts, but also requires some knowledge of the proposals to reform the operation of tribunals. The answer should include at least some of the following points:

- consideration of the usual advantages cited for tribunals – cheapness, speed and informality;
- consideration of the foregoing in the light of the disadvantages of the system;
- some note of the fact that the same areas can be cited as advantages and disadvantages, at one and the same time;
- comparison of the operation of tribunals with that of the courts;
- a conclusion suggesting whether, and if so how, the operation of tribunals can be improved (mention should be made of the review of tribunals conducted by Sir Andrew Leggatt);
- a consideration of the proposals contained in the **TCEA 2007** as far as they relate to tribunals.

Answer

The reason generally put forward for the establishment and growth of tribunals in Britain since 1945 is the need to provide a specialist forum to deal with cases involving conflicts between an increasingly interventionist welfare state, its functionaries, and the rights of private citizens. It is arguable, however, that the large-scale development of this special area of dispute resolution marks a diminishment in the general rule of law, to the extent that it has led to a transfer of power from the ordinary courts. A number of advantages are usually cited in favour of the use of tribunals, rather than the ordinary court system. These advantages relate to the cost, speed, efficiency, privacy and the lack of formality involved in such proceedings. It is important, however, that these supposed advantages are not simply taken at face value for, although they do no doubt represent significant improvements over the operation of the ordinary court system, it is at least arguable that some of them are not necessarily as advantageous as they appear at first sight and that others represent potential (if not actual) weaknesses in the tribunal system.

The ordinary system of courts, with the important exception of the magistrates' courts, are staffed by people who have had a specifically legal education and training, as may be seen from the requirement for judges to be qualified legal practitioners of some standing. With regard to the tribunal system, however, this is not the case.

Tribunals are usually made up of three members, only one of whom, the chair, is expected to be legally qualified. The other two members require no specific legal qualification or expertise. The lack of legal training is not considered a drawback, given the technical administrative, as opposed to specifically legal, nature of the provisions they have to consider. Indeed, the fact of there being two lay representatives on tribunals provides them with one of their perceived advantages over courts, for, to the extent that the non-legal members may provide specialist knowledge, they enable the tribunal to base its decision on actual practice as opposed to abstract legal theory, and thus enable decisions to be taken on practical grounds rather than on the basis of mere legal formalism.

An example of this can be seen in respect of the tribunals responsible for deciding matters relating to employment under the **Employment Rights Act 1996**. In practice, such tribunals are normally made up of a legally qualified chairperson, a representative of employers and a representative of employees. As a consequence, the tribunal has access to the practical experience of the lay members, together with knowledge of the circumstances involved in any particular dispute from both sides of the employment relationship. Such practical experience and expertise provides a basis for the decisions of the tribunal and gives such decisions a degree of pragmatic legitimacy.

A lack of formalism is also evident in the general procedure of tribunals, with the intention of making them less intimidating than full-blown court cases. Informality is shown in the fact that the strict rules relating to evidence, pleading and procedure, which apply in courts, are not binding or applied in tribunal proceedings. An example of this relaxation of strict court procedure is evident in the fact that tribunals are not bound by the strict rules of precedent. Of equal importance is the perhaps conflicting, if not contradictory, need for consistency of treatment, which is one of the major justifications of the system of precedent.

When these matters relating to the lack of formality are linked with the fact that tribunal proceedings tend not to be accusatorial, they generally lead to the conclusion that complainants do not need to be represented by a lawyer in order to present their grievance. They may represent themselves or be represented by a more knowledgeable associate, such as a trade union representative or a friend.

The fact that complainants do not have to rely on legal representation, in turn, makes the tribunal procedure less expensive than using the traditional court system, and this reduction in expense is further enhanced by the additional facts that there are no court fees involved in relation to tribunal proceedings and that costs are not normally awarded against a party who loses the case.

A further perceived advantage of the tribunal system is the speed of its operation, together with the certainty that a dispute will be heard on a specific date.

The final advantage usually cited is the fact that proceedings can be taken before a tribunal without necessarily triggering the publicity that might follow from a court case.

All of these factors, making the use of the tribunal system less intimidating as well as much less expensive than using the normal court system, serve to encourage individuals to pursue their grievances in circumstances where they might not be willing to take action in the courts and, thus, they can be seen as serving the praiseworthy function of increasing access to the law and legal remedies.

Having examined the supposed advantages of the tribunal system, its shortcomings remain to be considered. The first of these arises with regard to the uncertainty and lack of uniformity that exists in relation to appeals from tribunals. Rights of appeal from decisions of tribunals and the route of such appeals depend on the provision of the statute under which a particular tribunal operates and, where they exist, may be exercised variously, to a further tribunal, a minister or a court of law. Prior to the Franks Committee Report (Cmnd 218, 1957), tribunals were not required to provide reasons for their decisions and this prevented appeals in most cases. Subsequent to the Franks Report, however, most tribunals, although still not all of them (and this remains a major bone of contention), are required to provide reasons for their decisions under s 12 of the **Tribunals and Inquiries Act 1971**. The importance of this provision is that in cases where a tribunal has erred in its application of the law, the claimant can appeal to the High Court for an application for judicial review, to have the decision of the tribunal set aside for error of law on the face of the record.

Second, it has generally been accepted that the lack of publicity in relation to the majority of tribunal proceedings is an advantage, but the alternative possibility has to be considered: that such lack of publicity is, in fact, a distinct disadvantage, because it has the effect that cases involving issues of general public importance are not given the publicity and consideration that they might merit.

The major weakness as regards the operation of tribunals, however, is that except for Land Tribunals and the Commons Commissioners, people pursuing cases before tribunals were not entitled to legal aid to finance their cases. The effect of the replacement of legal aid by the Community Legal Service fund under the **Access to Justice Act 1999** remains to be seen. It is probably accurate to say, however, that in this particular area, it certainly cannot make matters worse and that the establishment of Community Legal Service Partnerships may well improve the availability of quality advice for those with problems to be decided by tribunals.

The foregoing has stated that the major advantages of the tribunal system are to be found in its lack of formality and its non-legal atmosphere, but research has shown that individual complainants fare better where they are, in fact, represented by lawyers. Additionally, it is, perhaps, one of the unintended consequences of the Franks Report that the appointment of legally qualified chairpersons has led to an increase in the formality of tribunal proceedings. As a consequence, non-law experts find it increasingly difficult in practice to represent themselves effectively. This difficulty is compounded when the body which is the object of the complaint is itself legally represented, for although the parties to hearings do not have to be legally represented, equally, there is nothing to prevent them from being so represented, no doubt to their advantage.

If tribunals are becoming increasingly important in determining individual rights and are, at the same time, becoming formalistic, then the refusal of assistance to fund legal representation to those seeking to use tribunals is tantamount to refusing them access to justice.

In August 2001, Sir Andrew Leggatt published his review of the tribunal system and after commenting on the lack of coherence in the system, his most important recommendations were as follows:

- to make the present 70 separate tribunals into one Tribunals System;
- to ensure that the tribunals operate independently of their sponsoring departments by having them administered by one Tribunals Service. Sir Andrew felt that tribunals neither appeared to be independent, nor were independent in fact, from their department of state;
- to improve the training of chairpersons and members in the interpersonal skills peculiarly required by tribunals;
- to clarify the appeals procedure. At present, routes of appeal from tribunal decisions are extremely confusing;

- Leggatt recommended that there should be a right of appeal on a point of law, by permission, on the generic ground that the decision of the tribunal was unlawful:

  (a) from the first-tier tribunals in each Division to its corresponding appellate tribunal;

  (b) from appellate tribunals to the Court of Appeal;

- to consider the effectiveness of lay members. It was felt that there is no justification for any members to sit, whether expert or lay, unless they have a particular function to fulfil, as they do in Employment Tribunals. In all other Divisions, the President (or Regional or District Chairmen) should have a discretion concerning whether lay members should sit in any particular case or category of cases.

Subsequently, in March 2003, the Lord Chancellor's Office announced the Government's intention to follow Sir Andrew Leggatt's recommendations and to institute a new unified Tribunals Service. The new organisation formally came into being in April 2005 and was launched operationally in April 2006.

According to its mission statement, the Tribunals Service will be focused on delivering real benefits to tribunal users, including:

- ensuring that tribunals are manifestly independent from those whose decisions are being reviewed;
- helping to provide better information to users and potential users;
- delivering greater consistency in practice and procedure;
- making better use of existing tribunal resources.

It will also have a wider mission to work in partnership with other government departments to improve the standard of decision-making, so that fewer disputes arise.

The Tribunals, Court and Enforcement Act 2007

In pursuance of the Leggatt review, the stated intention of this piece of legislation (**TCEA 2007**) was the creation of a new, simplified, statutory framework for tribunals, which was to be achieved not just by the bringing together of existing tribunal jurisdictions but by the provision of a new structure of jurisdiction and new appeal rights.

- *Unified structure*

  The Act provides for the establishment of a new unified structure to subsume all tribunals, except the for the Employment and Asylum and Immigration tribunals which will remain independent. This unification is to be achieved through the creation of two new tribunals, the First-tier Tribunal and the Upper Tribunal and in pursuit of that end the Act gives the Lord Chancellor power to transfer the jurisdiction of existing tribunals to the two new tribunals. The Act also provides for the establishment within each tier of 'chambers' so that exiting jurisdictions may be grouped together appropriately. Chambers at the first-tier level will hear cases initially and the role of the upper chambers will be mainly, but not exclusively, to hear appeals from the first tier. Each chamber will be headed by a Chamber President and the tribunals' judiciary, as the legal members of tribunals will now be entitled, will be headed by a Senior President of Tribunals.

- *Appeals*

    The Act specifically recognises and attempts to deal with the previous unclear and unsatisfactory routes of appeal in relation to tribunals' decisions. Under its provisions, in most cases, a decision of the First-tier Tribunal may be appealed to the Upper Tribunal and a decision of the Upper Tribunal may be appealed to a court. However, it also provides that any such appeal must relate to a point of law and may only be exercised with permission from the tribunal being appealed from or the tribunal or court being appealed to.

- *Administration*

    The Act restates and reinforces the role of the Tribunal Service in the successful operation of the new unified system.

- *Supervision*

    Whereas the previous tribunals had come under the purview of the Council of Tribunals, the new act replaced that body with the Administrative Justice and Tribunals Council (AJTC) an important new institution with responsibility, not just for tribunals as was the remit of the previous body, but with a wider overview and input into the operation of the administrative justice system as a whole.

- *Enforcement*

    In relation to enforcement, at present, tribunals have no enforcement powers of their own. Consequently if a monetary award is not paid then the claimant must register the claim in the county court before seeking enforcement. Under **TCEA 2007** claimants will be able to go directly to the county court or High Court for enforcement.

Question 42

Explain the operation of the ombudsman system.

> **Answer plan**
>
> The Parliamentary Commissioner for Administration (PCA) is better known as the ombudsman, whose function under the **Parliamentary Commissioner Act (PCA) 1967** is to investigate complaints relating to maladministration. The PCA deals with problems in relation to central government and the health service, but other ombudsmen have been appointed under the **Local Government Act (LGA) 1974** to oversee the administration of local government in England and Wales. In dealing with this question, the following points should be addressed:
>
> - a brief history of the concept of ombudsmen;
> - the statutory basis of the PCA's powers;
> - the meaning of maladministration;
> - the filter role of MPs;
> - the powers of the PCA;
> - criticisms/limitations of the system;
> - the spread of the system to other areas.

Answer

The actual concept of the ombudsman is Scandinavian in origin and the function of the office holder is to investigate complaints of maladministration: that is, situations where the performance of a government department has fallen below acceptable standards of administration.

As with tribunals, so the institution of the ombudsman reflects the increased activity of the contemporary state. The ombudsman procedure, however, is not just an alternative to the court and tribunal system; it is based upon a distinctly different approach to dealing with disputes. Indeed, the **PCA 1967**, which established the position of the first ombudsman, provides that complainants with rights to pursue their complaints in either of those arenas will not be able to make use of the ombudsman procedure. This prohibition is subject to the discretion of the ombudsman and, in practice, it is interpreted in a generous manner in favour of the complainant, so as to allow investigations.

The first ombudsman, appointed in 1967 under the aforementioned legislation, operated – and the present PCA, Ann Abraham, still operates – under the title of the PCA and was empowered to consider central government processes only. Since that date, under the **LGA 1974** a number of other ombudsmen have been appointed to oversee the administration of local government in England and Wales. Scotland and Northern Ireland have their own local government ombudsmen fulfilling the same task. Initially a separate ombudsman was appointed to oversee the operation of the health service but that role has subsequently been assumed by the Parliamentary Commissioner. In 1994, an ombudsman for the Prison Service was appointed to cover that area. Additionally, the ombudsman role has proved popular in commercial areas and ombudsmen have been appointed in relation to legal services, banking, building societies, insurance and pensions. This proliferation of ombudsmen has led to some confusion about which one any particular complaint should be taken. This can be especially problematic where the complaint concerns more than one public body. In order to remedy this potential difficulty, a Cabinet Office review recommended in April 2000 that access be made easier through the establishment of one new Commission, bringing together the ombudsmen for central government, local government and the health service. The body subsequently established is the Commission of Local Administration, although the Parliamentary and Local Government ombudsmen still operate independently.

The procedure for making use of the various ombudsmen and their powers differs according to the particular field they cover and the manner in which they were established, that is, whether under statutory authority or purely as a voluntary procedure under commercial codes of conduct. As regards the PCA, the following points are worthy of mention.

Although maladministration is not defined in the **PCA 1967**, it has been taken to refer to an error in the way a decision was reached, rather than an error in the actual decision itself. Indeed, **s** 12(3) of the **PCA 1967** expressly precludes the PCA from questioning the merits of particular decisions taken without maladministration. Maladministration, therefore, can be seen to refer to a procedure used to reach a result, rather than the result itself. In an illuminating and much-quoted speech introducing the 1967 Act, Richard Crossman, the then leader of the House of Commons, gave an indicative, if non-definitive, list of what might be included within the term maladministration, and included within it: bias, neglect, inattention, delay, incompetence, ineptitude, perversity, turpitude and arbitrariness.

Members of the public do not have the right to complain directly to the PCA, but must channel any such complaint through an MP. Complainants do not have to provide precise details of any maladministration; they simply have to indicate difficulties they have experienced as a result of dealing with an agency of central government. It is the function of the PCA to discover whether the problem arose as a result of maladministration. There is a 12-month time limit for raising complaints, but the PCA has discretion to ignore this.

The powers of the PCA to investigate complaints are similar to those of a High Court judge: to require the attendance of witnesses and the production of documents; wilful obstruction of the investigation is treated as contempt of court. On conclusion of an investigation, the PCA submits reports to the MP who raised the complaint and to the principal of the government office which was subject to the investigation. The PCA has no enforcement powers, but, if his recommendations are ignored and existing practices involving maladministration are not altered, he may submit a further report to both Houses of Parliament, in order to highlight the continued bad practice. The assumption is that on the submission of such a report, MPs will exert pressure on the appropriate minister of state to ensure that any necessary changes in procedure are made. Annual reports are laid before Parliament and a Parliamentary Select Committee exists to oversee the operation of the PCA.

Two reports from the PCA are worthy of particular consideration. The first one, issued in January 1995, related to the much criticised Child Support Agency (CSA), which was established in an attempt to ensure that absent parents, essentially fathers, would have to accept financial responsibility for the maintenance of their children as determined by the agency. The PCA's report followed complaints referred to him by 95 MPs, covering the time from when the CSA started its operations until the end of 1994. The conclusion of the PCA was that the CSA was liable for maladministration, inexcusable delays and slipshod service. In response to the report, the chief executive of the CSA wrote to the PCA, informing him that steps were being taken to deal with the problems highlighted in the report and, pre-empting a significant alteration in the operation of the CSA implemented subsequently, the Junior Minister for Social Security promised alterations to improve quality, accuracy and customer service.

The second report, issued in February 1995, related to the effect of the delays in determining the route for the Channel Tunnel rail link. As a consequence of the four-year delay on the part of the Department of Transport in deciding on a route, the owners of properties along the various possible routes found the value of their properties blighted and the properties themselves even unsaleable. The situation was not finalised until the Department announced its final selection in 1994. According to the PCA:

> The effect of the Department of Transport's policy was to put the project in limbo, keeping it alive when it could not be funded.

As a consequence, he held that the Department:

> ... had a responsibility to consider the position of such persons suffering exceptional or extreme hardship and to provide redress where appropriate.

The unusual thing about this case, however, was the reaction of the Department of Transport, which rejected the findings of the PCA and refused to provide any compensation. It was this refusal which led the PCA to issue his special report, consequent upon a situation where an 'injustice has been found which has not or will not be remedied'. Even then, the Department of Transport did not give way, until pressured to do so by the Parliamentary Select Committee on the PCA. Eventually, payments of £5,000 were made to those owners whose houses had suffered from property blight.

In offering an evaluation of the ombudsman procedure, it may be claimed that, all in all, the system appears to work fairly well within its restricted sphere of operation, but there are major areas where it could be improved. The more important of the criticisms levelled at the PCA relate to:

(a) the retention of MPs as filters for complaints. It is generally accepted that there is no need for such a filter mechanism;

(b) the restrictive nature of the definition of maladministration. It is possible to argue that any procedure that leads to an unreasonable decision must involve an element of maladministration and that therefore, the definition as currently stated is not overly restrictive. However, even if such reverse reasoning is valid, it would still be preferable for the definition of the scope of the PCA's investigations to be clearly stated and be stated in wider terms than at present;

(c) the lack of publicity given to complaints. If more people were aware of the procedure and what it could achieve, then more people would make use of it, leading to an overall improvement in the administration of governmental policies;

(d) the reactive role of the ombudsmen. This criticism refers to the fact that the ombudsmen are dependent upon receiving complaints before they can initiate investigations. It is suggested that a more proactive role, under which the ombudsmen would be empowered to initiate investigation on their own authority, would lead to an improvement in general administration, as well as an increase in the effectiveness of the activity of the ombudsmen.

Question 43

Explain the content and effect of the **Arbitration Act 1996**.

Answer plan

This question is very straightforward and simply tests the candidate's knowledge of this important piece of legislation. In answering it, candidates should be aware of the changes introduced by the Act; essentially, the shift from a court-based system to a voluntary, party-based system, and should be able to provide a clear analysis of the major statutory provisions. An explanation of the reasons for the change and its origin would also be beneficial. The following structure would provide a framework for answering the question adequately:

- introduction – principles behind and reasons for the Act;
- freedom of the parties to choose what suits them best;
- arbitrators and their powers;
- role and powers of the court.

Answer

The **Arbitration Act 1996** was given Royal Assent in June 1996, and the majority of its provisions were brought into force by January 1997. The Act repeals **Pt I** of the **Arbitration Act 1950** and the whole of the **Arbitration Acts** of 1975 and 1979. The Act follows the Model Arbitration Law adopted in 1985 by the United Nations Commission on International Trade Law (UNCITRAL).

Section 1 of the Act states that it is founded on the following principles:

(a) the object of arbitration is to obtain the fair resolution of disputes by an impartial tribunal without necessary delay or expense;

(b) the parties should be free to agree how their disputes are resolved, subject only to such safeguards as are necessary in the public interest;

(c) in matters governed by this part of the Act the court should not intervene except as provided by this part.

This statement of general principles, which should inform the reading of the later detailed provisions of the Act, is unusual for UK legislation, but may be seen as reflecting the purposes behind the Act. One major purpose was to ensure that London did not lose its place as a leading centre for international arbitration. As a consequence of the demand-driven nature of the new legislation, it would seem that court interference in the arbitration process has had to be reduced to a minimum and replaced by party autonomy. Under the Act, the role of the arbitrator has been increased and that of the court has been reduced to the residual level of intervention where the arbitration process either requires legal assistance, or else is seen to be failing to provide a just settlement.

In analysing the operation of the Act, and contrasting it with the way in which the previous legislation operated, it is useful to consider it in three distinct parts:

(a) autonomy of the parties; (b) powers of the arbitral panel; and (c) court powers.

Autonomy

As has been stated already, the main thrust of the Act is to empower the parties to the dispute and to allow them to decide how the matter is best decided. In pursuit of this aim, the mandatory parts of the Act only take effect where the parties involved do not agree otherwise. It is even possible for the parties to agree that the dispute should not be decided in line with the strict legal rules, but rather in line with commercial fairness, which might be a completely different thing.

Whilst it is possible for there to be an oral arbitration agreement at common law, **s 5** provides that **Pt I** of the Act only applies to agreements in writing. What this means in practice, however, has been extended by **s 5(3)**, which provides that where the parties agree to an arbitration procedure which is in writing, that procedure will be operative, even though the agreement between the parties is not itself in writing. An example of such a situation would be where a salvage operation was negotiated between two vessels at sea on the basis of Lloyd's standard salvage terms. It would be unlikely that the actual agreement would be reduced to written form, but nonetheless, the arbitration element in those terms would be effective.

Section 6 provides that an arbitration agreement means an agreement to submit to arbitration present or future disputes, whether contractual or not.

Arbitrators and their powers

The arbitration tribunal may consist of a single arbitrator, or a panel, as the parties decide (**s 15**). If one party fails to appoint an arbitrator, then the other party's nominee may act as sole arbitrator (**s 17**).

Under **s 20(4)**, where there is a panel and it fails to reach a majority decision, then the decision of the chair shall prevail.

Section 28 expressly provides that the parties to the proceedings are jointly and severally liable to pay the arbitrators such reasonable fees and expenses as appropriate. Previously, this was only an implied term. And **s 29** provides that arbitrators are not liable for anything done or omitted in the discharge of their functions, unless the act or omission was done in bad faith.

It is also for the tribunal to decide all procedural and evidential matters. **Section 30** provides that unless the parties agree otherwise, the arbitrator can rule on questions relating to its own jurisdiction, that is, in relation to:

(a) whether there actually is a valid arbitration agreement;

(b) whether the arbitration tribunal is properly constituted;

(c) what matters have been submitted to arbitration in accordance with the agreement.

Parties may be represented by a lawyer or any other person, and the tribunal may appoint experts or legal advisers to report to it. **Section 33** provides that the tribunal has a general duty:

(a) to act fairly and impartially between the parties, giving each a reasonable opportunity to state their case; and

(b) to adopt procedures suitable for the circumstances of the case, avoiding unnecessary delay or expense.

Section 35 provides that, subject to the parties agreeing to the contrary, the tribunal shall have the following powers:

(a) to order parties to provide security for costs (previously, a power reserved to the courts);

(b) to give directions in relation to property subject to the arbitration;

(c) to direct that a party or witness be examined on oath and to administer the oath. The parties may also empower the arbitrator to make provisional orders (s 39).

Section 46 states that the arbitral tribunal must decide the dispute:

(a) in accordance with the law chosen by the parties; or

(b) in accordance with such other considerations as the parties have agreed.

Section 48 again states that, unless agreed otherwise, the tribunal shall have the following powers:

(a) to make a declaration about any matter to be determined in the proceedings;

(b) to order payment of money;

(c) to order a party to refrain from doing anything;

(d) to order specific performance of a contract;

(e) to order rectification, setting aside or cancellation of a deed or any other document.

Section 49 empowers the awarding of interest, either simple or compound, and **s 50** allows for the extension of the time for making an award. **Section 58** provides that any award made is final and binding on the parties, and **s 66** provides that any such award can be enforced in the same manner as a court judgment.

Role of the court

Where one party seeks to start a court action, in contradiction to a valid arbitration agreement to the contrary, then the other party may request the court to stay the litigation in favour of the arbitration agreement under **ss 9–11** of the Act. Where, however, both parties agree to ignore the arbitration agreement and seek recourse to the litigation, then, following the party consensual nature of the Act, the original agreement may be ignored.

Under s 12, the courts may grant an extension to any set time limit for starting proceedings, but only on the limited exceptions stated, that is, what is reasonable and in the interests of justice.

The courts may order a party to comply with an order of the tribunal, and may also order parties and witnesses to attend and to give oral evidence before tribunals (s 43).

Under s 18, the court has power to revoke the appointment of an arbitrator, on application of any of the parties, where there has been a failure in the appointment procedure, and it also has powers to revoke authority under s 24, on the application of one of the parties, where the arbitrator:

(a) has not acted impartially;
(b) does not possess the required qualifications;
(c) does not have either the physical or mental capacity to deal with the proceedings;
(d) has refused or failed:
  (i) to conduct the proceedings properly; or
  (ii) has been dilatory in dealing with the proceedings or in making an award, to the extent that it will cause substantial injustice to the party applying for their removal.

Section 32 allows any of the parties to raise in court preliminary objections to the substantive jurisdiction of the arbitration tribunal, but provides that they may only do so on limited grounds, which requires either the agreement of the parties concerned, or the permission of the arbitration tribunal and the agreement of the court. Leave to appeal will only be granted where the court is satisfied that the question involves a point of law of general importance.

Under s 45, the court may, on application by one of the parties, decide any preliminary question of law arising in the course of the proceedings.

Appeals

Once the decision of the arbitral panel has been made, there are only limited grounds for appeal to the court. The first ground arises under s 67, in relation to the substantive jurisdiction of the arbitral panel, although this right may be lost if the party attempting to make use of it took part in the arbitration proceedings without objecting to the alleged lack of jurisdiction.

The second ground for appeal to the courts is on procedural grounds, under s 68, on the basis that some serious irregularity affected the operation of the tribunal. By serious irregularity is meant:

(a) failure to comply with the general duty set out in s 33;
(b) failure to conduct the tribunal as agreed by the parties;

(c) uncertainty or ambiguity as to the effect of the award;
(d) failure to comply with the requirement as to the form of the award.

Under **s 69**, parties may also appeal on a point of law arising from the award. However, the parties can agree beforehand to preclude such a possibility and, where they agree to the arbitral panel making a decision without providing a reasoned justification for it, they will also lose the right to appeal.

The issue of rights to appeal under **s 69** has been considered in a number of cases by the Court of Appeal. In 2002 in *North Range Shipping Ltd v Seatrams Shipping Corporation* (2002) it confirmed that there was no further right of appeal against a judge's refusal to grant permission for an appeal against an arbitrator's decision, except on the grounds of unfairness. In *CMA CGM SA v Beteiligungs KG* (2002) it insisted that judges in the High Court should not be too hasty in allowing appeals. In the case in point, the Court of Appeal decided that the present appeal should not have been allowed. In reaching this decision the court set out the new standard that had to be met to justify an appeal, that 'the question should be one of general importance and the decision of the arbitrators should be at least open to serious doubt'. This standard was higher than that applied under the previous test as stated in *Antaios Compania Naviera SA v Salen Redereierna AB* (1985).

In *BLCT Ltd v J Sainsbury plc* (2003) the Court of Appeal held that the case not only had no real prospect of succeeding in its appeal but also rejected the argument that by curtailing the right of appeal, **s 69** was incompatible with **Art 6** of the **European Convention on Human Rights**.

The foregoing sets out the main provisions of the **Arbitration Act 1996** in such a way as to demonstrate the shift from a court-based system to a voluntaristic arbitration-based system, in line with the expressed wishes of commercial enterprises.

Question 44

Explain what is meant by 'ADR', paying particular attention to the following types:
(a) arbitration;
(b) mediation; and
(c) conciliation.

Answer plan

This question is more general than the previous ones, in that it introduces arbitration and asks for a consideration of the processes of mediation and conciliation. Detail is necessarily less, but the question still requires a substantial understanding of the processes. The following structure might prove satisfactory:

- consider the operation of arbitration as compared to the ordinary courts (refer specifically to the **Arbitration Act 1996**);
- consider the distinction between mediation and conciliation, as well as detailing how and when they are likely to be used;
- conclude by placing these various ADR mechanisms within the framework of the general legal system.

Answer

Arbitration

It is generally recognised that the formal atmosphere of the ordinary courts is not necessarily the most appropriate one in which to determine all disputes which might need adjudication. In recognition of this fact, various alternatives have been developed specifically to avoid the perceived shortcomings of court procedure.

The first and oldest of these alternative procedures is arbitration. Arbitration is the procedure whereby parties in dispute refer the issue under contention to a third party for resolution, rather than institute legal proceedings in the courts. This practice is well established in commerce and industry; its legal effectiveness has long been recognised by the court. In contemporary business usage, it is a matter of common practice for commercial contracts to contain express clauses referring any future disputes to arbitration.

Arbitration proceedings are now governed by the **Arbitration Act 1996**, which repeals previous legislation. This Act (which is dealt with in detail in Question 43, above) significantly alters the relationship between the parties, the arbitrator and the courts. Whereas, previously, the courts ultimately dominated the procedure, now their role has been reduced to providing safeguards against improper actions on the part of the arbitrator, and the determination of points of law. So, now the parties to any dispute are at liberty to provide their procedures for resolving it.

It is possible for arbitration agreements to specify in advance who will act as arbitrator in the event of any dispute. Such a person may be a legal practitioner, or an expert in the particular field of commerce to which the contract relates. There are also specialist institutions which deal with arbitration, and it is quite common for the agreement simply to refer the dispute to such an institution to select an appropriate arbitrator.

There are numerous advantages to be gained from using arbitration rather than the court system. First, arbitration tends to be a private procedure and this has the twofold advantage that outsiders do not get access to any potentially sensitive information and, further, that the parties to the arbitration do not run the risk of any damaging publicity arising out of reports of the proceedings.

Second, the use of arbitration lessens the likelihood of protracted litigation, although it has to be admitted that where one of the parties makes use of the available grounds to challenge an arbitration award, the prior costs of the arbitration will have been largely wasted.

This previous point leads to a consideration of the actual costs of the arbitration process. It is generally asserted that arbitration is a much cheaper procedure than taking a case to the normal courts, but the costs of arbitration and the use of specialist arbitrators should not be underestimated, for they can in themselves be considerable.

Cost is usually in direct proportion to the time taken to decide a case and, here again, the arbitration procedure has distinct advantages over the usual court procedure, for it is distinctly quicker in delivering a decision on the case in point.

A further point which follows from the use of a specialist arbitrator is that the parties to the arbitration can rely on that person having an expert knowledge of the actual practice within the area that constitutes the ground of the dispute, and can count on the arbitrator delivering a decision in line with accepted practice.

Small claims

The type of arbitration scheme considered above tends to relate to large business contracts, but it should be noted that, since 1973, an arbitration service has been available within the county court specifically for the settlement of small claims. Any dispute involving a sum of £3,000 or less was automatically referred to this procedure and claims involving more than £3,000 could be referred to the procedure with the approval of the parties involved. As with arbitration, the aim of this procedure was to provide a cheap, informal mechanism for dealing with small claims and, specifically, consumer complaints, usually under the supervision of a district judge. In pursuit of those ends, the county court rules actually provided that, in relation to the arbitration process, any such hearing should be informal and that the strict rules of evidence should not apply.

This previous procedure has been replaced, following **Pt 27** of the **Civil Procedure Rules 1998**. Under the new rules, the concept of an 'arbitration' disappears and is replaced by a small claims hearing, although there is no longer any 'automatic' reference to the small claims track. Other consequential changes to the handling of small claims include:

- an increase in the jurisdiction from £3,000 to no more than £5,000, with the

exception of claims for personal injury and for housing disrepair where the limit remains at £1,000;
- where a judge thinks that paper adjudication may be appropriate, that is, without the parties having to attend, then they will be asked to say whether or not they have any objections within a given time period. If a party does object, the matter will be given a hearing in the normal way;
- parties need not attend the hearing, but the court will take into account any written evidence that a party has sent to the court;
- parties, with the court's approval, can consent to use the small claims track, even if the value of their claim exceeds the normal value for that track;
- parties will also be restricted to a maximum one day hearing.

Aspects of the old small claims procedure which are retained include their informality, the interventionist approach adopted by the judiciary, the limited costs regime and the limited grounds for appeal (misconduct of the district judge, or an error of law made by the court).

Although the use of legal representation is not forbidden, it is effectively discouraged by the fact that the normal rule as to costs following the event is not applicable under the arbitration process; this 'no costs' rule provides that expenses are not awarded to the successful party in such a case. The general attempt to provide an informal atmosphere is further encouraged by the wide discretion afforded to the courts as to the manner in which they pursue the arbitration procedure, to the extent that they can assume an inquisitorial approach to the hearings before them in order to elicit information on which to base their decisions.

Mediation

Mediation and conciliation are the most informal of all ADR procedures. Mediation is the process where a third party acts as the conduit through which two disputing parties communicate and negotiate in an attempt to reach a common resolution of a problem. Mediation has an important part to play in family matters, where it is felt that the adversarial approach of the traditional legal system has tended to emphasise, if not increase, existing differences of view between individuals and has not been conducive to amicable settlements. Thus, in divorce cases, mediation has traditionally been used to enable the parties themselves to work out an agreed settlement, rather than having one imposed on them from outside by the courts. It is important to realise that there are potential problems with mediation. The assumption that the parties freely negotiate the terms of their final agreement in a less than hostile manner may be deeply flawed, to the extent that it assumes equality of bargaining power and knowledge between the parties to the negotiation. Mediation may well ease pain, but, unless the mediation procedure is carefully and critically monitored, it may gloss over and perpetuate a previously exploitative relationship, allowing the more powerful participant to manipulate and dominate the more vulnerable, and force an inequitable agreement. Establishing entitlements on the basis of clear legal advice may be preferable to apparently negotiating those entitlements away in the non-confrontational, therapeutic atmosphere of mediation.

Conciliation

Conciliation takes mediation a step further and gives the mediator the power to suggest grounds for compromise and the possible basis for a conclusive agreement. Both mediation and conciliation have been available in relation to industrial disputes, under the auspices of the Government-funded Advisory Conciliation and Arbitration Service (ACAS), and have an important part to play in family matters. The essential weakness in these two procedures, however, lies in the fact that although they may lead to the resolution of a dispute, they do not necessarily achieve that end. Where they operate successfully, they are excellent methods of dealing with problems, as essentially the parties to the dispute determine their own solutions and, therefore, feel commitment to the outcome. The problem is that they have no binding power and do not always lead to an outcome.

In conclusion, the foregoing has considered a variety of alternative mechanisms for dealing with legal problems which have been developed in response to particular shortcomings in the ordinary court system and, perhaps, they point to a fundamental need to reform the operation of those law courts and to regularise the whole provision of dispute resolution devices under the law.

Chapter 8

The Rule of Law, Judicial Review and Human Rights

INTRODUCTION

The questions in this chapter may not appear in all English Legal System syllabuses. It is true that this chapter touches on material that will, traditionally, be considered more fully in other courses, such as public or constitutional and administrative law, civil liberties options, or, indeed, some legal theory courses. The fact is, however, that the English legal system simply cannot be fully understood or placed in its contemporary context without a consideration of the points raised hereafter, and many syllabuses look to students to have at least a passing acquaintance with the matters that are considered in this chapter.

The English legal system cannot be treated as static; it is continuously responding to changes that take place in society as a whole. As was stated in the introduction to Chapter 1 of this text, to deny the relevance of European law in an English Legal System course would not only be restrictive, it would be wrong, to the extent that it ignores an increasingly important factor in the formation and determination of UK law. The same can be said of the change in the form and content of law that took place in the course of the twentieth century and which can be linked to the emergence of the interventionist state. Equally, the same can be said with regard to the increase in applications for judicial review. Arguably, this may be seen as the judges fighting a reactionary rearguard action against the forces of the all-encompassing state, or it can be seen as the judges valiantly endeavouring to curtail excesses of that state in the defence of individual liberties. In either case, it represents a political struggle between the judiciary and the executive and one that has fundamental implications for not only the English legal system, but also the constitution of the UK.

The incorporation of the **European Convention on Human Rights (ECHR)** into UK law through the **Human Rights Act (HRA) 1998** has had profound implications for the operation of the English legal system and the relationship of the judiciary to the legislature and executive. Although how it finally works out remains to be seen, it can already be seen to have had a substantial effect since its implementation in October 2000.

Checklist

- What is actually meant by the term 'the rule of law'?
- Does everyone agree as to the meaning?
- To what extent has the meaning changed over time?
- Is there an identifiable core meaning to 'the rule of law'?
- What is judicial review and what remedies does it offer?
- Why have applications for judicial review increased so remarkably?
- Is law an end in itself, or simply a means to an end?
- What does the **HRA 1998** provide?
- What are the implications of the **HRA 1998**?

Question 45

Section 1 of the **Constitutional Reform Act 2005** specifically provides that it 'does not adversely affect the existing constitutional principle of the rule of law . . .'.

Explain what is meant by the 'rule of law' and its relevance in contemporary society.

Answer plan

This question asks for a general consideration of the rule of law and, importantly, questions its relevance in contemporary times. Candidates must know what is understood by the concept and must offer an opinion as to its continued relevance; but they must be careful to substantiate any opinion and not resort to mere assertion and amorphous waffle. One way (and it is only one of many ways) to answer this question is as follows:

- offer a general definition of the rule of law, before going on to examine particular versions of the idea;
- explain AV Dicey's understanding of the concept;
- outline historical criticisms of Dicey;
- give an account of Friedrich von Hayek's view of the rule of law;
- describe Raz's critique of Hayek and his version of the rule of law;

> - conclude by considering the possibility of there being some core meaning within the idea of the rule of law.

Answer

The rule of law has been described by DM Walker, in *The Oxford Companion to Law* (1980), as a 'concept of the utmost importance but having no defined, nor readily definable, content'. Although there is certainly an element of truth in what Walker states, it is suggested that it is possible to establish a core meaning in relation to the idea of the rule of law, although the complete meaning of the concept does tend to be more ambiguous and subject to change, depending on the political outlook of the person using the term and the time period in which it is being considered.

In considering the meaning of the concept 'the rule of law', one is immediately drawn into a consideration of the work of the nineteenth-century writer on the English constitution, AV Dicey, whose *Law of the Constitution* was first published in 1885. According to the chauvinistic Dicey, the rule of law was one of the key features which distinguished the English constitution from its continental counterparts. (The other essential element in the English constitution was the sovereignty of Parliament, an idea not completely compatible with the rule of law, for the idea that Parliament is sovereign and recognises no restraint is in conflict with a notion of the rule of law which sees it as primarily about controlling executive power.)

Whereas foreigners were subject to the exercise of arbitrary power, the Englishman was secure within the protection afforded him by the rule of law. In setting out what was actually meant by the rule of law, Dicey considered three distinct elements. First, it involved an absence of arbitrary power on the part of the Government. Under the rule of law, the extent of the state's power and the manner in which it exercises such power is limited and controlled by law. This control is aimed at preventing the state from acquiring and using wide discretionary powers, because Dicey recognised that inherent in discretion is the possibility of its being used in an arbitrary manner.

The second of Dicey's elements related to equality before the law; the fact that no person is above the law, irrespective of rank or class, together with the related fact that functionaries of the state are subject to the same law and legal procedures as private citizens. Thus, the law, as represented in Dicey's version of the rule of law, ignores substantive differences and treats everyone as formally equal. In other words, the law is blind to real, concrete differences between people, in terms of wealth or power or connection, and treats them all the same as possessors of abstract rights and duties.

The third component of the rule of law for Dicey related to the fact that the rules of the English constitution were the outcome of the ordinary law of the land and were based on the provision of remedies by the courts, rather than on the declaration of rights in the form of a written constitution.

It is essential to recognise that Dicey was writing not just at a particular historical period but, perhaps more importantly, he was writing from a particular political perspective. He was a committed believer in the free operation of the market and was opposed to any increase in state activity, particularly with regard to any attempt by the state to regulate the economy. It is at least arguable that at the time Dicey wrote his *Law of the Constitution*, he was misrepresenting changes that had already occurred in the UK polity, in a desire to curtail the burgeoning activity of the state and, at the same time, to justify that political stance on the basis of a spurious constitutional history. Certainly, by 1933 and in the light of the increased role that the state had assumed in organising society in general and the economy in particular, Sir Ivor Jennings, in his book *The Law and the Constitution* (5th edn, 1959), could express the view that if Dicey's version of the rule of law:

> ... means that the state exercises only the functions of carrying out external relations and maintaining order, it is not true. If it means that the state ought to exercise these functions only, it is a rule of policy for Whigs (if there are any left) [Whigs were a former political party].

If there were no Whigs as such, their attitudes towards the free market lived on in the work of such social thinkers as Friedrich von Hayek. Although Hayek's work has become increasingly influential with the coming to power of the Thatcher Conservative government in 1979, it has to be said that in 1944, when his *The Road to Serfdom* was first published, he was almost a lone voice crying in the wilderness. As regards the rule of law, it is not surprising that Hayek followed Dicey in emphasising its essential component as the absence of arbitrary power in the hands of the state. According to Hayek:

> Stripped of all technicalities, the rule of law means that government in all its actions is bound by rules fixed and announced beforehand.

Hayek, however, went further than Dicey in setting out the actual form and, at least in a negative way, the actual content of legal rules, in order for them to be considered as compatible with the rule of law. As Hayek expressed it in *The Road to Serfdom*:

> The Rule of Law implies limits on the scope of legislation, it restricts it to the kind of general rules known as formal law; and excludes legislation directly aimed at particular people.

Nor should law be aimed at particular goals. In other words, the Government has no place in usurping the authority of individuals by deciding their course of action for them. Within clearly defined and strictly controlled legal parameters, individuals should be left to act as they choose. The job of law is to set the boundaries of personal action, not to dictate the course of such action. Laws should not be particular in content or application, but should be general in nature, applying to all and benefiting no one in particular.

It is important to note that Hayek did not suggest that rules are not laws; they are legal, as long as they are enacted through the appropriate and proper mechanisms; they simply are not in accord with the rule of law. Hayek may very well have agreed with Karl Mannheim, whom he quoted, that the rule of law only operated during the classical liberal competitive phase of capitalism, but he certainly regretted and condemned the change that had taken place in the form and function of law. His regret and condemnation arose from two sources. First, from the economic perspective, as only the particular individual concerned can fully know all the circumstances of his situation, the state should, *as a matter of efficiency*, leave that individual to make his own decisions. Second, from the moral perspective, to the extent that the all-encompassing interventionist/welfare state leaves individuals less room to make decisions as to their actions, it reduces their freedom.

Other legal philosophers have recognised the need for, and have come to terms with, state intervention in the pursuit of substantive as well as merely formal justice and have provided new ways of understanding the rule of law as a means of controlling discretion, without attempting to eradicate it completely. Joseph Raz, for example, took Hayek to task for disguising a socio-economic argument as a legal one, in order to strike at policies of which he did not approve as being contrary to the rule of law, and he suggested that such reasoning was in danger of identifying the 'rule of law' with the rule of 'good law', that is, law/policy of which Hayek approved.

If both Dicey and Hayek laid great emphasis on government by law, rather than by men, Raz recognises the need for the government of men as well as of laws and that the pursuit of social goals may require the enactment of both general *and particular* laws. Indeed, he suggests that it is actually inconceivable for law to consist solely of general rules. Raz claims that the basic requirement from which the wider idea of the rule of law emerges is the requirement that the law must be capable of guiding the individual's behaviour. On that basis, he lists some of the most important principles that may be derived from the general idea. These are as follows:

(a) laws should be prospective rather than retroactive, for the reason that people cannot be guided by and expected to obey laws which have not as yet been introduced. The laws should also be open and clear, in order to enable people to understand/guide their actions in line with them;

(b) laws should be relatively stable and should not be changed too frequently, as this might lead to confusion as to what actually is covered by the law;

(c) there should be clear rules and procedures for making laws;

(d) the independence of the judiciary has to be guaranteed, to ensure that it is free to decide cases in line with the law and not in response to any external pressure;

(e) the principles of natural justice should be observed, requiring an open and fair hearing to be given to all parties to proceedings;

(f) the courts should have the power to review the way in which the other principles are implemented, to ensure that they are being operated as demanded by the rule of law;
(g) the courts should be easily accessible, as they remain at the heart of the idea of making discretion subject to legal control;
(h) the discretion of the crime prevention agencies should not be allowed to pervert the law.

Raz recognises the validity of, and the need to use, discretionary powers and particular goal-oriented legislation in contemporary society and, to that extent, he differs from both Dicey and Hayek. Yet, he also sees the rule of law as essentially a negative value, acting to minimise the danger that can be consequent upon the exercise, in an arbitrary manner, of such discretionary power. In seeking to control the exercise of discretion, he shares common ground with Dicey and Hayek.

Question 46

Assess Lord Bingham's contribution to the contemporary debate as to the meaning and content of the concept of 'the rule of law'.

Answer plan

This question clearly requires the respondent to have a detailed knowledge of Lord Bingham's *Sir David Williams Lecture* on the rule of law, but as this is likely to form a central component of any English Legal System module dealing with the rule of law, the specific nature of the question is not unexpected.

A structure for answering the question would be as follows:

- introduce the concept with a brief reference to the context in which the lecture was delivered;
- deal with each of Lord Bingham's sub-rules in some detail, but being careful to précis the content so as to keep the answer within the necessary limitations of length;
- provide a critical analysis/commentary on each of the points made in the lecture;
- finish with a general conclusion as to the relevance and success of the lecture.

Answer

The **Constitutional Reform Act 2005** provides, in **s 1**, that the Act does not adversely affect 'the existing constitutional principle of the rule of law'. That provision is further reflected in the oath to be taken by Lord Chancellors under **s 17(1)** of the Act, to respect the rule of law and defend the independence of the judiciary. However, as Lord Bingham has pointed out, the Act does not actually define what is meant by the rule of law, or indeed the Lord Chancellor's role in relation to it. Whilst he recognised the difficulty in fixing a single meaning to the principle, citing various different academic references to it, Lord Bingham nonetheless felt it appropriate to offer his own understanding of the rule of law in the sixth *Sir David Williams Lecture* delivered at the Centre for Public Law at the University of Cambridge.

According to Lord Bingham, at the core of the concept of the rule of law is the idea that:

> all persons and authorities within the state, whether public or private, should be bound by and entitled to the benefit of laws publicly and prospectively promulgated and publicly administered in the courts.

However, the vital element is the detail that Lord Bingham introduces through his consideration of the eight implications, or sub-rules, that he holds are particular aspects of the general principle of the rule of law. These sub-rules are:

- *The law must be accessible and so far as possible intelligible, clear and predictable*
  The reasoning behind this requirement is that if everyone is bound by the law they must be able without undue difficulty to find out what it is, even if that means taking advice from their lawyers. Equally the response should be sufficiently clear that a course of action can be based on it. However, for this to be achieved there has to be an end to what Lord Bingham refers to as the legislative hyperactivity which appears to have become a permanent feature of our governance. This excessive legislation, exacerbated by baffling parliamentary draftsmanship, is particularly problematic in relation to the 'torrent of criminal legislation', not all of which is 'readily intelligible'.

- *Questions of legal right and liability should ordinarily be resolved by application of the law and not the exercise of discretion*
  Lord Bingham does not share Dicey's complete antipathy to the exercise of discretion, and cites immigration law as an example where it has been advantageous. Nonetheless he does believe that the essential truth of Dicey's insight stands and that:

  > the broader and more loosely-textured a discretion is, *whether conferred on an official or a judge*, the greater the scope for subjectivity and hence for arbitrariness, which is the antithesis of the rule of law.

However, he is satisfied of the need for discretion to be narrowly defined, and its exercise to be capable of reasoned justification are requirements which UK law almost always satisfies.

- *The laws of the land should apply equally to all, save to the extent that objective differences justify differentiation*

    However, if the law is to apply to all, then governments should also accept the converse, that the rule of law does not allow for any distinction between British nationals and others. Unfortunately, the second part of the reciprocal link did not appear to have been considered when parliament passed **Pt 4 of the Anti-terrorism, Crime and Security Act 2001**, which was held to be incompatible with the **Human Rights Act 1998** in the *Belmarsh* case (*A v Secretary of State for the Home Department* (2004)).

- *The law must afford adequate protection of fundamental human rights*

    This sub-rule goes beyond the formalistic approaches of both Dicey and Raz to insist that the rule of law does in fact connote a substantive content, although Lord Bingham is less certain as to the particular detail of that content. However, he still maintains that:

    > within a given state there will ordinarily be a measure of agreement on where the lines are to be drawn, and in the last resort (subject in this country to statute) the courts are there to draw them.

    Consequently the rule of law must require the legal protection of such human rights as are recognised in that society.

- *Means must be provided for resolving, without prohibitive cost or inordinate delay, bona fide civil disputes which the parties themselves are unable to resolve*

    As a corollary of the principle that everyone is bound by and entitled to the benefit of the law is the requirement that people should be able, in the last resort, to go to court to have their rights and liabilities determined. In stating this sub-rule Lord Bingham makes it clear that he is not seeking to undermine arbitration, which he sees as supremely important, rather he is looking to support the provisions of a properly funded legal aid scheme, the demise of which he clearly regrets, as may be seen from the following:

- *Ministers and public officers at all levels must exercise the powers conferred on them reasonably, in good faith, for the purpose for which the powers were conferred and without exceeding the limits of such powers*

    As Lord Bingham saw it:

    > The historic role of the courts has of course been to check excesses of executive power, a role greatly expanded in recent years due to the increased complexity of government and the greater willingness of the public to challenge governmental (in the broadest sense) decisions. Even under our constitution the separation of powers is crucial in guaranteeing the integrity of the courts' performance of this role.

This judicial role has of course been met through judicial review.

- *Adjudicative procedures provided by the state should be fair.*

    In Lord Bingham's view decisions must be taken by adjudicators who are:

    > independent and impartial: independent in the sense that they are free to decide on the legal and factual merits of a case as they see it, free of any extraneous influence or pressure, and impartial in the sense that they are, so far as humanly possible, open-minded, unbiased by any personal interest or partisan allegiance of any kind.

    However, a second element is involved, which relates to the presumption that any issue should not be finally decided against a person until they have had an adequate opportunity for their response to the allegation to be heard. In effect this means that:

    > a person potentially subject to any liability or penalty should be adequately informed of what is said against him; that the accuser should make adequate disclosure of material helpful to the other party or damaging to itself; that where the interests of a party cannot be adequately protected without the benefit of professional help which the party cannot afford, public assistance should so far as practicable be afforded; that a party accused should have an adequate opportunity to prepare his answer to what is said against him; and that the innocence of a defendant charged with criminal conduct should be presumed until guilt is proved.

- *The existing principle of the rule of law requires compliance by the state with its obligations in international law*

    This particular section of Lord Bingham's lecture is interesting for the indirect way in which he examined the involvement of the UK in the ongoing war in Iraq whilst, as he said:

    > not for obvious reasons touch[ing] on the vexed question whether Britain's involvement in the 2003 war on Iraq was in breach of international law and thus, if this sub-rule is sound, of the rule of law.

    The way he achieved this was through a comparison between the procedures followed in 2003 and those followed at the time of the Suez invasion of 1956. Whilst he concluded that the comparison suggests that over the period the rule of law has gained ground in the UK it also allowed him to make some pointed comments in relation to the way the current war was initiated.

    In conclusion, Lord Bingham correlated the rule of law with a democratic society based on:

    > an unspoken but fundamental bargain between the individual and the state, the governed and the governor, by which both sacrifice a measure of the freedom and power which they would otherwise enjoy. The individual living in society implicitly accepts that he or she cannot exercise the unbridled freedom enjoyed by Adam in the Garden of Eden, before the

creation of Eve, and accepts the constraints imposed by laws properly made because of the benefits which, on balance, they confer. The state for its part accepts that it may not do, at home or abroad, all that it has the power to do but only that which laws binding upon it authorise it to do. If correct, this conclusion is reassuring to all of us who, in any capacity, devote our professional lives to the service of the law. For it means that we are not, as we are sometimes seen, mere custodians of a body of arid prescriptive rules but are, with others, the guardians of an all but sacred flame which animates and enlightens the society in which we live.

Question 47

What are the prerogative orders available under judicial review, and what is the procedure for achieving such remedies?

Answer plan

This is a fairly straightforward question that looks to assess candidates' knowledge of not just the remedies available under judicial review, but also the impact of the Woolf reforms on the procedure for applying for judicial review. Candidates must be aware of the new **Pt 54** of the **Civil Procedure Rules (CPR)** and must be prepared to explain them in detail. A suggested plan for dealing with the question is as follows:

- consider the three prerogative orders in turn, explaining the effect of each of them;
- explain the genesis of **Pt 54** of the new **CPR**, paying particular attention to the Bowman Report;
- consider the provisions of **Pt 54** in some detail;
- pay particular attention to the changes introduced under **Pt 54**;
- in particular, consider permission, standing and pre-action protocols.

Answer

The remedies available against a public authority are the three prerogative orders: a quashing order, a prohibiting order and a mandatory order.

A *quashing order*, formerly known as *certiorari*, is the mechanism by means of which decisions of inferior courts, tribunals and other authoritative bodies are brought before the High Court to have their validity examined. Where any such decisions are found to be invalid, they may be set aside. An example of this can be seen in *Ridge v Baldwin* (1964). The Chief Constable of Brighton had been charged with conspiracy to obstruct the course of justice, but was acquitted. On the basis of criticisms made of him by the trial judge, he was subsequently dismissed from his post, by the local Watch Committee responsible for the supervision of the local police force, without a hearing. The House of Lords eventually held that the denial of a hearing was contrary to natural justice and, therefore, that his dismissal had been carried out in an improper manner. The House of Lords also rejected the argument that *certiorari* did not lie in this case, as the Watch Committee was exercising an administrative rather than a judicial function: it was emphasised that the important issue was the consequence of the decision, not whether it was administrative or judicial.

A *prohibiting order* is similar to a quashing order, in that it relates to invalid acts of public authorities, but it is pre-emptive and prescriptive with regard to any such activity, and prevents the authority from taking invalid decisions in the first place. An example of the use of the prohibition order arose in *Telford JJ ex p Badham* (1991), in which committal proceedings in relation to a rape charge were discontinued on the grounds that the alleged offence had taken place some 15 years previously and the lapse of time could not but seriously prejudice the defendant in the preparation of his defence.

A *mandatory order*, previously referred to as *mandamus*, is an order issued by the Queen's Bench Division of the High Court, instructing an inferior court, or some other public authority, to carry out a duty laid upon them. Such an order is frequently issued in conjunction with an order of *certiorari*, to the effect that a public body is held to be using its powers improperly and is instructed to use them in a proper fashion. An example of how the order of *mandamus* operates and an example of the consequences of ignoring such an order arose in the infamous cases involving the Poplar Borough Council in 1922 (*Poplar BC (Nos 1 and 2)* (1922)). When the council refused to comply with a statutory requirement to levy rates in order to make a payment to the county council, an order of *mandamus* was awarded against it which instructed it to make the payment and, if need be, to levy a rate for that purpose. When the Labour Party majority on the council refused to comply with the order, an action for contempt of court was taken against them and some of the recalcitrant councillors were actually imprisoned.

The prerogative orders are so called because they were originally the means whereby sovereigns controlled the operation of their officials. As a consequence, the prerogative orders cannot be used against the Crown, but this shortcoming is not of major concern as the prerogative orders can be used against individual ministers of state, and it is to such people that powers are delegated.

In order to secure one of the above remedies, the procedure for judicial review as provided in **Pt 54** of the **CPR** must be followed. Alternatively, the non-prerogative remedies of declaration, injunction and damages are available against public authorities.

Until recently, the procedure for initiating an action for judicial review was made under **Ord 53** of the **Rules of the Supreme Court (RSC)**. Although in his report on the civil law system, Lord Woolf made recommendations as to how judicial review procedure should be altered, these were not put into effect. Instead, the old rules set out in **Ord 53** of the **RSC** were re-enacted, with minor amendments, in a schedule to the **CPR**.

However, the ever-increasing number of applications for judicial review, especially in the area of immigration, ensured that something had to be done about the system and in March 1999, the Lord Chancellor appointed a committee, under the chairmanship of Sir Jeffrey Bowman, to examine the procedures of the Crown Office List, which dealt with judicial review.

The Bowman Committee proposed two crucial amendments to the system. First, the permission stage was to become an *inter partes* procedure rather than an *ex parte* one, with the defendant being given full notice of the application. Second, consideration of permission applications should be a paper-based exercise only. The Committee also considered that a pre-action protocol, which required communication between the parties even before the making of a claim to the court, would assist in bringing settlements forward by focusing the parties on the issues in dispute and allowing them to consider the merits of the claim before legal proceedings were started.

The Lord Chancellor's Department subsequently issued a consultation paper and new draft rules on the procedure for judicial review. The outcome of this is that **Ord 53** has been abolished and replaced by **r 54** of the **CPR**.

The new rules adopt many of the recommendations of the Bowman Report and bring judicial review procedure fully within the style and purposes of the **CPR**.

Permission

Access to the public law remedies has never been directly open to the public, and the new **Pt 54** retains the requirement that claimants seek permission from the Administrative Court before they can pursue their action. Under the old **Ord 53** procedure, the application for permission to proceed acted as a filtering mechanism essentially to weed out unsustainable claims, but under **Pt 54**, in the pursuit of more economic use of the courts, it has been turned into a form of *inter partes* proceeding. A claim must be started not later than three months after the grounds to make the claim arose (**r 54.5**) and now, in order to get permission, the claim form must comply with the requirements of **r 8.2** of the **CPR** and *Practice Direction 54*. In particular, it must include a detailed statement of the claimant's grounds for seeking judicial review, the remedy they are seeking, a statement of facts relied on, copies of any document on which the claimant proposes to rely and a list of essential documents for advance reading by the court. The claim form must be served on the defendant, and any person the claimant considers to be an interested party, within seven days of the date of issue. Any person served with the claim form who wishes to take part in the judicial review must file an acknowledgment of service not more than 21 days after service of the claim form. If the defendant wishes to contest the claim, they must set out a summary of their grounds for doing so in the acknowledgment. Failure to acknowledge service does not, however, exclude the defendant from subsequent participation in the proceedings, although it might affect the court's decision in deciding costs.

The question of permission will generally be decided on the documents submitted without a hearing. However, where the court refuses permission, or grants it subject to conditions, the claimant may request a hearing. There is also a right to apply to the Court of Appeal for permission to appeal against any refusal and the Court of Appeal can give permission for judicial review to proceed, in which circumstances the case will proceed to a hearing in the High Court.

Standing

In order to pursue a claim for judicial review, the claimant must demonstrate that they have 'standing' (formerly referred to as *locus standi*). In other words, they must show that they are not just some officious bystander with no recognisable interest in the matter in question. Whether a person has sufficient interest is for the courts to decide on as a matter of law and fact, as decided in *IRC v National Federation of Self-Employed and Small Businesses Ltd* (1981). Standing to seek judicial review was extended to pressure groups with a particular interest in the matter at issue, and where it was unlikely that any other party would seek to raise the issue in *R v Inspector of Pollution ex p Greenpeace* (1994) and *R v Secretary of State for Foreign Affairs ex p World Development Movement* (1995).

The new rules say nothing about standing at all, so presumably the previous rules as to standing will apply. However, the issue of public interest is recognised in **r 54.17**, which gives the court power to permit any person to file evidence or make representations at the hearing of the judicial review. This follows with recent practice; thus, for example, Amnesty was allowed to participate in the hearing of the *Pinochet* case.

Pre-action protocol

In line with other **Civil Procedure Rules** and the specific recommendation of the Bowman Committee, the Lord Chancellor's Department issued a pre-action protocol in relation to judicial review, which came into effect on 4 March 2002.

It provides that before making a claim, the claimant should send a letter to the defendant using a standard format letter, which should contain the date and details of the decision, act or omission being challenged and a clear summary of the facts on which the claim is based. It should also contain the details of any relevant information that the claimant is seeking, and an explanation of why this is considered relevant. A claim should not normally be made until the proposed reply date given in the letter before the claim has passed, unless the circumstances of the case require more immediate action to be taken.

Defendants should normally reply within any reasonable time limit contained in the claimant's letter, once again using the standard format letter. Failure to comply with the pre-action protocol is to be taken into account by the court when making decisions on case management or costs.

Question 48

Consider the development of judicial review in the light of the judiciary's attempt to control the exercise of administrative discretion, and assess the likely impact of the **Human Rights Act (HRA) 1998** on this process.

Answer plan

This is a much more subtle and searching question than the previous one. It requires a consideration of modern forms of law, the rule of law, the constitutional role of the judiciary, as well as a knowledge of the procedure for judicial review. Consideration of the following will cover the above points well:

- the development of administrative law;
- the tension between the exercise of discretionary power and the rule of law;
- judicial review as the courts' means of curtailing abuse of discretion;
- the grounds for judicial review;
- the possibility of the doctrine of 'proportionality' as the means of extending judicial review in the area of substantive administrative decisions;
- judges' competence to make policy decisions;
- the constitutional situation of the judiciary.

Answer

According to AV Dicey, in *Law of the Constitution*, published in 1885, the UK knew no such thing as administrative law as distinct from ordinary law. In Dicey's exposition, it was essential that all activities be open to the ordinary law of the land for the maintenance of the rule of law. Whether or not he was correct when he expressed this opinion, and there are substantial grounds for doubting the accuracy of his claim even at the time he made it, it can no longer be denied that there is now a large area of law that can be properly called administrative, that is, related to the pursuit and application of particular policies, usually within a framework of statutory powers, although the powers under question may be derived from the common law. The lack of a more precise definition reflects the extent to which the state and state-appointed bodies intervene in contemporary life and the multiplicity of areas in which they act. It is certainly true that the twentieth century saw a large scale increase in the power of the state – both central and local – and its various functionaries and appointed bodies to intervene in the day-to-day lives of its citizens. The question that arises is whether such activity is subject to judicial control and, if it is, how such control is to be exercised.

Dicey described the concept of the rule of law as one of the two fundamental elements of the English polity, the other being Parliamentary sovereignty, or, in other words, the undisputed supremacy of central government. The former was aimed at controlling arbitrary power, but the latter could, within this constitutional structure, make provision for the granting of such arbitrary power by passing appropriate legislation. The historical reality is that in the course of the twentieth century, with the emergence and development of the interventionist welfare state, the Government increasingly took over the regulation of many areas of social activity and delegated wide-ranging discretionary powers to various people and bodies, in order to implement its policies and to deal with particular problems as they arose. It has been suggested by some that in fact, the rule of law has been reduced to a matter of procedure, to the mere requirement that legislation be passed in the prescribed manner and that the most arbitrary of party political decisions can, thus, be readily cloaked with legality.

Dicey did not resolve the potential conflict between the rule of law, as represented by the decisions of the ordinary courts of the land, and the sovereignty of Parliament, nor can it be claimed, as yet, that such tensions have been resolved. Indeed, it might be argued that the tension between the two principles has not only continued, but has intensified with the growth in state activity. There are significant indications that the higher judiciary may well be attempting to reassert at least a measure of control over the executive, but, if this is the case, it is not, in itself, unproblematic and has important constitutional implications for the UK. The importance of this process was not lost on the former Master of the Rolls, Sir Thomas Bingham, who described it in an interview (*The Observer*, 9 May 1993) as follows:

> Slowly, the constitutional balance is tilting towards the judiciary. The courts have reacted to the increase in powers claimed by the Government by being more active themselves.

Judicial review may be seen as one of the ways in which the courts have attempted to maintain a measure of control over such activity, in an endeavour to reassert the dominance of the rule of law ideal. Of all areas of law, judicial review is the one in which most growth was apparent, before the enactment of the **Human Rights Act 1998**, as can be seen from the fact that in 1980, there were only 525 applications for judicial review, but in 2007, there were 6,690 such applications, more than a twelve-fold increase in 27 years.

Judicial review may be seen, therefore, as the means to curtail the power of the executive and as a counter to the use of discretionary forms of regulation. The grounds of application can be considered under two traditional heads: *procedural ultra vires* and *substantive ultra vires*. Procedural *ultra vires*, as its name suggests, relates to the failure of a person, or body provided with specific authority, to follow the procedure established for using that power, or to follow the requirements of natural law. Substantive *ultra vires* occurs where someone does something that is not actually authorised by the enabling legislation, and its most interesting area of operation relates to areas where it is sought to challenge the substance of a decision.

In *Associated Provincial Picture House v Wednesbury Corp* (1947), which concerned a local authority's decision to impose a condition on a licensing of a cinema, Lord Greene MR established the possibility of discretionary decisions being challenged on the basis of their being unreasonable. As Lord Greene pointed out:

> ... the decision of the local authority can be upset if it is proved to be unreasonable in the sense that the court considers it to be a decision *that no reasonable body could have come to*.

Lord Greene's approach was endorsed and refined by Lord Diplock in *Council of Civil Service Unions v Minister for the Civil Service (the GCHQ case)* (1984), where he established the three grounds for judicial review to be:

(a) illegality;

(b) irrationality; and

(c) procedural impropriety.

In delivering his judgment, however, Lord Diplock, intriguingly, introduced the possibility of a much wider-ranging reason for challenging administrative decisions. The additional ground for applying for judicial review was based on the doctrine of 'proportionality', which looks at the substance of a decision, rather than simply the way in which it is reached.

The applicability of the concept of proportionality was at least uncertain under judicial review, but it has been given direct relevance under the **HRA 1998**. Under that Act, the courts have been given the power to intervene in situations where public authorities have acted in such a way as to breach any of the rights provided to individuals under the **European Convention on Human Rights**. However, not all the rights provided under the **HRA** are absolute, and in some situations the state can interfere with them, as long as it acts in a proportionate manner. In other words, the courts are given the power to decide whether the state has taken more action than is necessary to deal with a particular problem. Thus, the doctrine of proportionality requires the courts to engage in what are essentially political decisions. Similarly, under the **HRA**, the courts have the power to declare secondary legislation, such as statutory instruments, invalid and although they cannot exercise the same power with regard to primary legislation, they can make a declaration that such legislation is incompatible with the **European Convention**. Once again, this can be seen as introducing the judiciary into the political arena in a much more direct way than was possible under the restricted approach of judicial review.

The increased participation of the judiciary in the socio-political arena raises a number of important issues.

First, there is the question of the competency of the judiciary to overrule substantive decisions. Judges are experts in law; they are not expert in the questions of policy that come before them in the guise of legal cases. They may disagree with particular decisions, but it has to be, at least, doubted that they are qualified to take such policy decisions. A classic example of this arises from the infamous 'fares fair' case, *Bromley LBC v GLC* (1982), in which the courts held that a policy to subsidise transport within London was not legal. When an amended scheme came before the court in *London Transport Executive ex p GLC* (1983), it was decided that the Greater London Council could instruct the London Transport Authority to implement policies that would effectively reduce its revenues. Thus, the courts could reject schemes, but could not replace them with other ones.

There is also the wider question that in interfering with substantive decisions, the judiciary involves itself in political matters and, therefore, exceeds its constitutional powers. It has to be remembered that judges are unelected and unaccountable. The question as to their suitability to take such essentially political decisions cannot but be brought into question. As Farquharson LJ commented in *The Observer* interview:

> We have to be very careful: the executive is elected. We have a role in the constitution, but if we go too far, there will be a reaction.

In conclusion, if judicial review has firmly placed the judiciary in the political arena, the introduction of the **HRA 1998** can only increase that process of overt politicisation, in that it expressly gives judges the duty and power to protect individuals' rights from attack from public authorities. The question that remains to be answered, especially in the light of criticisms directed at the conservative nature of the judiciary, levelled by some commentators on the political left, is whether the judiciary are the right people to be given such power.

Question 49

Explain the background and content of the **Human Rights Act (HRA) 1998**.

> ### Answer plan
>
> This question asks candidates to provide a brief consideration of the incorporation of the **European Convention on Human Rights (ECHR)** into UK law, through the mechanism of the **HRA 1998**. It requires a basic knowledge of the content and effect of the **HRA 1998**. The following points should be covered:
>
> - explain what the **ECHR** is;
> - explain the disadvantages of the UK's relationship to the Convention prior to the **HRA 1998**;
> - list the various Articles that have been incorporated by the Act;
> - consider the effect of the Act on public bodies;
> - explain what is meant by a declaration of compatibility in relation to legislation;
> - assess the role of the courts in relation to the Act;
> - explain fast-track remedial action for legislation that is found to be incompatible.

Answer

The UK was one of the initial signatories to the **European Convention on Human Rights (ECHR)** in 1950, which was created in post-war Europe as a means of establishing and enforcing essential human rights. In 1966, the UK recognised the power of the European Commission on Human Rights to hear complaints from individual UK citizens and, at the same time, recognised the authority of the European Court of Human Rights to adjudicate in such matters. It did not, however, at that time incorporate the **ECHR** into UK law.

The consequence of non-incorporation was that the Convention could not be directly enforced in English courts. In *R v Secretary of State for the Home Department ex p Brind* (1991), the Court of Appeal decided that ministerial directives did not have to be construed in line with the **ECHR**, as that would be tantamount to introducing the Convention into English law without the necessary legislation. UK citizens were therefore in the position of having to pursue rights, which the state endorsed, in an external forum, rather than through their own court system and, in addition, having to exhaust the domestic judicial procedure before they could gain access to that external forum. Such a situation was expensive, time consuming and extremely unsatisfactory, and not just for complainants under the Convention. Many members of the judiciary, including the former Lord Chief Justice, Lord Bingham, were in favour of incorporation, not merely on general moral grounds, but equally on the ground that they resented having to make decisions in line with UK law which they knew full well would be overturned on appeal to the European Court. Equally, there was some discontent that the decisions in the European Court were being taken, and its general jurisprudence was being developed, without the direct input of the UK legal system.

The **HRA 1998** corrected this anomalous situation by incorporating the rights enshrined in the **ECHR**, together with the protocols to it, into UK law. The Act received Royal Assent on 9 November 1998, but was only brought fully into force on 2 October 2000. The reason for the delay was so that the courts, from the magistrates all the way up to the House of Lords, could be adequately trained in the consequences of the Act.

The rights incorporated are listed in **Sched 1** to the Act, and cover the following matters:

- a general commitment to human rights (**Art 1**);
- right to life (**Art 2**);
- freedom from torture and inhuman or degrading treatment or punishment (**Art 3**);
- freedom from slavery and forced or compulsory labour (**Art 4**);
- right to liberty and security of person (subject to a derogation applicable to Northern Ireland) (**Art 5**);
- right to a fair and public trial within a reasonable time (**Art 6**);
- freedom from retrospective criminal law and no punishment without law (**Art 7**);
- right to respect for private and family life, home and correspondence (**Art 8**);
- freedom of thought, conscience and religion (**Art 9**);
- freedom of expression (**Art 10**);
- freedom of assembly and association (**Art 11**);
- right to marry and found a family (**Art 12**);
- prohibition of discrimination in the enjoyment of the Convention rights (**Art 14**);
- right to peaceful enjoyment of possessions and protection of property (**Art 1, Protocol 1**);
- right to education (subject to a UK reservation) (**Art 2, Protocol 1**);
- right to free elections (**Art 3, Protocol 1**);

- right not to be subjected to the death penalty (**Arts 1 and 2, Protocol 6**).

The above rights can be relied on by any person, non-governmental organisation or group of individuals. Importantly, it also applies where appropriate to companies which are incorporated entities and, hence, legal persons and other bodies. It cannot be relied on by governmental organisations, such as local authorities.

The general list of rights are not all seen in the same way. Some are absolute and inalienable and cannot be interfered with by the state, or, at least, only to a limited and tightly circumscribed degree. Others are merely contingent and are subject to derogation, that is, signatory states can opt out of them in particular circumstances. The absolute rights are those provided for in **Arts 2, 3, 4, 7 and 14**. All the others are subject to potential limitations; and, in particular, the rights provided for under **Arts 8, 9, 10** and **11** are subject to legal restrictions, such as are:

> ... necessary in a democratic society in the interests of national security or public safety, for the prevention of crime, for the protection of health or morals or the protection of the rights and freedoms of others [**Art 11(2)**].

In deciding the legality of any derogation, courts are required not just to be convinced that there is a need for the derogation, but they must also be sure that the state's action has been proportionate to that need. In other words, the state must not overreact to a perceived problem by removing more rights than is necessary to effect the solution. With further regard to the possibility of derogation, **s 19** of the Act requires a minister, responsible for the passage of any Bill through Parliament, either to make a written declaration that it is compatible with the Convention or, alternatively, to declare that although it may not be compatible, it is still the Government's wish to proceed with it.

The **HRA 1998** has profound implications for the operation of the English legal system. **Section 2** of the Act requires future courts to take into account any previous decision of the European Court of Human Rights. It was at first thought that this provision would have a major impact on the operation of the doctrine of precedent within the English legal system, as it was thought effectively to sanction the overruling of any previous English authority that was in conflict with a decision of the European Court of Human Rights. However, in *Price v Leeds City* (2006) the House of Lords distinguished between decisions of the European Court of Justice and those of the European Court of Human Rights: the former are binding, while the latter are not. As Lord Bingham put it:

> The mandatory duty imposed on domestic courts by **s 2** of the **1998 Act** is to take into account any judgment of the Strasbourg Court and any opinion of the Commission. Thus they are not strictly required to follow Strasbourg rulings, as they are bound by **s 3(1)** of the **European Communities Act 1972** and as they are bound by the rulings of superior courts in the domestic curial hierarchy.

As a consequence the House of Lords decided that the normal rules of precedent should apply, and lower courts should follow the House of Lords, even when their decisions have been overturned by the ECtHR. This does not apply, however, where the previous authority had been set without reference to the **Human Rights Act**.

Also, **s 3**, requiring all legislation to be read so far as possible to give effect to the rights provided under the Convention, has the potential to invalidate previously accepted interpretations of statutes which were made, by necessity, without recourse to the Convention. Thus in *Mendoza v Ghaidan* (2002), the Court of Appeal used **s 3** to extend the rights of same-sex partners to inherit a statutory tenancy under the **Rent Act 1977**. In *Fitzpatrick v Sterling Housing Association Ltd* (1999), the House of Lords had extended the rights of such individuals to inherit the lesser assured tenancy by including them within the deceased person's family. However, it declined to allow them to inherit statutory tenancies, on the grounds that they could not be considered to be the wife or husband of the deceased as the Act required. In *Mendoza*, the Court of Appeal held that the **Rent Act**, as it had been construed by the House of Lords in *Fitzpatrick*, was incompatible with **Art 14** of the **ECHR** on the grounds of its discriminatory treatment of surviving same-sex partners. The court, however, decided that the failing could be remedied by reading the words 'as his or her wife or husband' in the Act as meaning 'as if they were his or her wife or husband'. The Court of Appeal's decision and reasoning was subsequently confirmed by the House of Lords in 2004.

Section 6 declares it unlawful for any public authority to act in a way which is incompatible with the Convention, and **s 7** allows the 'victim of the unlawful act' to bring proceedings against the public authority in breach. **Section 8** empowers the court to grant such relief or remedy against the public authority in breach of the Act, as it considers just and appropriate. However, where a public authority is acting under the instructions of some primary legislation, which is itself incompatible with the Convention, the public authority will not be liable under **s 6**.

It can be seen that the Act reflects a move towards the entrenchment of rights recognised under the Convention, but the Act expressly states that the courts cannot invalidate any primary legislation, essentially Acts of Parliament, which are found to be incompatible with the Convention. The courts can only make a declaration of such incompatibility and leave it to the legislature to remedy the situation through new legislation (s 4). The Act requires that the Crown be given notice of a case where a declaration might be given, and the Crown is given a right to intervene in the case. This will enable the Crown to argue that the provision can be interpreted compatibly with the Convention rights. It also ensures that the Crown is in a position to respond quickly where a declaration of incompatibility is made. In this respect, the Act provides for the provision of remedial legislation through a fast-track procedure. This fast-track procedure gives a minister of the Crown the power to alter primary legislation by way of statutory instrument. This power is also available to implement judgments of the Strasbourg Court against the UK which are made after the coming into force of the **HRA 1998**. It is also available in urgent cases, where subordinate legislation has been quashed or declared invalid.

Question 50

Assess the impact of the **Human Rights Act (HRA) 1998** on the separation of powers.

Answer plan

This question requires an examination of the way in which the courts have made use of the powers extended to them under the **HRA 1998** within the context of the separation of power, which should briefly be explained at the outset. Although many other cases and examples could be used to answer the question, the suggested answer focuses on the specific area of anti-terrorist legislation, which has highlighted the issue most clearly.

A possible structure could take the following form:

- briefly explain what is meant by the separation of powers;
- set out the courts' powers under the **HRA 1998**, making specific reference to the duty under **s 3** to interpret legislation in line with the **European Convention on Human Rights (ECHR)**, and **s 4** declarations of incompatibility;
- consider the doctrine of proportionality;
- consider case examples where the courts have made use of these powers;
- conclude with an assessment of the effect of the provisions in the **HRA 1998**.

Answer

Although the idea of the separation of powers can be traced back to ancient Greek philosophy, it was advocated in early modern times by the English philosopher Locke and the later French philosopher Montesquieu, and found its practical expression in the constitution of the US. The idea of the separation of powers is posited on the existence of three distinct functions of government (the legislative, executive and judicial functions) and the conviction that these functions should be kept apart in order to prevent the centralisation of too much power (essentially a system of checks and balances). Establishing the appropriate relationship between the actions of the state and the legal control over those actions crucially involves a consideration of whether there is any absolute limit on the authority of the government of the day. Answering that question inevitably involves an examination of the general constitutional structure of the UK and, in particular, the inter-relationship of two doctrines: Parliamentary sovereignty and judicial independence, in that although the courts have always operated free from direct interference from either parliament or the government, nonetheless it has always retained the right to make such laws as it considers fit, without limit and without the interference of the courts. However it is at least arguable that this historical relationship has been altered by the implementation of **HRA 1998**, which has caused no little friction between the judiciary and the executive, but which has also increased the powers of the courts *vis à vis* the legislature.

Section 3 of the **HRA** requires all legislation to be read so far as possible to give effect to the rights provided under the Convention. This section provides the courts with new and extended powers of interpretation. Where a court cannot interpret a piece of primary legislation in such a way as to make it compatible with the Convention, it cannot declare the legislation invalid but, under **HRA s 4**, it can make a declaration that the legislation in question is not compatible with the rights provided by the Convention. In deciding whether or not a piece of legislation is compatible with the **ECHR** the courts will assess whether or not it represents a proportionate response to the particular problem that it is intended to address. Without doubt the clearest and sharpest conflict between the judiciary and the executive and Parliament, in relation to the powers given to the courts under the **HRA 1998**, has arisen in connection with anti-terrorist legislation and the treatment of those suspected by the authorities of being terrorists. This conflict highlights not only the tensions between these branches of the constitution but also the way in which the courts will use the powers previously mentioned under the **HRA 1998** and their willingness to use those powers in the face of political opposition.

Anti-Terrorism, Crime and Security Act 2001

Following the terrorist attack on the World Trade Centre on 11 September 2001, the UK Parliament introduced the **Anti-Terrorism, Crime and Security Act (ACSA) 2001**. This Act allowed for the detention, without charge, of non-UK citizens suspected of terrorist activities, but who could not be repatriated to their own countries because of fear for their well-being.

Under **s 21(1)**, the Home Secretary was given the power to issue a detention certificate in respect of a person if he reasonably:

(a) believes that person's presence in the UK is a risk to national security; and

(b) suspects that the person is a terrorist.

While a person who would otherwise be detained was free to leave the UK, the Act provided that a person certificated as a suspected international terrorist under **s 21** might be detained in circumstances where their safe removal or departure from the UK was not practical (**s 23(1)**). Such a provision was clearly contrary to **Art 5** of the **ECHR**. Consequently, the government was required to enter a derogation from the Convention by virtue of the **Human Rights Act 1998 (Designated Derogation) Order 2001**, the justification for the derogation being that the prospect of terrorism following 11 September 2001 threatened the life of the nation. As a result of the **HRA 1998** and the limited derogation, the Home Secretary's power under the **ACSA 2001** could only be exercised in relation to individuals who were suspected of being a risk to national security because of their connection to the public emergency cited in the derogation – namely the threat posed by Al Qa'ida and its associated networks. Consequently, it was not enough that the detained person might have had connections with a terrorist organisation. It must be a terrorist organisation that had links with Al Qa'ida.

In July 2002, the Special Immigration Appeals Commission, SIAC, held that the **ACSA 2001** was not in compliance with the anti-discriminatory provisions of **Art 14** of the **ECHR**, to the extent that it treated non-nationals differently from UK nationals. When the case eventually came before the House of Lords (*A & Ors v Secretary of State for the Home Department* (2004)), it resulted in a crushing judgment against the Act, the Court holding, by a majority of eight to one, that the **ACSA 2001** was incompatible with the provisions of the **ECHR**. Although the House of Lords recognised the deference due to the government and parliament and accepted that the government had been entitled to conclude that there was a public emergency, it nonetheless concluded that the response to the perceived threat had been disproportionate and incompatible with the rights under the **ECHR**. It held that the prohibition on grounds of nationality or immigration status under **Art 14** had not been the subject of derogation. Further, it held that the decision to detain one group of suspected international terrorists, defined by nationality or immigration status, and not another, could not be justified, and violated **Art 14** of the **ECHR**. The House of Lords also held that **ss 21** and **23** of the Act were disproportionate for the general reason that the provisions did not rationally address the threat to the security of the UK presented by Al Qa'ida terrorists and that consequently **s 23** of the **ACSA 2001** was incompatible with **Arts 5** and **14** of the **ECHR**. The House of Lords appropriately quashed the derogation order, as it was secondary rather than primary legislation.

Prevention of Terrorism Act (PTA) 2005

This Act, which replaced the **ACSA 2001**, dealt with one of the shortcomings of the **earlier Act** by widening the provisions of the previous legislation to control all terrorist-related activity, *irrespective of nationality* and replaced the detention without trial regime under the **ACSA 2001** with a new system of 'control orders'. These control orders were to be of two distinct types: derogating and non-derogating, in relation to the **ECHR**.

Derogating control orders require derogation from **ECHR** because they deprive the person affected of their liberty by requiring them to remain in a particular place at all times. It is equivalent to house arrest and consequently it clearly infringes the person's rights under **Art 5** of the **ECHR**. Non-derogating control orders, however, allow the Home Secretary to impose a range of controls over people's activities, such as the imposition of curfews and the use of tagging for the purposes of monitoring those curfews. They also allow for the restriction and control of the movement of the individuals concerned, or restrictions on association with other named individuals. They also provide for the possibility of a ban on the use of mobile phones or the Internet. The government claimed that, even if the non-derogational control orders affected other Convention rights, such as the right to private and family life (**Art 8**), the right to freedom of expression (**Art 10**), or the right to freedom of association (**Art 11**), as they very well might, nonetheless they would not require derogation because they did not engage the right to liberty (**Art 5**).

The **PTA 2005** retains the role of the *special advocate,* who is expected to support the interests of the suspect in regard to material to which neither the accused nor his chosen legal representatives is allowed access.

The legal effect of non-derogation control orders issued under the **PTA 2005** was considered by the House of Lords in four related appeals, the decisions in which were delivered in three judgments at the end of October 2007.

In the first (*Secretary of State for the Home Department* v *JJ and others* (2007)) the majority of the House of Lords held that a control order imposing an 18-hour curfew amounted to a deprivation of liberty contrary to **Art 5**. Subsequently, in *Secretary of State for the Home Department v MB & AF* (2007) the House of Lords unanimously held that a curfew of 14 hours did not amount to a deprivation of liberty. However, the majority also held that the reliance on undisclosed material could not be supported in cases where the accused had no possibility of responding to allegations charged against them, and that the special advocate system did not validate such a system. Rather than issue a declaration of incompatibility the majority preferred to interpret the provisions of the **PTA 2005** to ensure the provision of a fair trial, but in complete contradiction to the actual wording of the Act.

Whether one approves of the House of Lords' decisions in the above cases probably depends on one's political perspective, and that is specifically the point, for it emphasises that the judges were engaged in taking essentially political decisions. In using their powers under the **HRA 1998**, it is arguable that that the House of Lords did not just subvert the policy of the executive, but rewrote the express provisions of parliament. In doing so it is also arguable that they may have overstepped their limited role within the UK constitution. Such a possibility was not lost on Lord Bingham who, in *A v SSHD* (2004), justified the courts' new status thus:

. . .Parliament has expressly legislated in **section 6** of the 1998 **Act** to render unlawful any act of a public authority, including a court, incompatible with a Convention right, has required courts (in **section 2**) to take account of relevant Strasbourg jurisprudence, has (in **section 3**) required courts, so far as possible, to give effect to Convention rights and has conferred a right of appeal on derogation issues. The effect is not, of course, to override the sovereign legislative authority of the Queen in Parliament, since if primary legislation is declared to be incompatible the validity of the legislation is unaffected (**section 4(6)**) and the remedy lies with the appropriate minister (**section 10**), who is answerable to Parliament. The 1998 **Act** gives the courts a very specific, wholly democratic, mandate.

INDEX

access to justice 222; appeal system 55
Acts of Parliament *see* legislation
Advisory Conciliation and Arbitration Service (ACAS) 216
alternative dispute resolution (ADR) 36, 181–2, 197, 212–13; arbitration 198, 207–12, 213–15; conciliation 213, 216; mediation 197, 213, 215–16; ombudsman system 204–7; tribunals 197, 198–203
anti-social behaviour orders 47
appeals 37–8, 54–6; against refusal of bail 155; arbitration 211–12; civil 37, 56, 60–3, 69–70, 179; criminal 37, 55, 56–60, 70, 116, 138; Criminal Cases Review Commission (CCRC) 59, 63–6, 116, 193; leave to appeal 55; tribunals 203
appointment of judges 93, 94–6
arbitrary power 219
arbitration 198, 207–12, 213–15
arrest 116–17, 147–50; access to legal advice and 129–33; caution on arrest/detention 120–1, 137; informing friend/relative of arrest 132; resisting 149
assault 133–8; on police officer 142, 143–4
Attorney-General: appeal to 37
Auld Report 38, 59, 109, 110, 154, 156, 160

bail 150–6
balancing of interests 46–51; evidence and 84, 88–9
bias 98–9, 100; excusal of judge from case on grounds of possible partiality 100–4
Blackstone's Commentaries (1765) 5
Bowman Committee 37, 60–1, 228
Brodrick Committee 44
burglary 89, 129–33; going equipped 142, 144–6

bylaws 4, 19

care, duty of 39–40
case management 36, 177, 180, 181, 182
caution on arrest/detention of suspect 120–1, 137
challenging jurors 108, 109
children/young people: in criminal justice system 115–16, 128; *doli incapax* 74–5; evidence given by 84, 86
Civil Justice Council 167
civil law system 167–9; administrative staff 167–8; appeals 37, 56, 60–3, 69–70, 179; conditional fee arrangements (CFAs) 169; CPR reforms 35–6, 62, 168, 178–83; expert witnesses 192–6; judicial review *see* judicial review; negligence by courtroom advocates 56, 186–92; 'out of court' settlements 36, 173–8, 191–2
cloning 79
Commission of Local Administration 205
Commission of the EU 24
common law 1, 10; defects 9; doctrine of precedent *see* precedent; Henry II as father of 5–9; presumption against alteration of 82; as source of law 1, 4–5
Community Legal Service (CLS) 36, 169, 201
compensation: wrongful conviction 116
computerisation 36, 175–6
conciliation 213, 216
conditional bail 152, 154, 155
conditional fee arrangements (CFAs) 169
confessions 84, 88, 116, 125–8
context: interpretation and 83–4
control orders 240–1
convictions: evidence of previous convictions 85–6
coroners' courts 42–6

243

corporate manslaughter 45
costs 35, 174, 180, 182, 183; expert witnesses 193; interest on 36; tribunals and 200
Council of the EU 22–3
county courts 35, 167–8
Court of Appeal 35, 68; civil appeals 37, 55, 60–1, 69–70; criminal appeals 37, 55, 57, 59, 70, 116
Court of First Instance 25
courts 35–7, 222; appeals *see* appeals; arbitration and 210–11; balancing of interests 46–51; computerisation 36, 175–6; development of common law and 6–9; equity 10, 11; hierarchy of 68, 69; rules of procedure 19; silence in 116, 117, 118, 119–23; *see also* trials; individual courts
Criminal Cases Review Commission (CCRC) 59, 63–6, 116, 193
criminal justice system 115–16; appeals 37, 55, 56–60, 70, 116, 138; bail 150–6; expert witnesses 192–6; plea bargaining 116, 156–61; preparation of witnesses 162–5; presumption of innocence 121, 122, 150; right to silence *see* silence right; witnesses *see* witnesses
Criminal Law Revision Committee 1, 14, 122
criminal offences: mental element 82–3; previous convictions 85–6; *see also* individual offences
Criminal Records Bureau 37
cross-examination 51–4
Crown 10; non-applicability of legislation to 83
Crown Court 35, 70
custom 6; as source of law 2, 5

damages remedy 187
de minimis rule 143–4
death: coroners' courts 43–5
defamation 47
defendants: absence of accused in magistrates' courts 115; evidence unduly prejudicial to 84, 85–6, 125
delays in legal system 175, 178, 180, 181
delegated legislation 2, 18–21; as source of law 1, 3–4
Department for Constitutional Affairs 36
Divisional Court 70
DNA evidence 89
documentary hearsay 87
doli incapax 74–5
drugs offences 87
duty of care 39–40
duty solicitors 130, 131–2

ejusdem generis rule 83–4
embryology 79
employment tribunals 199
enforcement: tribunal awards 203
equality before the law 219, 224
equity 1, 9–13
European Court of Human Rights 68, 70, 75, 236
European Union (EU) 21–2; Commission 24; Council 22–3; Court of First Instance 25; European Court of Justice 2, 24–5, 68, 70; European law 1, 2–3, 19, 22, 217; European Parliament 23
evidence 11, 84–9; appeals and 55, 56, 58–9; balancing of interests and 84, 88–9; children 84, 86; confessions 84, 88, 116, 125–8; hearsay 84, 86–8; previous convictions 85–6; unduly prejudicial to defendant 84, 85–6, 125
expert witnesses 192–6
expressio unius exclusio alterius rule 84

fair trial right 52, 121
false imprisonment 147, 149
fast-track procedure 36
feudalism 6–9
foreign prisoners 37
Franks Committee 200
free speech 46, 47
friends: informing of arrest 132

going equipped to steal 142, 144–6
government: legislation and *see* legislation
gross negligence: manslaughter 45
guilty pleas: plea bargaining 116, 156–61

Hansard 81–2
hearsay evidence 84, 86–8
Henry II: as father of common law 5–9
High Court 35, 70
Home Office 36, 37
Home Secretary: appeal to 37
House of Lords 4, 15, 16, 56, 60, 68–9, 93; overruling previous decisions 4, 38–42, 69
human rights issues 17, 21, 31, 79, 121, 153, 217, 224, 232–3, 234–42

information technology 175–6
informers 88
inheritance: intestate 32
innocence: presumption of 121, 122, 150
inquests 43–5

insanity defence 32, 57
interest on costs 36
international law 83, 225
interpretation of statutes 75–6; context and 83–4; extrinsic assistance 80, 81–2; golden rule 77, 78; intrinsic assistance 80, 81; literal rule 77, 78; mischief rule 77–8; presumptions 80, 82–4; purposive approach 78–9
intestate inheritance 32

judges 91, 92; appointment 93, 94–6; bound by precedent *see* precedent; case management 36, 177, 180, 181, 182; deciding on guilt 56; excusal from case on grounds of possible partiality 100–4; independence of 221; ineligibility for jury service 106, 111; judicial reasoning 67, 75; law reform and 31; plea bargaining 116, 156–61; social composition of judiciary 91, 97–100; statutory interpretation *see* interpretation of statutes; Supreme Court 93–6
judicial review 170–3, 217, 225, 230–3; permission 228–9; pre-action protocol 229–30; remedies 226–8; standing 229
juries 9, 91–2, 104–5, 110–11, 116; challenging jurors 108, 109; disqualification/excusal from jury service 106–8, 112–14; ineligibility 106–7, 110, 111–12; inquests 44; racial composition 108–9; selection of potential jurors 105–10; vetting 109

Law Commission 1, 2, 14, 29, 31–4, 87, 153
Law Reform Committee 1, 14, 30
law reforms 29–34; CPR reforms in civil law system 35–6, 62, 168, 178–83; right to silence 119–23
Law Society 19
leave to appeal 55
legal advice *see* solicitors/legal advisers
legal aid *see* public funding
Legal Services Commission (LSC) 169, 194
Leggatt Committee 201–2
legislation 13; delegated *see* delegated legislation; human rights issues 17, 21, 31, 79; law reforms 29–34; preamble 81; presumption against retrospective legislation 83, 221; process of 13, 14–16; Royal Assent 1, 15, 16; schedules 81; as source of law 1, 3–4; sources of 13–14; statutory interpretation *see* interpretation of statutes; types 13, 17
level crossings 32

liberty: presumption against deprivation of 83
life sentences 115
limitation periods 40–2
Local Government Ombudsman 205
Lord Chancellor 36, 95–6, 202

magistrates' courts 35; absence of accused 115; appeals from 55
mandatory order 227
manslaughter 45; refusal of bail and conviction for 152–3
marriage: pre-nuptial contracts 32; rape within 31, 33, 72
mediation 197, 213, 215–16
medical negligence 194
mental element in criminal offences 82–3
mental illness: ineligibility for jury service 106, 111; insanity defence 32, 57
Ministry of Justice 36, 37, 115
miscarriages of justice 56, 57–8, 59, 63, 195
monarch *see* Crown
murder: refusal of bail and conviction for 152–3

National Audit Office 37
National Health Service (NHS) 46, 47–8
National Offender Management Service (NOMS) 36, 37
natural justice 221
negligence: by courtroom advocates 56, 186–92; medical negligence 194
nemo judex in causa sua 100, 101
noscitur a sociis rule 83

obiter dicta 68, 71, 73
obstruction of police 134–5
occupiers: duty of care 39–40
offers of settlement *see* 'out of court' settlements
ombudsman system 204–7
oppression 84, 88, 127–8
Orders in Council 3–4, 19
'out of court' settlements 36, 173–8, 191–2; *see also* alternative dispute resolution (ADR)

Parliament 20; *Hansard* 81–2; ombudsman 204–7; sovereignty of 1, 17, 82, 219; *see also* legislation
Parliamentary Commissioner for Administration (PCA) 204–7
Part 36 payments 174, 176–7, 180
personal injuries 174; liability for injury to trespasser 39–40; limitation periods 40–2

245

plea bargaining 116, 156–61
police: arrest by *see* arrest; assault on police officer 142, 143–4; confessions to 84, 88, 116, 125–8; disciplinary charges 122; ineligibility of police officers for jury service 106, 111–12; informers 88; obstruction of 134–5; oppression by 84, 88, 127–8; refusal to answer police questions 118–19, 120, 131, 134–5; searches by 139–42, 144–6; suspects' access to legal advice while in custody 129–33
pre-action protocols 179; judicial review 229–30
preamble to statutes 81
precedent 4, 28, 67, 68–75; advantages 68, 71; disadvantages 68, 71–2; distinguishing 74–5; *obiter dicta* 68, 71, 73; overruling 4, 38–42, 69, 74, 75, 236–7; *ratio decidendi* 4, 68, 71, 73–84
pre-nuptial contracts 32
preparation of witnesses 162–5
prerogative orders 226–8
presumptions: bail 152, 153, 154; innocence 121, 122, 150; interpretation of statutes 82–4
previous convictions 85–6
privilege: legal professional privilege 84, 88, 183–6
Privy Council 19; Judicial Committee 35
prohibiting order 227
proportionality 232–3
public funding 169, 194, 224; tribunals 201
public interest: evidence and 84, 88–9

quashing order 226–7
Queen's Bench Divisional Court 70
questions: cross-examination of witnesses 51–4

racial composition of juries 108–9
racial hatred 47
railway level crossings 32
rape 89; within marriage 31, 33, 72
ratio decidendi 4, 68, 71, 73–84
res gestae 87
resisting arrest 149
retrospective legislation: presumption against 83, 221
rights: balancing of interests 46–51; *see also* human rights issues
robbery 138–42
Royal Assent 1, 15, 16
Royal Commissions 1, 29, 30, 55
rule of law 218–26
Runciman Commission 30, 37, 63, 116, 119–20, 156, 157, 160

Salaried Defence Service 169
schedules to statutes 81
searches by police 139–42, 144–6
secondary legislation *see* delegated legislation
selection of potential jurors 105–9
sentencing 115; plea bargaining 116, 156–61
separation of powers 238–42
sex discrimination 28
shoplifting 146–50
silence right 116, 117–23; in court 116, 117, 118, 119–23; law reforms 119–23; refusal to answer police questions 118–19, 120, 131, 134–5
small claims 36, 198; arbitration 214–15
social care 32
social composition of judiciary 91, 97–100
social conditions: changing law and 39
solicitors/legal advisers: access to 129–33; duty solicitors 130, 131–2; legal professional privilege 84, 88, 183–6; negligence by courtroom advocates 56, 186–92; preparation of witnesses 162–5; regulation of 19
sources of law 1; common law 1, 4–5; custom 2, 5; delegated legislation 1, 3–4; European law 1, 2–3; legislation 1, 3–4
sovereignty of Parliament 1, 17, 82, 219
standing: judicial review 229
stare decisis see precedent
statutes *see* legislation
statutory instruments 4, 19, 21
stay in proceedings 177
strict liability 82–3
suicide 44
Supreme Court 92–4
sureties 154

technological developments 175–6
terrorism 48–50, 81, 99, 239–42
textbooks 5
theft: going equipped to steal 142, 144–6; robbery 138–42; shoplifting 146–50
treasure trove 43
trespass: liability for injury to trespasser 39–40
trials: cross-examination of witnesses 51–4; fair trial right 52, 121; trial centres 36; *see also* evidence
tribunals 197, 198–203
trusts 9, 11

ultra vires 21, 171, 232
unfair commercial practices 32

unfitness to plead 32

vetting of juries 109
vexatious litigation 47, 48

Winn Committee 173
witnesses 189; children 84, 86; cross-examination 51–4; expert 192–6; hearsay evidence 84, 86–8; preparation 162–5; statements 177–8
Woolf Report 30, 35, 62, 169, 175, 177, 194, 228
writs: common law 8
wrongful conviction 116

Youth Conditional Cautions 116
Youth Rehabilitation Orders 115–16